PENGUIN BOOKS

A TREASURY OF ROYAL SCANDALS

Michael Farquhar is a writer and editor at *The Washington Post* specializing in history. He is coauthor of *The Century: History as It Happened on the Front Page of the Capital's Newspaper*, and his work has been published in *The Chicago Sun-Times, Chicago Tribune, Dallas Morning News, Reader's Digest*, and Discovery Online.

Henry VIII

A Treasury of Royal Scandals

The Shocking True Stories
of History's Wickedest, Weirdest,
Most Wanton Kings, Queens, Tsars,
Popes, and Emperors

MICHAEL FARQUHAR

PENGUIN BOOKS

PENGUIN BOOKS
Published by the Penguin Group
Penguin Putnam Inc., 375 Hudson Street,
New York, New York 10014, U.S.A.
Penguin Books Ltd, 80 Strand,London WC2R 0RL, England
Penguin Books Australia Ltd, 250 Camberwell Road,
Camberwell,Victoria 3124, Australia
Penguin Books Canada Ltd, 10 Alcorn Avenue,
Toronto, Ontario, Canada M4V 3B2
Penguin Books India (P) Ltd, 11 Community Centre,
Panchsheel Park,New Delhi – 110 017, India
Penguin Books (N.Z.) Ltd, Cnr Rosedale and Airborne Roads,
Albany,Auckland, New Zealand
Penguin Books (South Africa) (Pty) Ltd, 24 Sturdee Avenue,
Rosebank, Johannesburg 2196, South Africa

Penguin Books Ltd, Registered Offices:
Harmondsworth, Middlesex, England

First published in Penguin Books 2001

9   10   8

Copyright © Michael Farquhar, 2001
All rights reserved

Illustration credits
Frontispiece (iii), pages 28, 54, 1000, 126, 172, 202, 260:
The Granger Collection, New York.
Page 2: © Leonard de Selva/CORBIS.
Page 222: © Christel Gerstenberg/CORBIS.

LIBRARY OF CONGRESS CATALOGING IN PUBLICATION DATA
Farquhar, Michael.
A treasury of royal scandals : the shocking true stories of history's wickedest, weirdest,
and most wanton kings, queens, tsars, popes, and emperors / Michael Farquhar.
p.   cm.
ISBN 0 14 02.8024 3 (pbk. : alk. paper)
1. Kings and rulers—Conduct of life—History.
2. Heads of state—Conduct of life—History.   3. Scandals.   I. Title.
D107 .F32 2001
920.02—dc21   2001024575

Printed in the United States of America
Set in Adobe Garamond • Designed by Manuela Paul

This book is dedicated with love to my grandmother, Claire O'Donnell Donahue Courtney. What a life!

All I say is, kings is kings and you got to make allowances.
—Mark Twain, *The Adventures of Huckleberry Finn*

Contents

Contents

Introduction

The twentieth century was a slaughterhouse for European monarchy. Across the continent, scores of kings and queens were swept from their thrones in a frenzy of war and revolution. Those managing to cling to their crowns, meanwhile, have been rendered either faceless and bland, as in, say, Norway, or, as in Britain, regarded as little more than inane tabloid fodder.

Maybe the decline of monarchy is for the best. After all, the notion that one individual—no matter how stupid or depraved—should by some fluke of birth hold dominion over all others is ridiculous and well past its prime. Still, there's a void now. People with unlimited power and an inbred sense of their own superiority tended to misbehave. Royally. Democratically elected presidents and prime ministers—not to mention constitutionally constrained monarchs—simply can't compete. Consequently, things are a lot duller these days, and what passes for scandal is almost laughable.

So what if Charles and Diana were miserably married? He never slammed the doors of Westminster Abbey in her face, or buried pieces of her boyfriend under the floorboards of his palace. That was behavior typical of a bygone era celebrated in this treasury—a time of lusty kings and treacherous queens; of murderous tsars, insane emperors, and unholy popes (once the supreme monarchs in Europe). Toe sucking aside, Fergie and the rest of this generation's royals can't hold a scandal to their for-bears. Not one of them has delivered anything worthy of the name, and are thus excluded from this collection.

Some of the stories that do appear here are no doubt famil-iar to readers of history. But they are classics, and no anthology of royal bad behavior would be complete without them. Others have been mined from the past, largely unexposed. All of the sto-ries showcase the rich assortment of scandals that once flour-ished across Europe. And, thanks to the generations of royals who unwittingly created them, they remain immensely enter-taining.

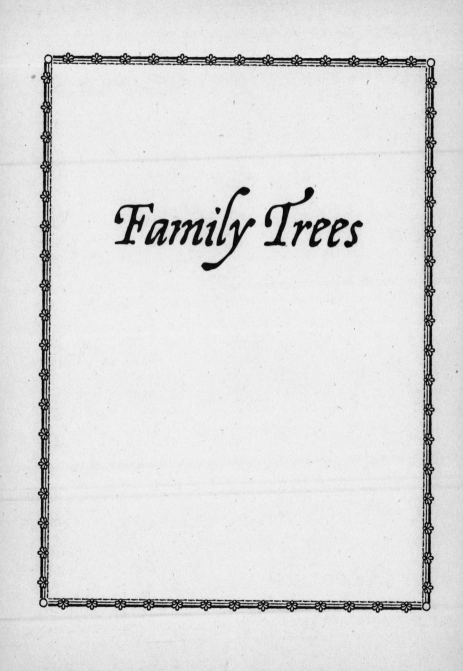

Family Trees

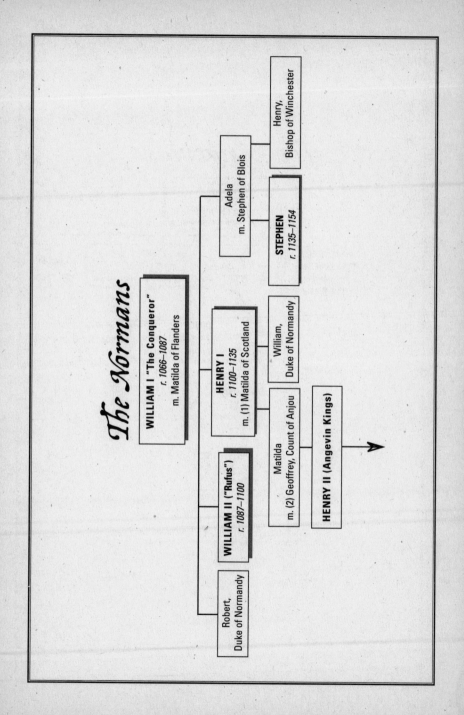

The Normans

WILLIAM I "The Conqueror"
r. 1066–1087
m. Matilda of Flanders

Robert,
Duke of Normandy

WILLIAM II ("Rufus")
r. 1087–1100

HENRY I
r. 1100–1135
m. (1) Matilda of Scotland

Adela
m. Stephen of Blois

William,
Duke of Normandy

Matilda
m. (2) Geoffrey, Count of Anjou

HENRY II (Angevin Kings)

STEPHEN
r. 1135–1154

Henry,
Bishop of Winchester

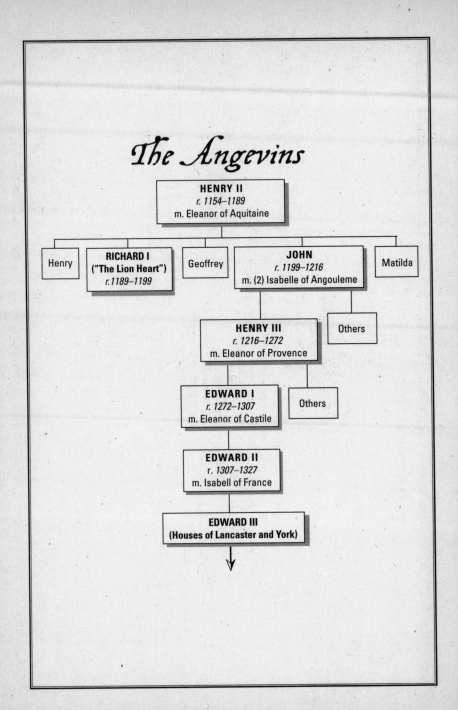

The Angevins

HENRY II
r. 1154–1189
m. Eleanor of Aquitaine

Henry

RICHARD I
("The Lion Heart")
r.1189–1199

Geoffrey

JOHN
r. 1199–1216
m. (2) Isabelle of Angouleme

Matilda

Others

HENRY III
r. 1216–1272
m. Eleanor of Provence

EDWARD I
r. 1272–1307
m. Eleanor of Castile

Others

EDWARD II
r. 1307–1327
m. Isabell of France

EDWARD III
(Houses of Lancaster and York)

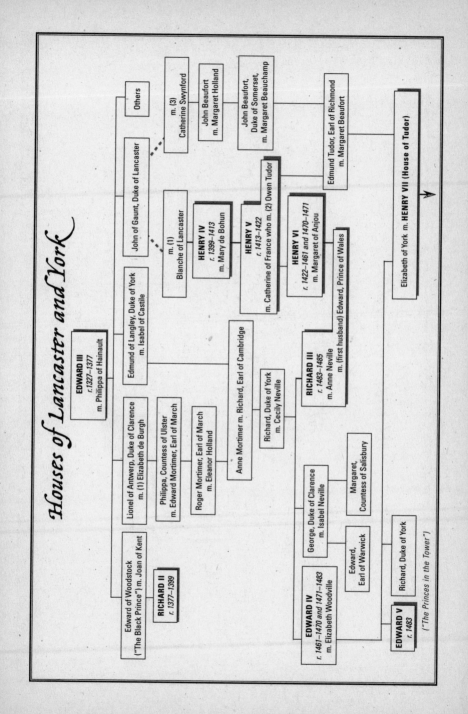

Houses of Lancaster and York

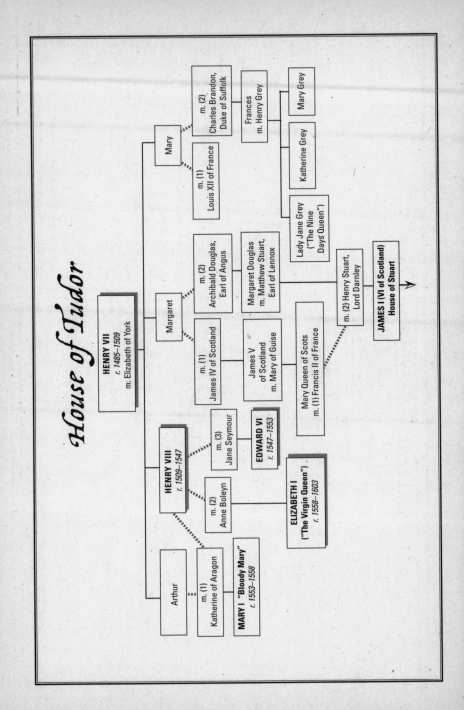

House of Tudor

HENRY VII
r. 1485–1509
m. Elizabeth of York

Arthur

Margaret

Mary

HENRY VIII
r. 1509–1547

m. (1)
Katherine of Aragon

m. (2)
Anne Boleyn

m. (3)
Jane Seymour

MARY I "Bloody Mary"
r. 1553–1558

ELIZABETH I
("The Virgin Queen")
r. 1558–1603

EDWARD VI
r. 1547–1553

m. (1)
James IV of Scotland

m. (2)
Archibald Douglas,
Earl of Angus

m. (1)
Louis XII of France

m. (2)
Charles Brandon,
Duke of Suffolk

James V
of Scotland
m. Mary of Guise

Margaret Douglas
m. Matthew Stuart,
Earl of Lennox

Frances
m. Henry Grey

Mary Queen of Scots
m. (1) Francis II of France

m. (2) Henry Stuart,
Lord Darnley

Lady Jane Grey
("The Nine
Days Queen")

Katherine Grey

Mary Grey

JAMES I (VI of Scotland)
House of Stuart
→

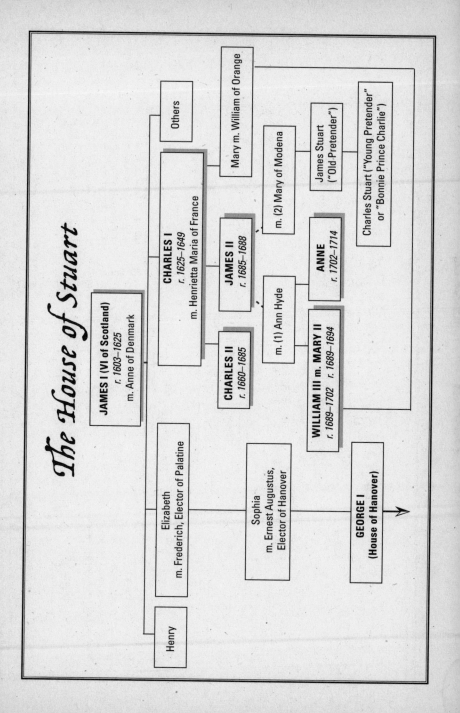

The House of Stuart

JAMES I (VI of Scotland)
r. 1603–1625
m. Anne of Denmark

Henry

Elizabeth
m. Frederich, Elector of Palatine

CHARLES I
r. 1625–1649
m. Henrietta Maria of France

Others

Mary m. William of Orange

CHARLES II
r. 1660–1685

JAMES II
r. 1685–1688

m. (1) Ann Hyde

m. (2) Mary of Modena

Sophia
m. Ernest Augustus, Elector of Hanover

WILLIAM III m. MARY II
r. 1689–1702   r. 1689–1694

ANNE
r. 1702–1714

James Stuart
("Old Pretender")

GEORGE I
(House of Hanover)

Charles Stuart ("Young Pretender"
or "Bonnie Prince Charlie")

House of Hanover

GEORGE I
r. 1714–1727
m. Sophia Dorothea of Brunswick

GEORGE II
r. 1727–1760
m. Caroline of Anspach

Frederick, Prince of Wales
m. Augusta of Saxe, Gotha-Attenburg

GEORGE III
r. 1760–1820
m. Sophia Charlotte of Mecklenberg

GEORGE IV
r. 1820–1830
m. (2) Caroline of Brunswick

Charlotte

Frederick

WILLIAM IV
r. 1830–1837
m. Adelaide of Saxe-Coburg

Edward, Duke of Kent
m. Victoria of Saxe-Coburg

VICTORIA
(House of Saxe-Coburg-Gotha)

Others

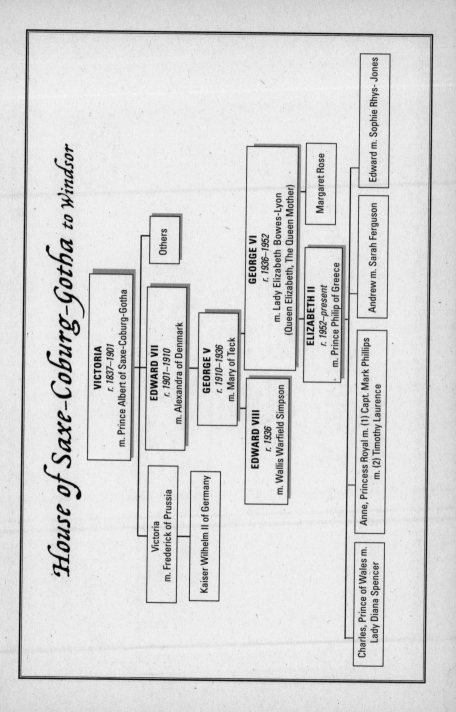

House of Saxe-Coburg-Gotha to Windsor

VICTORIA
r. 1837–1901
m. Prince Albert of Saxe-Coburg-Gotha

Victoria
m. Frederick of Prussia

Kaiser Wilhelm II of Germany

EDWARD VII
r. 1901–1910
m. Alexandra of Denmark

Others

GEORGE V
r. 1910–1936
m. Mary of Teck

EDWARD VIII
r. 1936
m. Wallis Warfield Simpson

GEORGE VI
r. 1936–1952
m. Lady Elizabeth Bowes-Lyon
(Queen Elizabeth, The Queen Mother)

ELIZABETH II
r. 1952–present
m. Prince Philip of Greece

Margaret Rose

Charles, Prince of Wales m.
Lady Diana Spencer

Anne, Princess Royal m. (1) Capt. Mark Phillips
m. (2) Timothy Laurence

Andrew m. Sarah Ferguson

Edward m. Sophie Rhys-Jones

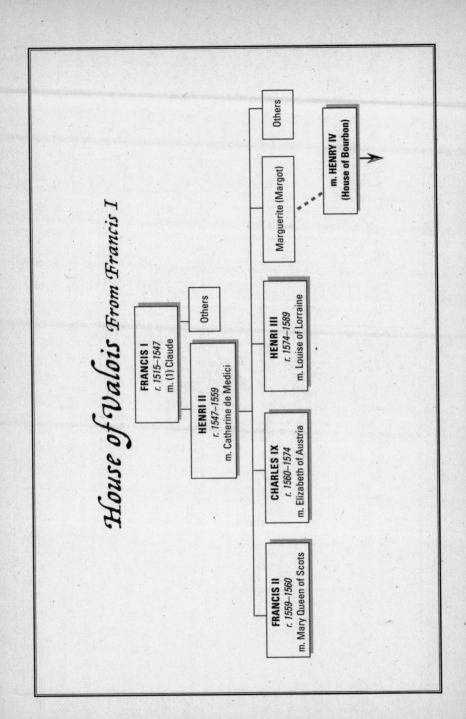

House of Valois From Francis I

FRANCIS I
r. 1515–1547
m. (1) Claude

Others

HENRI II
r. 1547–1559
m. Catherine de Medici

FRANCIS II
r. 1559–1560
m. Mary Queen of Scots

CHARLES IX
r. 1560–1574
m. Elizabeth of Austria

HENRI III
r. 1574–1589
m. Louise of Lorraine

Marguerite (Margot)

Others

m. **HENRY IV**
(House of Bourbon)

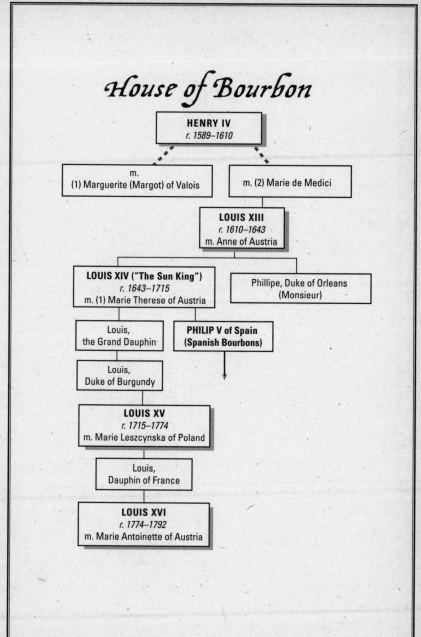

House of Bourbon

HENRY IV
r. 1589–1610

m.
(1) Marguerite (Margot) of Valois

m. (2) Marie de Medici

LOUIS XIII
r. 1610–1643
m. Anne of Austria

LOUIS XIV ("The Sun King")
r. 1643–1715
m. (1) Marie Therese of Austria

Phillipe, Duke of Orleans
(Monsieur)

Louis,
the Grand Dauphin

**PHILIP V of Spain
(Spanish Bourbons)**

Louis,
Duke of Burgundy

LOUIS XV
r. 1715–1774
m. Marie Leszcynska of Poland

Louis,
Dauphin of France

LOUIS XVI
r. 1774–1792
m. Marie Antoinette of Austria

House of Romanov *(from Alexis)*

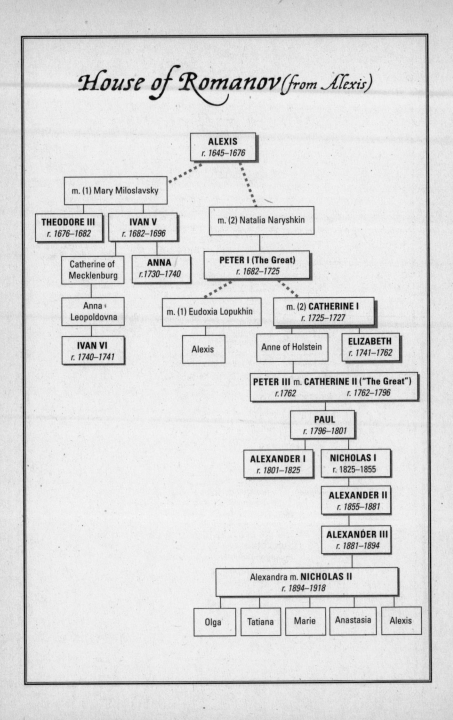

ALEXIS
r. 1645–1676

m. (1) Mary Miloslavsky

m. (2) Natalia Naryshkin

THEODORE III
r. 1676–1682

IVAN V
r. 1682–1696

PETER I (The Great)
r. 1682–1725

Catherine of Mecklenburg

ANNA
r.1730–1740

Anna Leopoldovna

m. (1) Eudoxia Lopukhin

m. (2) **CATHERINE I**
r. 1725–1727

IVAN VI
r. 1740–1741

Alexis

Anne of Holstein

ELIZABETH
r. 1741–1762

PETER III m. **CATHERINE II ("The Great")**
r.1762   *r. 1762–1796*

PAUL
r. 1796–1801

ALEXANDER I
r. 1801–1825

NICHOLAS I
r. 1825–1855

ALEXANDER II
r. 1855–1881

ALEXANDER III
r. 1881–1894

Alexandra m. **NICHOLAS II**
r. 1894–1918

Olga

Tatiana

Marie

Anastasia

Alexis

The Spanish Habsburgs

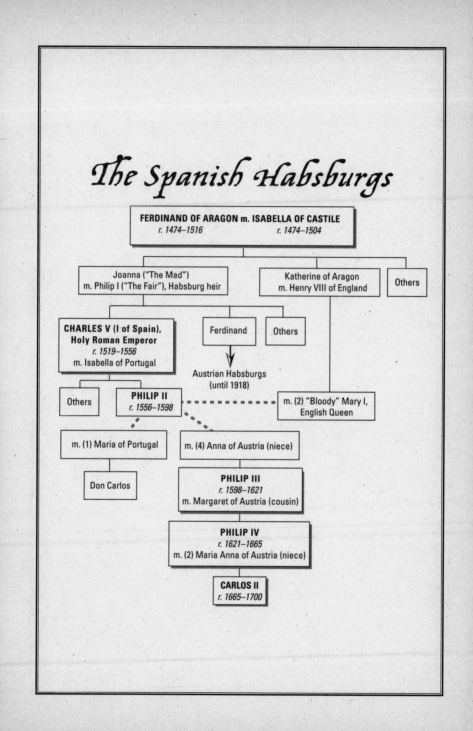

FERDINAND OF ARAGON m. ISABELLA OF CASTILE
r. 1474–1516   *r. 1474–1504*

Joanna ("The Mad")
m. Philip I ("The Fair"), Habsburg heir

Katherine of Aragon
m. Henry VIII of England

Others

CHARLES V (I of Spain),
Holy Roman Emperor
r. 1519–1556
m. Isabella of Portugal

Ferdinand

Others

Austrian Habsburgs
(until 1918)

Others

PHILIP II
r. 1556–1598

m. (2) "Bloody" Mary I,
English Queen

m. (1) Maria of Portugal

m. (4) Anna of Austria (niece)

Don Carlos

PHILIP III
r. 1598–1621
m. Margaret of Austria (cousin)

PHILIP IV
r. 1621–1665
m. (2) Maria Anna of Austria (niece)

CARLOS II
r. 1665–1700

PART I

The Lust Emperors

"Lust's passion will be served," the French libertine and novelist Marquis de Sade once wrote. "It demands, it militates, it tyrannizes." The Marquis might have added that this relentless vice has always been oblivious to social status. So, the whole theory behind royalty—that it conferred a certain exalted status over ordinary mortals; a place closer to God in the hierarchy of the universe—was compromised somewhat by the fact that kings and queens proved themselves to be every bit as sex-driven as the peons who served them. The only difference was that, from their positions of power, royal folk were able to serve the demands of lust more creatively and energetically than most.

Henri III preening amongst his minions.

1

From Russia with Lots of Love

Catherine the Great loved horses. She also loved sex. Contrary to popular legend, however, she never managed to unite the two passions. Still, the autocratic empress of Russia brought all the enthusiasm of a vigorous ride to her extremely busy bedroom.

After ridding herself of her imbecile husband Peter III in 1762,[1] Catherine grabbed the Russian crown and came to dominate her kingdom for the next thirty-four years. Boldly indulging herself as she grew more secure in her position, the empress consumed handsome young lovers with an appetite that sometimes shocked her contemporaries. "She's no woman," exclaimed one, "she's a siren!"

The empress relished her weakness for men, abandoning herself to a giddy romanticism that belied her cold and pragmatic rule. She loved being entertained, even into old age, by a succession of well-formed young studs eager to please her. "It is my misfortune that my heart cannot be content, even for one hour, without love," she wrote.

Sharing the empress's bed brought ample rewards, not the least of which was an intimate proximity to power, but getting

---

[1] Find out just how much Catherine hated Peter in Part III, Chapter 4.

there wasn't easy. A good body and a pleasant face, combined whenever possible with wit and intelligence, were merely starters. Potential lovers also had to have the right pedigree and pass a crucial test. Catherine had several ladies-in-waiting—test drivers of sorts—whose job it was to ensure that all candidates for their mistress's bed were up to the highly demanding task of satisfying her.

The applicants were most often supplied by the empress's one-eyed ex-lover—the man many assumed to be her secret husband—Gregory Potemkin. She had fallen in love with this rough, hulking officer relatively early in her industrious sexual career, overcome by his brash courage, quick wit, and almost primitive sexuality. Wasting little time disposing of Alexander Vassilzhikov, her boyfriend at the time, Catherine was delighted the first night Potemkin came to her bedroom, naked under his nightshirt and ready for action. "I have parted from a certain excellent but very boring citizen," the empress wrote to a confidante, "who has been replaced, I know not how, by one of the greatest, oddest, most amusing and original personalities of this Iron Age."

Because of his long greasy hair, and brutish unwashed body, many women found Potemkin repulsive. Catherine, however, reveled in his strength, charm, and sexual domination. She couldn't get enough of this strange man who made her forget her royal dignity. Whenever they were parted, even for a few hours, she regaled him with an avalanche of feverish love notes, each peppered with at least one of her special pet names: "My marble beauty," "my darling pet," "my dearest doll," "golden cock," "lion of the jungle," "my professional bon bon."

In one letter, she pretended to be shocked at the intensity of her passion and tried to get hold of herself: "I have issued strict orders to my whole body, down to the smallest hair on my head, not to show you the least sign of love. I have locked my love inside my heart and bolted it ten times, it is suffocating there, it is constrained, and I fear it may explode." In other letters she gloried in his good company: "Darling, what comical stories you told me yesterday! I can't stop laughing when I think of them . . . we spend four hours together without a shadow of boredom, and it is always with reluctance that I leave you. My dearest pigeon, I love you very much. You are handsome, intelligent, amusing."

Of course Catherine loved the sex, and in her exultation could sound much more like a bad romance novelist than the authoritarian empress of all the Russias:

—"There is not a cell in my whole body that does not
yearn for you, oh infidel! . . ."
—"I thank you for yesterday's feast. My little Grisha fed
me and quenched my thirst, but not with wine. . . ."
—"My head is like that of a cat in heat. . . ."
—"I will be a 'woman of fire' for you, as you so often
say. But I shall try to hide my flames."

Moody and temperamental, subject to bouts of black depression and fits of jealousy, Potemkin was sometimes lovingly scolded by his royal mistress: "There is a woman in the world who loves you and who has a right to a tender word from you, Imbecile, Tatar, Cossack, infidel, Muscovite, *morbleu!*" The relationship was so physically intimate that Catherine did not hesitate to share even the most unflattering of ailments with him: "I have some diarrhea today, but apart from that, I am well, my adored one. . . . Do not be distressed because of my diarrhea, it cleans out the intestines."

There is no surviving evidence to support the rumor that

Catherine secretly married Potemkin, although she often referred to him in her letters as "my beloved spouse," or "my dearest husband." Married or not, the relationship certainly transcended the bedroom as it evolved into a close political partnership. Catherine shared her vast kingdom with Potemkin as if he were her king. She consulted with him on all affairs of state, working closely with him on her ambitious plans to expand Russia's borders and crush the Muslim Turks.

The empress's powerful lover is perhaps best remembered for the legendary "Potemkin Villages" he is said to have created for her benefit as she embarked on a grand tour of all the newly Russianized lands he had conquered for her. These "villages," it was said, were little more than elaborate stage sets of prosperous towns, populated by cheerful serfs, all of which were quickly collapsed and set up again at the next stop on Catherine's carefully plotted itinerary. The artificiality of the Potemkin Villages came to represent in the minds of many, Catherine's superficial and halfhearted attempts to reform and liberalize her kingdom.

Though the relationship with Potemkin endured until his death in 1791, the sexual intensity between them dimmed after only a few years. No longer champion of the empress's boudoir, Potemkin resolved to retain her favor by pimping his replacements. He handpicked a steady succession of new lovers for his erstwhile mistress—all of whom paid him a handsome brokerage fee for the privilege of servicing her. There was Zavadovsky, followed by Zorich, followed by Rimsky-Korsakov, followed by Lanskoy, followed by Ermolov, followed by Mamonov and so on and on, and on.

After being installed in the official apartment set aside for Catherine's lovers, each new favorite was feted and adored by the passionate monarch with almost girlish enthusiasm. But each, in turn, was eventually dismissed, either for boring Catherine or breaking her heart. Few, however, left her service without a handsome settlement. When Zavadovsky was dismissed in 1776, for example, Chevalier de Corberon, the French chargé d'affaires in Russia, wrote that "He has received from Her Majesty 50,000 rubles, a pension of 5,000, and 4,000 peasants in the Ukraine, where they are worth a great deal [serfs at the time were trade-able commodities, like cattle]. . . . You must agree, my friend, that it's not a bad line of work to be in here."

One ex-lover, Count Stanislas Augustus Poniatowski, was even given the crown of Poland, although Catherine did eventu-ally hack away huge chunks of his kingdom and absorb them into her own. All told, the generous payments to fallen lovers amounted to billions of dollars in today's currency. When her friend, the French philosopher Voltaire, gently chided Catherine for inconsistency in her love affairs, she responded that she was, on the contrary, "absolutely faithful."

"To whom? To beauty, of course. Beauty alone attracts me!"

2

French Kiss

Francis I was a true Renaissance monarch: warrior, grand patron of the arts, and skirt-chaser extraordinaire. This was a king who loved the ladies—lots and lots of ladies. "A court without women is a year without spring and a spring without roses," the promiscuous French ruler once remarked. Unfortunately, in his enthusiasm for plucking as many roses as possible, Francis gave his long-suffering queen a scorching case of syphilis. His son and heir, Henri II, was also a passionate adulterer. Rather than a sexually transmitted disease, though, he impetuously gave his favorite mistress, Diane de Poitiers, something else entirely: all the French crown jewels.

Henri's enchantment with Diane, who was old enough to be his mother, was in direct proportion to the distaste he had for his dumpy and unappealing queen, Catherine de Medici of Italy. Nevertheless, wife and mistress did develop a tenuous relationship of sorts. The queen quietly tolerated the affair, while her rival moved into the household and treated Catherine with a kind of contemptuous affection—even nursing her when she came down with scarlet fever. It was Diane who gently nudged the king out of her bed so he could sire legitimate children with his wife as duty demanded.

Despite her general composure in light of the odd arrangement, the queen's temper occasionally got the better of her.

Once, during an argument with the king and his mistress over Henri's policies toward her native land, Catherine disdainfully confronted Diane. "I have read the histories of this kingdom," she informed her rival, "and I have found in them that from time to time at all periods whores have managed the business of kings."

Years later, after Henri II's death in 1559,[1] Catherine wrote of her true feelings regarding the humiliating situation with her husband and his mistress. "I was hospitable to [Diane]; he was the king; yet even so I always let him know that it was to my great regret; for never has a woman who loves her husband liked his whore; for even though this is an ugly word for us to use, one cannot call her anything else."

❧

Given the atmosphere in which they grew up, it's not surprising that some of Henri and Catherine's children were a little unconventional when it came to sex. Henri III, who succeeded his father and two brothers in the Valois line of French kings, was an ostentatious transvestite who surrounded himself with an obsequious band of gay young men the French scathingly called *mignons.* The king and his male harem loved nothing more than dressing up and prancing around Paris in lace and ruffles, with long curls flowing from under dainty little caps. On special occasions, Henri dolled himself up magnificently, dripping with diamonds and swathed in silk. "One did not know whether it was a woman king or a man queen," a bewildered observer said at the time.

Historians have noted the peculiar affection Catherine de Medici had for her son Henri. The formidable woman the

---

[1] He was killed when a lance pierced through his visor during a joust and shattered into his face, a demise supposedly predicted by the famed seer Nostradamus.

French came to call "Madame Serpente," had consolidated her power after the death of her husband and, with three sons in a row reigning as kings of France, became history's ultimate Queen Mother. An avid disciple of Machiavelli's blueprint for power, *The Prince*, she considered her fellow Florentine almost a personal guru.

With a daunting combination of guile, treachery, and shrewd intelligence, this plump matron in her habitual black dress was ruthless in the struggle to maintain her family's power. Yet while Catherine orchestrated the lives of all of her other children, using them as pawns to achieve her political ends, Henri was special. Her devotion to him, in fact, bordered on the incestuous. She was certainly indulgent of his flamboyant lifestyle, even arranging lavish orgies for his royal pleasure. Henri, however, was completely controlled by his mignons, some of whom wielded enormous power. Fights often broke out among the perfumed favorites—sometimes to the death—as they vied for the king's affections.

Despite her overwhelming maternal devotion, Catherine was left out of the loop. With the kingdom shredded by religious wars, the government coffers empty and an attack by neighboring Spain a looming threat, Catherine begged for Henri's attention to the desperate situation she was trying so hard to remedy for him. "Things are in a worse state than they are thought to be," the ailing Queen Mother wrote in one of many long letters to the king while traveling around France in a vain attempt to generate support for him. "I beg you to control your finances very carefully in order to raise money for your service without having to rob your people, for you are on the brink of a general revolt . . . and whoever tells you otherwise deceives you."

All Catherine's tireless efforts on her beloved son's behalf were ignored, causing her no end of distress. King Henri was far too busy with his mignons to listen to his mother's barrage of pleas and warnings. The "King of Trifles," as his disgusted subjects called him, was more interested in finding new ways to entertain the boys than he was in the fate of France. There were occasions, though, when Henri was entirely overcome by a violent revulsion to his habitual frivolity. During these times he transformed himself into a religious fanatic—publicly flogging himself, walking barefoot in bizarre religious processions, and outfitting himself in monk's clothes with a rosary of small ivory skulls hanging from his waist. "I am frightened that everything is not golden here," Ougier de Busbecq wrote after witnessing the demonstration of Henri's unconventional piety.

During several of his manic bouts of religion, the king made pilgrimages to Chartres on foot, begging the Virgin Mary to give him a son and heir. Alas, even the Mother of God couldn't help him there. While he loved dressing up his wife, Queen Louise, doing her makeup and playing with her hair, he was rarely up to the task of sleeping with her.

⚜

Occupying almost as much of Henri III's time as his pretty boys and his alternating episodes of penance was his intense feud with his beautiful sister, Marguerite. Margot, as she was known, had a voracious appetite for men. Dating her, however, was often deadly, thanks to her despised brother. Actually, it was several members of the Valois royal family who arranged to make Margot's active love life lethal.

She was the youngest and most magnificent of the three daughters of Henri II and Catherine de Medici. When she was nineteen, her ambitious mother married her off to her Bourbon cousin, King Henry of Navarre. It was a cynical political match intended to shore up relations with the tiny kingdom wedged between France and Spain. Even if the newlyweds had loved one another, which they clearly did not, any happiness they might have shared was shattered only days after the wedding.

Margot's mother had been involved in a plot to assassinate a Huguenot leader. The murder was planned for just after the wedding, but the scheme failed. Fearing her role in it would be discovered and lead to a violent Protestant revolt, Catherine and her son (King Charles IX, who ruled just before Henri III) secretly initiated a sweeping slaughter of Huguenots who had gathered in Paris to celebrate the union of the Catholic French princess and the Protestant king of Navarre. The event, which became infamous as the St. Bartholomew's Day Massacre, was quite a wedding present. Although Margot, now queen of Navarre, was able to save her new husband from being murdered in the bloody frenzy, he was held prisoner in Paris, a situation that did not enhance the couple's already tenuous relationship. Both Margot and Henry were extraordinarily passionate people— just not for each other.

Desperate for satisfaction, Queen Margot took on the first of her many doomed lovers not long after she was married. His name was Joseph de Boniface de la Molle and her family hated him. Accused of conspiracy against King Charles IX, La Molle was hideously tortured. His fingernails were torn off and his bones crushed. He was then beheaded, but not before sending salutations to Margot from the scaffold. It was said that the distraught queen secretly ordered her lover's head removed from public display and brought to her for burial.

After La Molle's execution, Margot acquired several more lovers who were lucky enough to narrowly avoid her family's wrath. Then, wishing to escape her brother Henri, now king of France, and her estranged husband, the king of Navarre, Margot moved to the French town of Agen. Seeing the glamorous queen for the first time, a young officer by the name of Aubiac was entranced. "Let me be hanged," he exclaimed, "if I might only once sleep with that woman!" He would soon get both his wishes.

When the town of Agen was ransacked by the king's forces, Aubiac helped Margot escape. At some point they became lovers, for which he would pay dearly. After Aubiac was captured, Henri III announced that the Queen Mother had begged him to have Margot's lover "hung in the presence of this miserable woman, in the courtyard of the Castle of Usson, so that plenty of people may see him." The unfortunate lover was hung, upside down. Before he had even ceased breathing, Aubiac was cut down, tossed into a grave and buried alive.

Don Juan of Austria had once said of Margot: "She looks more like a goddess of Heaven than a princess of earth. Her charms are better suited to ruin men than to save them. Her beauty was sent to damn us." A succession of ill-fated lovers was proving Don Juan remarkably prescient.

Over time, Margot's once breathtaking beauty was fading, but then so was her tyrannical family. After the death of her mother and the assassination of her brother, Henri, both in 1589, she was the last of the Valois line. As French law barred women from inheriting the throne, it went to the nearest male relative. He happened to be Margot's long estranged husband, who became King Henry IV. With him began the Bourbon line of French kings. A genuine friendship developed between the childless couple and, for a fat settlement, Margot agreed to divorce Henry so he could remarry and start a family.

Obese and heavily made up as she aged, often sporting a little blonde wig, Margot started to look like a caricature of her former self. As she reveled in her freedom, her libido became exaggerated as well. Where once only noble gentlemen shared her bed, now she had her way with a series of virile young nobodies, among them the son of a local coppersmith, a shepherd, a strolling musician, and a son of a carpenter. The ex-queen took good care of her men, giving them positions and titles, and even sometimes arranging advantageous marriages for them. One, however, made her mad when he proved *too* devoted a husband to the maid she had chosen for him, leaving poor Margot out in the cold.

❦

The French monarchy reached its glorious pinnacle during the long reign of Henry IV's grandson, Louis XIV (1643–1715), only to sputter out completely in the years following Louis XVI's execution in 1793. If Louis XV—who reigned in between—had any idea he was occupying a throne teetering toward collapse, he wasn't about to let that ruin a good time. And a good time for Louis meant massive amounts of sex.

Successfully conquering a boyhood shyness around women, Louis XV became so insatiable that he had a private bordello established for himself at Versailles. This ensured a woman would be available whenever he needed one, which was most of the time. While over the years Louis had a number of official mistresses installed at court—including most famously Madame Pompadour, who wielded enormous power due to her influence on the king, and Madame Du Barry, a former prostitute plucked from obscurity to service him in splendor—they weren't always enough to satisfy this monarch's unrelenting libido. Certainly his homely and uninspiring Polish queen, Marie Leczinska, wasn't up to the task. She pooped out after giving Louis ten children in ten years.

At one point during the king's priapic career, he went through five sisters in succession—most of them already married. "Is it faithlessness or constancy to choose an entire family?" went a popular verse of the time. The first of the sisters, Madame de Mailly, was Louis XV's very first mistress. After she had initiated the king to the pleasures of adultery, she made the mistake of inviting her sister to court. "You bore me," Louis sniffed as he unceremoniously dismissed Madame de Mailly and replaced her with her sister, Madame de Vintimille. This one only had a brief tenure with Madame de Vintimille dying less than a year later while giving birth to the king's bastard. She was replaced by yet another sister, Madame de la Tournelle, who was somewhat wiser than her siblings. She demanded the title of duchess, a large apartment in Versailles, an unlimited allowance, public pregnancies, legitimatized bastards, and the exile of her already discarded sister, Madame de Mailly. She got everything she requested, but perhaps forgot to ask for protection from two more sisters waiting in the wings. They had their turn, too.

3

England Swings

*T*he British are rarely associated with blazing sensuality. Stiff upper lips, maybe, but that's about the extent of it. Considering the rich and nuanced sexual proclivities of a millennium's worth of British monarchs, this bland reputation hardly seems deserved.

Those meeting King Edward IV in the late fifteenth century often found him surprisingly affable and unaffected. "He was so genial in his greeting," noted contemporary chronicler Domenico Mancini, "that when he saw a newcomer bewildered by his regal appearance and royal pomp, he would give him courage to speak by laying a kindly hand on his shoulder." Maybe this was true for the guys. Most women, however, experienced something entirely different when they encountered the tall, handsome monarch.

"He was licentious in the extreme," Mancini reported. "It was said that he behaved very badly towards numerous women after seducing them because, as soon as he grew tired with the affair, much against their will he would pass the ladies on to other courtiers. He pursued indiscriminately married and unmarried, noble and low-born, though he never raped them. He overcame them all by money and promises and then, having had them, he got rid of them." It would be interesting to know how exactly Mancini defined rape, given his account of how King Edward threatened Elizabeth Woodville with a dagger when she had the audacity to resist him before they were married.

&

By royal standards of the time, Edward IV's grandson, Henry VIII, had relatively few mistresses. That's because he married most of them. Henry seems to have had a thing for the hired help, creating one hell of a hostile work environment. His second wife, Anne Boleyn (whose sister Henry also slept with) had been a lady-in-waiting to his first wife, Katherine of Aragon, while his third wife, Jane Seymour, had served both the first and the second. Then he met and fell in love with his fifth wife, Catherine Howard, while she was working for his fourth, Anne of Cleves. Two of these former employees would lose their heads.[1]

&

Sex and violent death were as closely intertwined in the psyche of Henry's younger daughter, Elizabeth I, as sleeping and dreaming. She was not yet three years old when her mother, Anne Boleyn, was executed for adultery, and she was nine when her young stepmother, Catherine Howard, was dragged away screaming to her own date with the headsman.

As a teenager, Elizabeth enjoyed the flirtatious attentions of Thomas Seymour—her first stepmother's brother who had married her last stepmother, Katherine Parr, after the death of Henry VIII in 1547. Seymour was beheaded, too, in part for his attempts to seduce her. Little wonder, then, that Elizabeth decided to stay single.

Despite her much lauded spinsterhood, a sexually charged aura attached itself to "The Virgin Queen" for most of her glorious reign. Elizabeth had an enduring passion for one Robert

---

[1] For a full account of Henry VIII and his six wives, see Part III, Chapter 2.

Dudley, going back to the days when they were both held prisoner in the Tower of London by her sister "Bloody" Mary I. As soon as she ascended the throne in 1558, the young, red-headed queen made Dudley her Master of the Horse, and eventually Earl of Leicester. She ordered his apartments at court moved closer to hers and flirted with him in public while enthusiastically extolling his virtues of body and mind. The Spanish ambassador reported that "Lord Robert has come so much into favor that he does whatever he pleases with affairs and it is even said that Her Majesty visits him in his chamber day and night."

This was a couple of centuries before Catherine the Great came to Russia's throne, and a time when female monarchs were rare and their sexuality expected to be beyond reproach. But the inevitable gossip arising from her dalliances with Lord Robert didn't faze this virgin queen in the least. When her old governess, Katherine Ashley, begged Elizabeth to be more circumspect in her dealings with her favorite, she denied any misbehavior by irritably pointing out the attendants who surrounded her at all times and made any secret dalliance nearly impossible. "Although," she concluded in a proud snit, "if I had the will . . . I do not know of anyone who could forbid me!"

Indeed, at twenty-five, the new queen was enjoying the intoxicating sensation of being free for the first time in her life to do exactly as she pleased. And although she was determined never to marry—or risk pregnancy by a fully realized affair—she was happy to wallow in the overtly sexual company of her handsome Master of the Horse, wagging tongues be damned. The fact that Dudley was married and came from humble origins with a tainted family history[2] posed no obstacle to the increasingly scandalous affair. Even the suspicious death of his wife,

---

[2]His grandfather, father and brother all were beheaded as traitors.

who ended up at the bottom of a stairway with a broken neck, was only a temporary damper. In fact, the intense relationship with the queen lasted until his death in 1588.

Devoted as she was to him, though, Dudley was by no means the only man in Elizabeth's life. She basked in the attention of foreign princes seeking her hand, and of increasingly younger courtiers like Sir Walter Ralegh and Robert Devereux, the Earl of Essex (Dudley's stepson), all of whom professed to worship her. Through it all, the queen played the wily coquette, absorbing all the professions of love yet never committing to anyone.

Inheriting the tremendous vanity of her father Henry VIII, she encouraged the ritualized cult that surrounded her as she grew older. Flattery was the name of the game and Elizabeth's suitors played to win, rhapsodizing endlessly about her magnificent beauty and glorious majesty. The courting rituals grew rather pathetic as the queen reached the end of her forty-four-year reign. Balding, with blackening teeth from too much sugar consumption and thick, white pancake makeup to cover her smallpox-scarred face, she was hardly England's rarest beauty. Yet the rewards were potentially great enough for men to attempt to convince her that she was.

⟨⟨❦⟩⟩

Elizabeth's cousin and heir, James I, also reveled in the attention received from handsome young courtiers. One of his favorites was George Villiers, whom he gave the title of Duke of Buckingham. A contemporary wrote about the king's relationship with Buckingham and his predecessor in the king's affections, Robert Carr, Lord Somerset: "Now, as no other reason appeared in favour of their choyce but handsomenesse, so the love the King shewed was as amorously conveyed as if he had mistaken their sex, and thought them ladies; which I have seene Sommerset and Buckingham labour to resemble in effiminatenesse of their dressings; though in W[horeson] lookes and wanton gestures, they exceeded any part of woman kind my conversation did ever cope with all."

It is perhaps ironic that those fundamentalists repulsed by homosexuality would condemn King James by citing the very Bible that bears his name. In any event, his preference for men was not uncommon among British kings. William II, Richard I—the lion-hearted hero-king of the Robin Hood legends—and Edward II were all reputed to have been gay.

❧

Charles II, King James's grandson, was anything but gay. He had a fleet of paramours that help explain his moniker, "The Merry Monarch." He wasn't choosy either, drawing his lovers from all levels of society and siring scads of bastards by them. "A king is supposed to be the father of his people and Charles certainly was father to a good many of them," noted George Villiers, son of the first Duke of Buckingham. Yet while his many mistresses bore him lots of children, his queen, alas, could not. With no legitimate heir to succeed Charles upon his death, the crown passed to his brother, James II, in 1685.

❧

Before she married and became half of the William and Mary comonarchy, James II's eldest daughter was a princess desperately in love—with another girl. She was Frances Apsley, the beautiful daughter of the king's hawks keeper and nine years Mary's senior. In her long string of passionate letters, the princess called Frances "Aurelia" and addressed her as "Husband."

"You shall hear from me every quarter of an hour if it were possible," Mary gushed in one letter, exclaiming in another that "all the paper books in the world would not hold half the love I have for you my dearest, dearest, dear Aurelia." While missives like these were filled with the frothy language of a girlish crush, others made it clear that Mary knew how to get down and dirty. "There is nothing in this heart or breast, guts or bowels, but you shall know it," she wrote, offering at one point to become Frances's "louse in bosom." Some of the letters were almost masochistic in their abasement: "[I am] your humble servant to kiss the ground where you go, to be your dog in a string, your fish in a net, your bird in a cage, your humble trout."

After a while, Mary's deluge of clingy love letters began to make Frances uncomfortable and she started to withdraw. As Frances's letters became more and more infrequent and her manner increasingly distant, Mary went into a desperate frenzy. "Oh have some pity on me and love me again or kill me quite with your unkindness for I cannot live with you in indifference, dear dearest loving kind charming obliging sweet dear Aurelia." Subtle she was not.

Her desperation grew worse when she heard the news that she was to be married to her cold, asthmatic cousin, William of Orange, and sent to live with him in Holland. Mary wept nonstop for a day and a half, lamenting her fate and loss of her "dear dearest Aurelia." Of course she eventually got over it, learning to love her wheezy mildly hunchbacked husband and helping him to usurp her father's throne in 1688.

❧

When Mary's sister Queen Anne died in 1714 with no surviving children, a relatively distant number of the royal family was imported from Germany to rule as King George I. Thus arrived the new House of Hanover, whose members would establish themselves as among the most wanton monarchs ever to rule Britain. No sooner had the English taken stock of their new king than they began to laugh at him. It was not just the fact that George I spoke barely a word of English nor his bizarre entourage and strange German customs. It was his penchant for fat and ugly mistresses.

Two of the most famous came over from Hanover with the king. To be fair, only one of these was grossly obese; the other was exceedingly thin. They were dubbed "The Maypole" and "Elephant and Castle." The essayist Horace Walpole recalled meeting the fat one—whom King George had given the title Countess of Darlington—when he was a young boy and being terrified of her enormous bulk: "Two fierce black eyes, large and rolling beneath two lofty arched eyebrows, two acres of cheeks spread with crimson, an ocean of neck that overflowed and was not distinguished from the lower part of her body, and no part restrained by a stay . . . no wonder that a child dreaded such an ogress, and that the mob of London were highly diverted at the importation of so uncommon a sergalio!"

Lord Chesterfield was particularly vicious in his assessment of King George's peccadillos: "The standard of His Majesty's taste, as exemplified in his mistresses, makes all ladies who aspire to his favour . . . strain and swell themselves, like the frogs in the fable, to rival the bulk and dignity of the ox. Some succeed, and others . . . burst."

The king's son, George II, inherited his father's tastes as well as his crown. "No woman came amiss to him," one contemporary snorted, "if she were but very willing and very fat." His queen, Caroline of Ansbach, shared the second George's lascivious interests, sometimes even arranging dalliances for him, but always making sure that any mistress she selected was uglier than she. When he was away visiting his Hanoverian homeland, the king always made sure he kept his wife apprised of his sexual exploits. Some of his letters, graphically detailing every conquest, reached thirty pages long! One paramour, Madame von Walmoden, so attracted the king that he determined to bring her back to England with him. "You must love Walmoden, for she loves me," he excitedly wrote the queen.

The British people had almost as much fun at this king's expense as they had at his father's. On one occasion, a beaten-down old horse was turned loose in the streets of London bearing a placard that read: "Let nobody stop me. I am the King's Hanover equipage going to fetch His Majesty and his whore to England."

⟨⟩

With his dull and dutiful monogamy, King George III set an entirely different tone from that of his two predecessors—except during his periodic bouts of madness.[3] Then he would shock those around him with his filthy mouth and unbridled libido, chasing terrified ladies of the court and begging them for sex. Ordinarily, though, George was a prude who thoroughly disapproved of the behavior of his large brood of dissolute sons. "They are the damndest millstones round the neck of any Government that can be imagined," the Duke of Wellington once said of them.

At one point, the boys, who included the future kings George IV and William IV, had given George III fifty-seven grandchildren—fifty-six of them bastards. William was by far the busiest. Before he finally settled down and married, the prince had fallen in love with an actress named Mrs. Dorothy Jordon, with whom he had ten children. They all lived together in domestic harmony until it became increasingly obvious that he would inherit the throne of his overindulged brother, George IV, and would have to marry an acceptable wife.

---

[3]The king's illness is examined in Part VI, Chapter 5.

As it was not expected that William would ever be king, he was never trained in the fine arts of courtly manners deemed necessary in a monarch. His boorish behavior sharply reflected this oversight. Writing his brother from the family's homeland of Hanover in 1785, William complained about the lack of suitable women with whom to have affairs. He was, he said, forced to perform "with a lady of the town against a wall or in the middle of the parade." He further added that he loathed "this damnable country, smoking, playing at twopenny whist, and wearing great big boots. Oh, for England and the pretty girls of Westminster; at least to such as would not clap or pox me every time I fucked."

William IV's successor and niece, Queen Victoria, may have left her name to an era of sexual repression and rigid morality in the nineteenth century, but within her marriage she was apparently quite the coquette. It was her husband, Prince Albert, who was actually the prude. Certainly her journal entries following her honeymoon give every indication that Victoria had enjoyed herself. Tremendously: "I NEVER NEVER spent such an evening!!! My DEAREST DEAREST DEAR Albert sat on a footstool by my side, and his excessive love and affection gave me feelings of heavenly love and happiness, I never could have *hoped* to have felt before! He clasped me in his arms, and we kissed each other again and again! His beauty, his sweetness and gentleness . . . really how can I ever be thankful enough for such a *Husband*!

"*His* love and gentleness is beyond everything," the gushing queen continued, "and to kiss that dear soft cheek, to press my lips to his, is heavenly bliss . . . Oh! was ever woman so blessed as I am!" Of course there's nothing remotely scandalous in these sweet passages written by a passionate woman so obviously in love. It's just fun to note that they came from such a notorious sourpuss, famous for her critique of a comedy she once attended: "We are *not* amused."

⚜

Victoria's great-grandson, Edward VIII, gave up his throne in 1936 to marry "the woman I love." That she was a screeching harridan bent on emasculating him didn't bother him a bit. In fact, he seems to have rather enjoyed it.

Historians have struggled for years to understand just what it was about Wallis Warfield Simpson that would make a king surrender his throne for her. The twice-divorced American was no beauty and, truth be told, something of a shrew. One of the more absurd theories put forth was that Mrs. Simpson practiced on Edward mysterious sexual techniques she had picked up in a Chinese brothel.

What appears most likely, though, is that he got a sexual charge out of being controlled and dominated by a strong woman. Ulick Alexander, a courtier close to the king, described him as being possessed by "the sexual perversion of self-abasement." Freda Dudley Ward, a former lover agreed. "I could have dominated him if I had wanted to. I could have done *anything* with him! Love bewitched him. He made himself the slave of whomever he loved and became totally dependent on her. It was his nature; he was a masochist. He *liked* being humbled, degraded. He *begged* for it!"

If this is what Edward really wanted, he found the perfect mate in Wallis. With her brash personality and sharp tongue, she treated the former king sometimes as an unruly child and other times with undisguised contempt, often reducing him to tears. "God, that woman's a bitch," Edward's friend, Edward "Fruity" Metcalfe, exclaimed after the abdication. "She'll play hell with him before long."

And indeed she did.

A group of dinner guests witnessed a particularly ugly scene, later related to Edward's biographer, Philip Ziegler. During the meal, the Duke of Windsor (his official title after the abdication) asked the butler to give the chauffeur a message about his needs for the following day. Hearing this, the duchess raised her hands high in the air and slammed them down on the table with a terrible crash. The guests were stunned into silence. "Never," she hissed, "never again will you give orders in my house!" Regaining her composure, she then turned to her neighbor at the table and tried to explain herself. "You see," she said, "the duke is in charge of everything that happens outside the house and I on the inside." Edward, meanwhile, sat quietly in his place, muttering incoherent apologies. He was used to this kind of treatment from her, having received it even before they were married. His equerry, John Aird, noted during the courtship that he "has lost all confidence in himself and follows W[allis] around like a dog." She led him to a life of stunning vacuity.[4]

---

[4]Just how vacuous is seen in Part II, Chapter 6.

PART II

Six Royals Sinning

While lust played a prominent role in the scandalous lives of royalty, the other deadly sins were by no means neglected. On the contrary, envy, pride, wrath, gluttony, covetousness, and sloth each were eagerly embraced by generations of royals—some of whom gave the vices a unique spin.

George IV: "A voluptuary under the horrors of digestion."

1

Envy: If Anyone Should Oppose This Union

Spinsterhood suited Elizabeth I just fine.[1] She loved being queen of England far too much to share her power with a man, as she would have been expected to do if she married. She much preferred to rule on her own and became one of Britain's greatest monarchs. "I am married to England," she was fond of proclaiming. But as much as Elizabeth gloried in the cult of the "Virgin Queen" that she encouraged to flourish around her, she bitterly resented any of the women in her service getting something she never would—namely, a fulfilling sex life. She was "angry with love," as Sir Edward Stafford later observed.

While it was considered a major social coup to be one of the queen's carefully selected ladies-in-waiting, these advantageous positions came at a hefty price. The women were expected to live like Elizabeth. This meant early exercise, long hours, and lonely nights. If any of them wished to marry, they had to obtain the queen's permission first. And this blessing was rarely granted without a series of grudging obstacles put into place by the jealous monarch. One couple had to wait nearly a decade before Elizabeth finally relented and let them wed.

---

[1] As explained in Part I, Chapter 3.

In another instance, young Mistress Arundel was foolish enough to remark to the queen that she favored a man and would marry him if only she could get her father's permission. To the surprise of those present, the queen benevolently answered, "You seem honest, in faith, and I will sue for you to your father." The girl, elated to have such a powerful advocate on her side, was convinced that her father could never deny her now. And sure enough, Sir Robert Arundel was called before the queen and eagerly gave his consent. Content, Elizabeth dismissed him, saying, "I will do the rest."

Mistress Arundel was then summoned and told that her father's cooperation had been obtained. "Then I shall be happy, and if it please Your Grace," the delighted girl replied in the belief that Elizabeth was about to grant her the husband of her choice. "So thou shalt, but not to be a fool and marry," the queen answered, a bitter edge rising in her voice. "I have his consent given to me and I vow thou shalt never get it into thy possession. I see thou art a bold one to own thy foolishness so readily." With this withering surprise, the stunned girl was waved away from the queen's presence.

Getting Elizabeth's seal of approval was difficult, but woe to the woman who risked bypassing the process altogether. When Mary Shelton secretly wed James Scudamore, the queen flew into such a rage upon hearing the news that in throttling her, she broke the bride's little finger. "No one ever bought her husband more dearly," remarked Eleanor Bridge, except possibly Elizabeth's cousin Katherine Grey, sister of the ill-fated "Nine Days Queen," Jane Grey.[2]

---

[2]Jane Grey's tragic career is examined in Part IV, Chapter 2.

Katherine Grey had been fortunate to not only have survived the executions of her sister and father with her reputation intact— albeit under reduced financial circumstances—but also to have found a prominent place in the court of "Bloody" Mary I, who had ordered the beheadings. There were no hard feelings and Katherine settled right in. But when Mary's sister Elizabeth came to the throne in 1558, Katherine's position at court was reduced somewhat. The new queen simply did not like her cousin, finding her arrogant and obnoxious. As a result, she rarely granted Katherine access to her royal person. Nevertheless, she kept a close eye on her. According to Henry VIII's will, Katherine was next in line to inherit the throne if Elizabeth failed to have children, and in such a position, she merited watching.

Proud as she was of her Tudor lineage, Katherine Grey inherited very little of that royal family's notable intelligence. While in the service of the queen she fell in love with Edward Seymour, son and namesake of the Lord Protector who had been beheaded for treason during the reign of his nephew and Elizabeth's brother, Edward VI. The two children of disgraced and executed fathers unwisely commenced a clandestine affair and eventually decided to marry in secret. On the day of the planned nuptials, Katherine and her future sister-in-law, Jane, claimed they were ill and thus were excused from accompanying the queen on a hunting trip scheduled for that day.

As soon as Elizabeth had ridden out of sight, the two women stole away from the palace and made their way under cover to Edward Seymour's home on the banks of the Thames River. There Katherine and Edward were privately married. The only witnesses were Jane and a clergyman borrowed from Westminster Abbey to officiate. In their haste to be wed, they forgot to ask his name. After a brief celebration that Katherine was too nervous to enjoy, the bride and her accomplice slipped back to the palace undetected. Incredibly, the wedding was kept secret for months. But then Jane died suddenly, and a month later Edward Seymour was sent on a diplomatic mission to France.

Soon after, Katherine discovered she was pregnant. With her secret husband away in France and the only witness to her wedding dead—the other being unknown—the poor woman went into a panic. It didn't help matters that she had lost the deed of jointure that made her marriage official. At a loss over what to do, she disclosed her secret to a woman of the court named Lady Saintlow. Knowing the queen as well as she did, Lady Saintlow berated Katherine not only for her stupidity but for telling her and thus putting *her* at risk. In a frightened rage, she ordered Katherine out of her chambers. Now almost hysterical with fear, Katherine went to the quarters of the queen's favorite, Robert Dudley, begging him to intercede for her. Aware that Elizabeth could burst into his room at any moment, as she was in the habit of doing, Dudley was eager to pacify the desperate woman and usher her out as quickly as possible. He reassured Katherine that he would do what he could and then sent her away.

Hearing the news from her beloved Dudley did nothing to soften Elizabeth's reaction. She was incensed. Not only had her impudent cousin defied and tricked her, which was bad enough, she was also close to the throne and any marriage within the royal family had to be approved by both Queen and Council. So Katherine's union with Edward Seymour had the additional taint of treason about it. And if Elizabeth begrudged marital bliss, she was even more jealous in protecting her own sovereignty.

Katherine Grey was immediately sent to the Tower of London, followed by Lady Saintlow for failing to reveal the matter when she first heard it. Shortly thereafter Edward Seymour, called back from France, joined them, though in an apartment separate from his wife's. A royal commission bombarded him with questions regarding his "infamous proceedings with the Lady Katherine Grey," but without a witness to the ceremony and the deed of jointure missing, he had little to back up his defiant assertion that it was a lawful union.

Katherine also was questioned, but the commission ceased temporarily when she gave birth to a son on September 21, 1561. Eight months later the resumed commission declared "there had been no marriage between [Seymour] and Lady Katherine Grey," making their son, in effect, a bastard. The little family was ordered to remain in the Tower at the queen's pleasure for their "undue and unlawful carnal copulation," but a sympathetic jailer allowed the couple to meet from time to time. As a result, another baby boy was conceived. Katherine was now beyond all hope of redemption. Though she was eventually released from the Tower and into the custody of her uncle, Lord John Grey, she was never to see her husband again. Bitter and unforgiven, she died of tuberculosis in 1568.

Katherine's dwarfish younger sister Mary apparently learned nothing from her sister's ordeal. In 1565, she secretly married Thomas Keyes, the Sergeant-Porter at court, who towered above her tiny, misshapen frame. "Here is the most unhappy chance and monstrous," wrote William Cecil, the queen's chief counsellor. "The Sergeant-Porter, being the biggest gentleman at this court, hath secretly married Lady Mary Grey, the least of all the court."

Enraged at being defied now by two cousins, Elizabeth sent Keyes to Fleet Prison and Mary into exile in the country, stating grimly that she would have "no little bastard Keyes" running around. After being widowed, Mary was allowed back at court, where she continued defiantly to sign her name "Mary Keyes." She died in 1578, unmourned by the perpetually single Queen Elizabeth I.

2

Pride: Here Comes the Sun King

*B*eing royal required a certain faith in one's inherent superiority over ordinary men. Few monarchs lacked it. Next to Louis XIV of France, though, even the most self-enamored of sovereigns came off looking neurotically insecure by comparison. In fact, Louis refused to be grouped with other kings under the term "Their Majesties" because, he explained, from that there might be deduced "an equality which does not exist."

For most of his seventy-two-year-reign (from 1643 to 1715, the longest in European history), Louis worked methodically to have all the glory and prestige of France embodied in himself. "I am the State," he proudly declared—even if the state needed six-inch heels to look taller. As an absolute monarch, Louis dictated nearly every facet of French life according to his own rarefied vision of how it should be. Nothing escaped his attention, from the national religion to tree maintenance. He even mandated a twenty-five-step itinerary to be followed by visitors to the gardens of Versailles. It was all about Louis.

Under him, there was no room for opposition. He and he alone decided what was good and what was right. "The subjugation of a monarch to the law of his people," he said, "is the last calamity which can befall a gentleman of our rank." Laws were initiated, aggressive wars pursued, and art and literature commissioned—all designed to make Louis look good. "My dominant passion is certainly love of glory," he once admitted.

For the royal emblem, Louis XIV adopted the sun because, as he explained in his *Memoirs*, "The unique quality of the brilliance which surrounds it, the light it communicates to other heavenly bodies which compose a kind of Court around it, the just and even allotment of its light among all the various tropics of the world, the good it does everywhere, endlessly producing on all sides life, joy, activity, its uninterrupted movement despite an always tranquil appearance, its constant and invariable path, from which it is never drawn or diverted, is assuredly the most beautiful and vivid image of a great monarch."

The "Sun King" put himself on dazzling display at Versailles, where in 1682 he permanently moved his court and the seat of government. The palace itself was designed to be a glittering reflection of its most regal inhabitant and everyone was welcome to come and observe him in his daily, unwavering routine. Onlookers were on hand every morning when the king arose, got dressed, and shaved. At meals, they could marvel at his dexterity with an egg as he clipped off the top with just one quick stroke of the spoon. A very privileged few even got to watch him as he sat perched on his *other* throne when nature called. "What price does even the most repulsive thing that comes from the king have in this country?" asked a shocked visitor from Italy after observing this unusual access.

The writer Jean de La Bruyere described how Louis worshiped at Mass under the adoring gaze of his subjects: "The great of the nation meet each day at a certain time in a temple called church . . . they form a vast circle at the foot of the altar, standing with their backs to the priest and the holy mysteries, their faces lifted toward their king, who can be seen kneeling at a tribune . . . one cannot help noticing in his usage a sort of subordination; for the people seem to be adoring the prince, who is adoring God."

Louis XIV was a genius at making Versailles appear to be the pinnacle of prestige and honor for the thousands of nobles who lived there, with himself as the radiant center of it all. In this way the king utterly obliterated their ancient power by having them chase the artificial gold that he created and dangled before them. The once mighty aristocracy fought for the honor of cramped rooms, handing the king his shirt in the morning, holding a candle for him, or accompanying him on a hunt.

Louis created hundreds of meaningless posts that the nobility were eager to snatch up at enormous costs, yet even he was surprised at how successful this venture became. "Who will buy them?" the king once asked his Minister of Finance, Desmarets, who wanted to create even more artificial offices. "Your Majesty ignores one of the finest prerogatives of the king of France," Desmarets replied, "which is that when a King creates an office God instantly creates a fool to buy it."

A rigid and highly nuanced code of etiquette flourished at Versailles, designed to flatter the nobility into worshipful and grateful complacency. People were thrilled to be granted the privilege to sit in the king's presence rather than stand, or to have him doff his hat at certain angles, which designated various levels of favor. "He substituted ideal rewards for real ones," wrote the Duc de Saint-Simon, an avid court observer and participant, "and these operated through jealousy, the petty preferences he showed many times a day, and his artfulness in showing them." One of the most coveted marks of favor was an invitation to the king's more intimate residence at Marley. According to Saint-Simon, "it was a crime not to ask for Marley either always or often, although this did not mean they would obtain it."

While Louis operated using an elaborate code of flattery toward the nobility, he demanded it for himself as well. He was surrounded by a sea of sycophants as a result. "Soon after he became master, his ministers, his generals, his mistresses and his courtiers noticed that he had a weakness for, rather than a love of, glory," Saint-Simon wrote. "They spoiled him with praise. Commendation and flattery pleased him to such a point that the most obvious compliments were received kindly and the most insidious were relished even more. It was the only way to approach him, and those who won his love knew it well and never tired of praising him. That is why his ministers were so powerful, for they had more opportunities to burn incense before him, attribute every success to him, and vow they had learned everything from him. The only way to please him was submissiveness, baseness, an air of admiring and crawling toadyism, and by giving the impression that he was the only source of wisdom."

And the ranks of the obsequious were legion. There was, for example, the subject who responded, when Louis asked for the time: "Whatever time Your Majesty desires." Or his son, the Duc du Maine, who said to his father after a long military campaign, "Ah, Sire, I will never learn anything. My tutor grants me a holiday each time you win a victory." Then there was the Superintendent of Buildings, the Duc d'Antin, who placed wedges under the statues at Versailles so the king would notice they were askew and d'Antin would get the chance to praise him for his keen perception.

The aura of majesty was so intoxicating that basking in it took absurd forms. When Louis suffered from a fistula, a deep ulcer of the rectum that required surgery, the ailment became ultra-chic and those fortunate enough to share the *operation du Roi* were much envied. The surgery carried so much prestige, in fact, that men without fistulas begged and bribed doctors to perform the procedure on them anyway—an entirely new spin on the fine art of kissing ass.

3

Wrath: Have an Ice Day

Indignatio principis mors est. The anger of the prince means death. Over the centuries countless executions by royal order proved this warning to be absolutely true. But with Empress Anna of Russia, the anger of the sovereign meant something else entirely: excruciating humiliation. This early eighteenth-century monarch had a knack for conjuring up the most embarrassing of punishments when she was displeased. In one case, three nobles who had managed to get on the empress's bad side were condemned to live like hens for a week. Dressed in feathers and made to roost in specially outfitted nests—complete with eggs— the unfortunate gentlemen were ordered to sit and cluck until the sentence was complete.

This was mild compared to the ordeal another noble, Prince Michael Alexsyevitch Golitsin, had to face. He had the nerve to marry a woman not to Anna's liking, and this made her angry. So angry, in fact, that she stripped him of his title and transformed the erstwhile aristocrat into a court jester. But this was just the beginning. When the wife he had chosen for himself died in 1740, Anna decided it was her turn to select a mate for him. She chose a woman who was reportedly one of the ugliest ladies in Russia. For the wedding party, Anna dug into her collection of deformed and freakish human beings to lead a procession of drunkards and other low lifes, all pulled in carriages by goats and pigs. The happy couple followed, in a cage, as the crowds gathered to watch.

After the wedding ceremony and breakfast reception, it was time for the honeymoon—no doubt one of the chilliest on record. The spot Anna had selected for them was right on the banks of the frozen Neva River. Her wedding present was a palace there made entirely of ice. It was a huge structure, complete with a honeymoon suite that included an ice bed and ice pillows. Outside, ice statues and ice trees were carved, with little ice birds perched upon them. There were even six ice cannons that actually fired. As the wedding party cheered them on, the newlyweds were forced inside the ice palace and ordered to bed down and consummate the marriage. Somehow they did, despite the frigid temperature.

Nine months later, ornery old Anna was dead. At about the same time, Golitsin's wife presented him with twin boys. Despite the circumstances of their less-than-fairy-tale union, it was said that the couple did in fact live happily ever after.

4

Gluttony: Eat, Drink, and Be Mocked

*G*eorge IV was a man of great wit and impeccable taste—a bon vivant noted for his elegant style, keen eye for fine art and architecture, and inclination toward grand generosity and warm amiability. Nevertheless, this early nineteenth-century British monarch was the perpetual target of savage lampoons and public ridicule. He could rarely ride out of the palace in his carriage without being hooted and jeered on the streets of London.

Some of the invective had to do with his shameless extravagance and enormous debts, his obvious greed for his sick father's throne, the undue credit he claimed for the British victory over Napoleon, and his flaunted love affairs and spectacularly disastrous marriage.[1] But it was George's status as an obese slob who drank too much—often spiking his liquor with heaping doses of laudanum—that inspired some of the most howling derision. Though he wasn't the fattest monarch ever to strain the British throne,[2] he was almost certainly the booziest—charming and dignified when sober; everything but, when drunk.

---

[1]George's hellish marriage is detailed in Part III, Chapter 5.
[2]Queen Anne, for one, was so obese that she had to be carried at her coronation because her legs couldn't support her.

He was still a young prince when his drinking started taking its toll on his appearance, giving him a premature look of dissipation and generating snickers among his subjects. His behavior at a ball given by Lady Hopetoun in 1787 was typical of his early carousing. According to one account, he "posted himself in the doorway, to the terror of everybody that went by, flung his arms round the Duchess of Ancaster's neck and kissed her with a great *smack*, threatened to pull Lord Galloway's wig off and knock out his false teeth, and played all the pranks of a drunken man upon the stage, till some of his companions called for his carriage, and almost forced him away."

Had he been a more popular prince, that kind of scene might have been thought delightfully eccentric or sympathetically ignored. But George was widely disliked, and his critics pounced on his all too apparent weaknesses. The *Times* of London condemned him as a hard-drinking, swearing, whoring man "who at all times would prefer a girl and a bottle to politics and a sermon," and whose only states of happiness were "gluttony, drunkenness, and gambling."

One of the most scathing images of the prince was the widely distributed caricature by James Gillray, portraying him as "a voluptuary under the horrors of digestion." George is shown picking his teeth with a fork as he recovers from an enormous meal, his guts bursting out of his trousers. Beneath his fat thighs are empty wine bottles and behind him are medicines for "the piles," "for stinking breath," and two contemporary cures for venereal disease, "Veno's Vegetable Syrup" and "Leeke's Pills."

If this ridicule wasn't enough, friends and family added to it with their own indictments. After one memorable binge, George's only (legitimate) child, Princess Charlotte, cracked that "too much oil was put into the lamp." And his tenuous friendship with the famous dandy of the period, Beau Brummell,

crashed to a mortifying public end at a ball
boring a lingering resentment over Brummell
to show proper deference to his royal person
mutual friend, Lord Alvanely, but pointedly ign
"Alvanely," the rebuffed Brummell shouted ad   ...oom,
"who is your fat friend?"

In an earlier era, heads would have rolled for such audacious
disrespect, but George presided over a monarchy—first as Prince
Regent during his father, George III's, mental incapacity, then as
king—that had been slowly losing its power over the years. As
much as he surely would have loved to order the executions of
his tormentors, there was little George could do to counter their
relentless assault, particularly since they were often right.

When *The Examiner* published a particularly nasty attack on
the Prince Regent in 1812—calling him, among other things, "a
violator of his word, a libertine head over ears in debt" and "a de-
spiser of domestic ties"—he was successful in having the author
and his brother, the paper's editor, arrested and charged "with
intention to traduce and vilify His Royal Highness, the Prince of
Wales, Regent of the United Kingdom." Writer and editor were
fined and jailed, but it was hardly a royal victory as the sentences
only made George more unpopular. It was during this time that
a devastating verse by Charles Lamb made the rounds:

> *Not a fatter fish than he*
> *Flounders round the polar sea.*
> *See his blubbers . . . at his gills*
> *What a world of drink he swills . . .*
> *Every fish of generous kind*
> *Scuds aside or shrinks behind;*
> *But about his presence keep*
> *All the monsters of the deep . . .*

> *Name or title what has he? . . .*
> *Is he Regent of the sea?*
> *By his bulk and by his size,*
> *By his oily qualities,*
> *This (or else my eyesight fails),*
> *This should be the Prince of Whales.*

Things didn't get much better when George became king in 1820, probably because he continued to give his critics fresh ammunition. They had a grand time with the king and his last mistress, Lady Conyngham, including the pamphleteer who distributed this verse:

> *Quaffing their claret, then mingling their lips,*
> *Or tickling the fat about each other's hips.*

A lifetime of debauchery started wrecking the king's body and mind toward the end of his life, and he became a recluse at Windsor Castle. His appetite, however, was little affected. His mode of living now was "really beyond belief," noted Mrs. Arbuthnot, who had chronicled other events in the life of the king. The Duke of Wellington was a frequent visitor at Windsor and noted the king's breakfast menu one day. He had "a pidgeon and beef steak pie of which he ate two pigeons and three beef-steaks, three parts of a bottle of Mozelle, a glass of dry champagne, two classes of port [and] a glass of brandy! He had taken laudanum the night before, again before this breakfast, again last night and again this morning." Not surprisingly, George IV died not long after.

It had been a life of great potential never realized, of appetites out of control. Of course the critics had the last word. "There never was an individual less regretted by his fellow-creatures than this deceased King," the *Times* of London editorialized the day after his funeral. "What eye has wept for him? What heart has heaved one throb of unmercenary sorrow ... for that Leviathan of the *haut ton*, George IV."

5

Covetousness: Hail Mary, Full of Greed

The kings of Spain once plundered the New World in their quest for gold. Britain's Queen Mary plundered living rooms. This early twentieth-century consort of King George V was quite a collector. Though she favored valuable little knickknacks and objects d'art, she didn't like paying for them. Mary had other ways of getting what she wanted and no home she visited was safe from her acquisitive glare.

"I am caressing it with my eyes," she would coyly whisper upon spotting a particular item she wanted, while lingering before it for added effect. This little routine was often enough for the owner in awe of royalty to insist immediately that she have it. But for those who didn't quite get the message, the marauding queen went a step further. Just before leaving the targeted home, Mary would make a dramatic pause at the doorstep and ask, "May I go back and say goodbye to that dear little [fill in the blank of whatever it was she wanted that day]?" With this less than subtle hint, the predatory queen usually got her prize. There were occasions, however, when actually paying became the only option left. If she happened to leave a home empty-handed, her thank-you note often included a request to purchase the coveted piece. Few could resist this final assault.

As Queen Mary's collection grew ever larger, those who regularly hosted her began to take precautions whenever she came for a visit. Anything they thought the queen might like was stashed away until the royal assault was over. Not everyone fell for the queen's charms, however. When she was collecting miniature items for her elaborate dollhouse, she persuaded famous authors of the time to donate tiny volumes of their works. A whole library was assembled, with one holdout. George Bernard Shaw rebuffed the queen's request, noted her daughter, "in a very rude manner." Basically he told her where she could stick her little book.

6

Sloth: An Idle Mind Is the Duchess's Playground

*I*f Edward VIII really was in cahoots with the Nazis, as has been alleged, it would prove that at least he was doing *something* after his abdication of the British throne in 1936. As it stands, however, the rumors of collaboration are almost certainly untrue, making the ex-king's life every bit as idle and vacuous as it appeared.

Led by his gasping, domineering duchess[1]—the woman for whom he set aside his crown to marry—the Duke of Windsor, as he was titled after the abdication, adopted a lifestyle almost totally devoid of purpose. His main preoccupation was social flitting with his wife between New York, Paris, and Palm Beach, always courting the rich and absorbing their hospitality. The only real responsibility the duke seemed willing to shoulder was the care and feeding of the couple's pet pugs.

He had given up the only job he was born to do, but he had nothing to replace it. Still, Edward insisted on retaining all of his royal dignity and prerequisites, and those he expected for his wife. The servants wore liveried uniforms, while portraits of the

---

[1]Wallis Warfield Simpson is introduced in Part 1, Chapter 3.

duke and duchess hung amidst those of his royal ancestors in their meticulously decorated homes and apartments. Without a kingdom to rule, Edward and Wallis presided over a small fiefdom of servants, chauffeurs, and cooks.

If Edward ever did expend any real energy—aside from his perpetual efforts to wring money out of the British government—it was in his almost obsessive desire to have Wallis granted a royal title. This had been refused her when she married Edward—sensibilities at the time utterly opposed to the brash, twice-divorced American from Baltimore being styled "Her Royal Highness." It was a snub bitterly resented by Edward and one that he never ceased trying to remedy.

His persistence on the issue drove deeper the wedge between the duke and his family—a relationship that was already strained because of the abdication crisis and the royal family's refusal to receive Wallis. "I cannot tell you how grieved I am at your brother being so tiresome about the HRH [Her Royal Highness]," Edward's mother Queen Mary wrote his brother George VI, who had ascended the throne in his place. "Giving *her* this title would be fatal, and after all these years I fear lest people think that we condone this dreadful marriage which was such a blow to us in every way."

Even as Britain was bravely facing Hitler's devastating onslaught during World War II and Buckingham Palace was being bombed, the former king was badgering the government and the royal family about the title he coveted for his wife. Taking time out from leading the nation's war effort, Prime Minister Winston Churchill offered the Duke a bit of advice on the issue. "Having voluntarily resigned the finest Throne in the world," Churchill wrote, "it would be natural to treat all minor questions of ceremony and precedence as entirely beneath your interest and your dignity."

Alas, it was not.

Vigorously pursuing the HRH issue was about as busy as Edward ever got during the war, which, sadly enough, was probably the most active period of his post-abdication career. He did serve as governor of the Bahamas during this time. With a world at war, this was not one of the most taxing assignments, yet Edward found it so unpalatable that he asked for a leave soon after he had arrived. It was August, after all, not the most pleasant month to settle on a tropical island. Churchill found the request for leave a tad premature. He was "very grieved to hear that you are entertaining such an idea," Walter Monckton wrote Edward. The prime minister hoped that, when the people of Britain were suffering so much, the duke "would be willing to put up with the discomfort and remain at your post until weather conditions made things less unpleasant."

Edward did reluctantly come around to his patriotic duty, but insisted that the accommodations in the Bahamas were unacceptable in their current state. "We found Government House quite uninhabitable," the duke told his friend and predecessor as governor, Bede Clifford, "and fled from the place after a week's picnic and sandflies." The money allotted for the home's upgrading was insufficient, Edward informed Colonial Secretary George Lloyd, and he requested additional funds to whip it into shape. Churchill's response to the request was succinct. "Comment is needless," he jotted on the memo.

After their grueling experience in the Bahamas, Edward and Wallis felt themselves entitled to a little leisure after the war. They spent the rest of their lives drowning in it. A typical day for the Duke consisted of a few rounds of golf, weather permitting, maybe a nap, then a drink—but never before 4 P.M. His main job was passing the duchess's orders to the help, or meekly following them himself, as she busily arranged for that evening's dinner and social activities.

In a moment of perhaps unintentional honesty, Edward revealed the sheer emptiness of his life. "You know what my day was today?" he said to the wife of an American diplomat. "I got up late, and then I went with the Duchess and watched her buy a hat, and then on the way home I had the car drop me in the Bois to watch some of your soldiers playing football, and then I planned to take a walk, but it was so cold that I could hardly bear it . . . When I got home the Duchess was having her French lesson, so I had no one to talk to, so I got a lot of tin boxes down which my mother had sent me last week and looked through them. They were essays and so on that I had written when I was in France studying French before the Great War . . . You know, I'm not much of a reading man."

PART III

Unholy Matrimony

Among royalty, love and marriage rarely went together like a horse and carriage—more like a mongoose and cobra. All too often royal unions were coldly calculated political arrangements, with some couples not even meeting until the wedding ceremony. If one did have a choice of mate, the desire to wed was not always mutual. Kings had a way with coercion, and woe to his queen when he became bored. The following is a selection of royalty's most miserable marriages.

Joanna the Mad still obsessing over Philip the Fair.

1

Mad About You

He was a dashing prince, heir to vast territories across Europe. They called him "Philip the Handsome," although "Philip the Heel" would have worked just as well. He treated his wife like a royal rash. She was the striking daughter of Spain's legendary co-monarchs, Ferdinand and Isabella. They called her "Joanna the Mad." Indeed, she was crazy about her husband—absolutely *nuts*, it turned out. Together, Joan and Phil forged one of the more pathetic unions in European royal history, where sexual dominance and relentless obsession endured to the grave—and well beyond.

As far as arranged royal marriages went, this one looked promising. Philip found Joanna quite alluring when he first saw her in 1496, a perk not to be underestimated in an era when strangers were wed to strangers without the slightest regard to compatibility. For her part, Joanna was immediately entranced by Philip's good looks and charm. Their first meeting went so well, in fact, that Philip insisted the wedding ceremony be arranged right away so he could bed his bride without delay.

Apparently the sex was fantastic and Joanna, who had been raised in the court of her ultra-conservative Catholic parents, was intoxicated. Philip, on the other hand, was a typical royal male who felt no particular allegiance to the marital bed. As Philip roamed, Joanna became more and more despondent. She breathed only for him, ignoring even the religious devotions that had once sustained her. Her neediness, however, only served to bring out Philip's inherent nastiness. He parceled out sex to his grateful wife, alternating it with threats of violence to subjugate her further. Joanna's familiar Spanish staff was sent away, and she was left isolated in Philip's hostile Flemish court. She was too paranoid even to write her parents.

Hopelessly in love and living in fear, Joanna was her husband's virtual prisoner. She was also becoming a bit unbalanced. Her maternal grandmother had died insane and Joanna, always dark and moody, was now exhibiting similar symptoms. Her plunge into madness was marked by one particularly disturbing episode in 1503. She and Philip had come to Spain so that Joanna could be sworn in as heir to her mother's kingdom of Castile. Philip, however, decided he hated his wife's homeland and promptly announced he was returning to his kingdom in the Low Countries (modern-day Belgium and the Netherlands).

Pregnant with their fourth child, Joanna was in no condition to travel. So while her beloved took off, she was stuck in Spain and miserable about it. Increasingly morose and withdrawn, she wept constantly and refused to eat. Even the birth of a healthy son failed to drag Joanna out of her neurotic malaise.

Then one night she simply lost it.

Barefoot, half-dressed, and raving, Joanna ran out of the castle where she was lodged, wailing in agony. Though the November night was freezing, she refused warm clothing and ignored desperate pleas to come back inside. Dressed only in her flimsy nightgown, she stayed out in the cold for thirty-six hours, clinging to the castle gates and hurling obscene insults at anyone who dared approach her. Though she was eventually coaxed back inside, the damage was done. As word of her behavior spread, "Juana la Loca" was on everyone's lips.

The strain was beginning to take its toll on her mother, Queen Isabella. Although this formidable monarch oversaw the Spanish Inquisition and cosponsored Columbus's voyages to the New World, her difficult daughter left her cowed. "She spoke to me very rudely," the queen wrote her ambassador in Flanders, "with such contempt and lack of respect that if I had not been aware of her mental condition, I would not have tolerated it in any way." Joanna was literally making her mother sick. "We believe that the Queen's life is endangered by her contact with Madame Princess," Isabella's doctors wrote King Ferdinand. "We pray that the fire that consumes [Joanna] disappears. Her life and condition has long affected the life and health of our Queen and Ladyship."

Meanwhile, back in Flanders, Philip, enjoying the extended respite from his clinging wife, was not pleased by the news of her impending return. His dread was soon confirmed when Joanna came home and went on a rampage with a pair of scissors. She attacked a young woman she suspected of sleeping with Philip, cutting off the poor woman's blond hair and slashing at her face. Fed up with his unstable spouse, Philip had her locked up in the apartments of his Brussels palace where it was rumored he took to slapping her around. He called her "the terror." She called him "the fairest of all husbands."

Not long after, in 1504, Queen Isabella died and Joanna and Philip were proclaimed the new rulers of Castile. Philip, however, died suddenly at age twenty-eight. Some suspected he was the victim of a poisoning plot by King Ferdinand of Aragon, who never was too fond of his son-in-law and certainly didn't want to share any power with him. Now Joanna really flipped. Plunged into deep despair, she refused to leave her dead husband's side. Jealous as ever of other women, she forbade any female to approach the corpse. Periodically, she would order

Philip's casket opened so that she might embrace his decaying remains.

Resolving to move the body for final burial, the grieving new queen commanded that the funeral train travel only at night because, she said, "a widow who has lost the sun of her own soul should never expose herself to the light of day." One night the procession came to rest at a convent, but Joanna didn't want any women near her man—even if they were nuns. She ordered the coffin taken from the monastery and out to the open fields, where she slept beside it all night.

A monk once told the grieving queen that her beloved husband would come back to life in fourteen years. Eager to believe him, Joanna waited patiently, but when the allotted time came and went with Philip still moldering in his casket, her mental condition deteriorated further. The demented behavior eventually became too much, and Joanna was confined in a Spanish castle until her death in 1555. Her legacy of madness, however, lived on, infiltrating her Habsburg descendants for generations to come.[1]

---

[1] That terrible legacy is detailed in Part VI, Chapter 2.

2

Until Divorce or Decapitation Do Us Part
(in Six Sections)

Katherine of Aragon

Living with Henry VIII was no picnic for the six women unfortunate enough to become his wives. And severed heads weren't necessarily the worst of it. Getting dumped after nearly twenty years of marriage was bad enough for Henry's first wife, Katherine of Aragon, but having the husband who once lovingly declared himself "Sir Loyal Heart" turn into a vicious cad devastated her.

The union looked auspicious when it began in 1509, just weeks after the nearly eighteen-year-old Henry became king of England. The young monarch was a vigorous and dazzling romantic who rescued Katherine from the life of misery she had been enduring under his cold and forbidding father, Henry VII.

The youngest daughter of Ferdinand and Isabella (and Joanna the Mad's kid sister), Katherine had come from Spain eight years earlier as the bride of Henry's sickly older brother, Arthur. That marriage ended almost as soon as it began, however, when fifteen-year-old Arthur died in 1502. The young widow was left in agonizing limbo. She was stuck in a strange land with no apparent future. Her father-in-law Henry VII used the poor girl as a pawn in his disputes with her father King Fer-

dinand over her dowry and other matters, depriving Katherine
of an allowance and leaving her nearly destitute. The situation
had grown so desperate that she was prepared to leave England
and become a nun.

Then suddenly it was all over. Henry VII died and his gal-
lant son immediately stepped in to marry his former sister-in-
law, who was six years his senior. It was a love match from the
beginning, with the happy newlyweds soon crowned together at
Westminster Abbey. The endless celebrations surrounding the
new king and queen seemed to usher in a new era of youth, vi-
tality, and Renaissance splendor.

The years that followed were happy for both of them. Henry
had a devoted queen who did everything from sew his shirts to
serve ably as regent while he was away fighting in France.
Katherine had a husband who respected her virtue, learning, and
piety. The marriage was, in the words of the great Dutch scholar
Erasmus, a true example of "harmonious wedlock." Harmonious, that is, until Katherine's looks faded, her girth expanded,
and it became increasingly obvious that she would be barren of
the boys Henry craved to carry on the Tudor family line.

After twenty years of marriage, the king's conveniently malleable conscience suddenly started gnawing at him. Didn't the
Bible clearly state in Leviticus that it was a sin against God for a
man to lie with his brother's widow? (Never mind that another
passage in Deuteronomy encouraged the very same thing.) It
was simple, he concluded. God never recognized the patently
sinful marriage, so it was cursed with only a daughter, Princess
Mary, and in fact never even existed.

But there was something else pricking the king besides his
conscience. He had fallen desperately in love with Katherine's
enchanting lady-in-waiting, Anne Boleyn. Unfortunately, this
dark-eyed lady with the graceful neck and sparkling wit was

withholding her favors until she had a guarantee that Henry would make her queen. Educated in the worldly court of the French King Francis I, Anne was nothing if not savvy. She had seen how quickly Henry discarded his handful of mistresses, including her own sister, so she wasn't about to become just another temporary treat. Henry didn't want this either. He was seeking a new wife who could provide him with legitimate sons as well as a good roll in the sack.

In a series of passionate love letters to Anne, "the woman in the world that I value most," Henry pleaded for patience, "assuring you that henceforth my heart will be dedicated to you alone, and wishing greatly that my body was so too." At the conclusion of another letter, the king's mounting lust was plain, "wishing myself in my sweetheart's arms, whose pretty ducks [breasts] I trust shortly to kiss." Before he could get his ducks in line, however, Henry had to confront an unexpected obstacle. Queen Katherine absolutely refused to step aside. Though she broke down and wept when her adored husband revealed that his suddenly troubled conscience was urging him out of the marriage, she didn't roll over and die. Behind the tears was a dignified determination that would forever alter the course of English history. "I am the king's true and lawful wife," she defiantly proclaimed when it was suggested that she quietly retire to a nunnery.

Katherine of Aragon may have been a submissive wife wishing only to please her man, but she was also a proud princess of Spain who would never willingly hand over her husband to the upstart Boleyn. Nor would the pious queen agree that twenty years of marriage had been a sinful sham in the eyes of the Church, making their daughter Mary a bastard. But there was something else compelling Katherine to stand up and fight. She was still in love with the dashing prince who had fallen in love with her two decades before.

Stunned by the obstinacy of the woman who had always shown herself to be so amenable, Henry realized that shedding his wife would not be so easy. Furthermore, he was confronted with something he had never encountered before—the unwelcome mutterings of a people unhappy with the prospect of seeing their beloved queen displaced. In what may be one of history's more disingenuous public speeches, the king attempted a bit of sixteenth-century spin control.

"If it be adjudged that the Queen is my lawful wife," he pronounced, "nothing will be more pleasant or more acceptable to me, both for the clearness of my conscience, and also for the good qualities and conditions I know her to be in . . . besides her noble parentage she is a woman of most gentleness, humility and buxomness; yea, and of all good qualities pertaining to nobility she is without comparison. . . . So that if I were to marry again, I would choose her above all women. But if it be determined in judgment that our marriage is against God's law, then shall I sorrow, parting from so good a lady and loving companion."

Henry had every intention of parting from the good lady, and concluded his speech on a rather sinister note. He shouted to the crowd that if anyone dared criticize him in the future, they would pay dearly. There was "no head so fine," he warned, that he would "not make it fly." This was a king who had grown accustomed to getting his way.

An ecclesiastical tribunal was convened to determine the validity of Henry's marriage to Katherine. One of the pope's two representatives assigned to hear the case happened to be the king's own chief minister, Cardinal Thomas Wolsey, so Katherine had little chance for a fair hearing. Nevertheless, she did show up to solemnly swear that her brief union with Prince Arthur had never been consummated, and as Henry well knew, she entered the marriage "as a virgin and an immaculate woman."

Falling to her knees, the queen made a dramatic public plea to her powerful husband that would inspire Shakespeare more than eight decades later. "Sir," Katherine began in her strong Spanish accent, "I beseech you for all the love that hath been between us, let me have justice and right, take of me some pity and compassion, for I am a poor woman, and a stranger born out of your dominion. I have no friend and much less indifferent counsel. I flee to you, as to the head of justice within this realm."

After reminding him of their life together, their shared tragedies and joys, Katherine concluded by returning to the heart of the issue. "And when ye had me at first, I take God to my judge, I was a true maid, without touch of man. And whether this be true or no, I put it to your conscience." With that, the proud queen made her way through the silenced crowd and walked out of the trial so clearly biased against her.

Henry never did overtly deny Katherine's declaration of virginity when entering the marriage, but he did allow evidence to be heard that no doubt would have mortified the deeply religious woman if she had hung around the courtroom to hear it. In what amounted to little more than teenage locker room testimony, a succession of witnesses claimed that the late Prince Arthur had indeed bedded his young bride. Sir Anthony Willoughby, for one, testified that he was there both when the prince had taken Katherine to bed and when he emerged from the wedding chamber the next morning. "Willoughby," he recalled Arthur saying, "bring me a cup of ale, for I have been this night in the midst of Spain."

Salacious testimony aside, the tribunal ended without a verdict. King Henry sincerely believed the case would be concluded quickly and that he soon would be able to marry Anne Boleyn, but it was not to be. Cardinal Wolsey may have been the king's man, but he wasn't the only one hearing the case. The other papal legate, Cardinal Lorenzo Campeggio, had come directly from Rome and was under strict orders from Pope Clement VII to delay a verdict at all costs.

The pope's motive was simple. Katherine's powerful nephew (and Joanna the Mad's son), the Habsburg Emperor Charles V,[1] had recently sacked Rome, and the pope was at his mercy. He could not allow the divorce without incurring Charles's wrath. Campeggio, exercising the order to delay, decided that the case was too important to be heard in England and referred it to Rome.

Hoping to be divorced and in bed with Anne by now, Henry was furious to find himself instead stuck in an intolerable position while the pope bided his time. The king was living with his wife and would-be wife in the same household, and none of them was happy about it. Katherine took every opportunity to remind her estranged husband that she was a virgin when she came to the marriage and that the union was true and legal. So relentless was the queen in defending her position that finally Henry exploded in anger. "I am content," he conceded impatiently on the issue of Katherine's maidenhood, "but you are not my wife for all that."

Henry found little relief from Katherine's haranguing in the arms of Anne Boleyn. His intended bride was growing tired of waiting around and didn't hesitate to let Henry know it. After one particularly nasty argument with Katherine, he rushed over to Anne's room where he got an unusually snappish reception. "Did I not tell you that whenever you disputed with the Queen, she was sure to have the upper hand?" Anne burst out. Then she began to cry, wailing that he would eventually return to his wife and leave her with nothing. "I have been waiting long and might in the meanwhile have contracted some advantageous marriage,

---

[1] He was also Charles I of Spain.

out of which I might have had issue, which is the greatest consolation in this world, but alas! Farewell to my time and youth spent to no purpose at all."

This was about all the drama Henry was going to take. A nagging wife and a nagging wife-in-waiting were proving to be too much. The pope had dragged his feet long enough and it was time to show him who was boss in his kingdom. Defying Pope Clement's order to put away Anne while the case was being decided, Henry instead banished Katherine forever from court. "Tell the Queen," he ordered a messenger, "that I do not want any of her goodbyes."

Henry had once been a faithful son of the Church, even receiving the title "Defender of the Faith"[2] from Pope Leo X for his scholarly defense of Rome against the theological attacks of Martin Luther, but he was now a defiant outsider. Threatened with the Church's ultimate punishment, Henry belligerently retorted, "I shall not mind it, for I care not a fig for all his excommunications." The pope could do as he pleased in Rome, the king snarled, "I will do here what I think best."

Henry VIII named himself Supreme Head of the Church in England, and one of his first actions was to secure at long last his divorce. Katherine was ordered to stop referring to herself as "Queen" and adopt the title "Princess Dowager" as she was nothing now but the widow of the dead Prince Arthur. She was also ordered to hand over all her jewels to her supplanter, Anne Boleyn, who had finally gone all the way with Henry and gotten pregnant in the process.

Soon after, the king married Anne and had her crowned Queen of England. This meant that Katherine's defiant use of the same title, and her refusal to acknowledge Henry's new role

---

[2] A title used by British monarchs ever since.

in the English Church, had to be dealt with. She was moved to increasingly desolate places of exile and deprived of any contact with her only child, Mary. Strain and illness were taking their toll as Katherine was battered into submission, but she never broke. She dictated a final letter to her once loving prince: "My most dear Lord, King and husband, the hour of my death approaching . . . I cannot choose, but out of love I bear you, advise you of your soul's health which you ought to prefer before all considerations of the world or flesh whatsoever. For which yet you have cast me into many calamities, and yourself into many troubles . . . I forgive you all, and pray God to do so likewise."

After pleading with Henry to treat their daughter kindly—a plea he ignored—she opened her heart for the last time, revealing just how much she loved the man who had so ruthlessly discarded her. "Lastly, I make this vow, that mine eyes desire you above all things. Farewell." The banished queen died in January 1536, of what was probably cancer, though many people then believed the cause was a broken heart. She would be followed only four months later by Anne Boleyn.

Anne Boleyn

Forbidden fruit tends to lose its flavor after a few bites, and so it was with Anne Boleyn. Though Henry had courted her passionately and defied Rome to marry her, he spit her out mercilessly when, like Katherine of Aragon before her, she failed to give him the son he desired far more than any wife's charms. Furthermore, the fiery temperament and quick tongue the king once found so captivating came across more like a roaring hangover as

Anne struggled to cling to the position that was rapidly slipping away from her. The glistening blade of a French sword would end it all in a very short time.

Anne Boleyn had never been popular with the English people. "The king's whore," they called her; a "naughty paike" [prostitute] who audaciously usurped the place of their adored Queen Katherine. Some were even bold enough to heckle the new queen at her coronation. They mocked, for example, the entwined initials of Henry and Anne that lined the magnificent coronation route. "HA! HA!," they snickered. Even members of her own family resented the haughtiness with which the queen wielded her newly acquired power. Fed up with her biting insults, Anne's powerful uncle, the Duke of Norfolk, began calling her *la grande putain*, the great whore, even as he reaped the vast rewards of her position.

Anne, however, blithely dismissed her enemies, some of them quite powerful. After all, she had the mighty king on her side—or so she thought. "That's how it's going to be," she was fond of saying in reaction to criticism, "however much people may grumble." It became her motto. Another was, "The Most Happy"—an unintentionally ironic choice considering the fate that awaited her when Henry turned on her and had her, quite literally, cut down to size.

Although she had no way of knowing it at the time—and neither did Henry for that matter—Anne Boleyn's fall was actually set into motion when she finally agreed to sleep with the king. Both took it for granted the child that resulted, with whom Anne was pregnant at her coronation, was going to be a boy. So confident were expectations that the official birth announcement, prepared in advance, joyfully proclaimed the blessed arrival of a prince.

It was a devastating surprise, then, when the much anticipated prince turned out to be an unwelcome princess—the future Elizabeth I. Obviously unaware that the child would grow up to embody the glory of Britain, Henry was violently disappointed. In a huff, he canceled a joust planned to celebrate the birth of his son. Had he gone through so much for this? Mesmerizing black eyes and tempestuous nature aside, Anne Boleyn was beginning to look like another Katherine of Aragon—especially when she miscarried a second baby.

Like Katherine before her, Anne was forced to put up with Henry's wandering eye. Unlike her predecessor, though, she was unable to contain her jealousy. She knew queens were disposable. After all, she was now sitting on another's throne. Having been a lady-in-waiting herself, she went ballistic when she found her own lady, Jane Seymour, sitting on her husband's lap. Far from being swayed toward monogamy by his wife's fits of fury, Henry became even more adamant about enjoying himself in any way he desired. There was a time when Anne's passionate temper had served as an enticing prelude to sex. Now it led only to bitterness and recriminations. The king told her angrily that she must shut her eyes and endure his affairs, as those who were better than she had done. Then he ominously reminded her that he could at any time "lower her as much as he had raised her."

In January 1536, Queen Anne Boleyn miscarried again—a boy. Aware that her declining fortunes could only be reversed by the birth of a son, she became hysterical with grief and fear over the loss. The good king provided little comfort. "I see God will not give me male children," he reportedly hissed. Turning to leave his stricken wife, he announced that he "would have no more boys" by *her.* Anne's fate was sealed.

King Henry began insisting that there was something sinister behind the exotic, Gypsy-looking creature who had so enchanted him. He claimed he had been bewitched by Anne

Boleyn, seduced and forced into this second marriage by means of "sortileges and charms." Picking up on Henry's lead, the queen's many enemies would take the wicked witch theme to absurd levels after her fall. She was hideously deformed, they claimed, "a goggle-eyed whore" covered with warts and moles, possessing a third breast and a sixth finger on one hand—enough to send the choosy king away screaming had they been even remotely accurate.

Henry's new minister, Thomas Cromwell, who had replaced Cardinal Wolsey, was too shrewd a politician to resort to attacks on Anne's appearance. He chose instead to assassinate her character. The scheming lord chancellor was determined to succeed where his predecessor had failed in expeditiously ridding his master of an unwanted wife. It took seven years, and Henry's ultimate break with Rome, to get rid of Katherine of Aragon, after which time Wolsey was stripped of all power and charged with treason for failing his sovereign. Cromwell would be much more efficient ensuring that Anne Boleyn would not be a lingering problem.

Henry VIII saw his wife for the last time on May Day, 1536. Like Katherine before her, there were no goodbyes. The queen was arrested the next day, charged with a variety of trumped-up crimes that included conspiracy to kill the king, committing adultery with a variety of men and even sleeping with her own brother. Cromwell left nothing to chance. Anne was taken by barge to the Tower of London, the same place she had prepared for her coronation only three years before. Terrified by what awaited her inside, the queen broke down and cried out, "I was received with greater ceremony last time I was here." The Constable of the Tower, Sir William Kingston, reassured her that she would be treated well and have comfortable quarters, not shoved into a dark dungeon. Awash with relief, the doomed lady fell on her knees. "It is too good for me," she wept before succumbing to a fit of laughter.

The manic transitions from tears to laughter, along with episodes of incoherent rambling—prompted no doubt by overwhelming stress and fear—characterized her stay in the Tower. She had every reason to be frightened. Cromwell, with the king's obvious complicity, was arranging a trial that would make certain the "poisoning whore," as Henry called her, would never come out alive.

Anne and her brother, George, were tried May 15 in a public spectacle that required special stands to be erected in order to accommodate the estimated 2,000 people in attendance. Sitting in judgment of the grossly maligned siblings were twenty-six peers of the realm, including their uncle, the Duke of Norfolk, who presided as High Steward. Anne was tried first. Arriving at the proceeding with cool dignity, she gave "wise and discreet answers to her accusers," according to a witness, but nothing she said mattered. The king wanted her dead, so the ridiculous evidence against her was solemnly heard with only one possible verdict. It was the same for George Boleyn, whose own wife testified to "undue familiarity" between brother and sister. Both were sentenced to death that very day—to be burnt or beheaded according to the king's pleasure.

Two days later, George and four other condemned men tried earlier were beheaded on Tower Hill. Anne had to wait a couple more days. After the dignity she had maintained during her trial, some of the erratic behavior returned as she waited to die. Upon hearing the news that she was going to be dispatched with a sword rather than the potentially messy ax, Anne remarked with a laugh that she had "heard say the executioner was very good." Then circling with her fingers her most famously graceful feature, she noted it was just as well since "I have a little neck."

It was a bright May morning when they came for her. The tears and hysteria were all gone now, replaced with a certain calm as she walked to the specially erected scaffold on Tower Green. To various witnesses, it seemed as if she welcomed death as a relief from all her troubles. Addressing the crowd that had gathered to watch a queen die, she spoke simply and pleasantly: "Masters, I here humbly submit me to the law as the law hath judged me, and as for mine offenses, I here accuse no man. God knoweth them; I remit them to God, beseeching him to have mercy on my soul."

She then spoke kindly of Henry, who not content with simply killing her, had divorced her as well several days earlier. Perhaps she was grateful that he did not order her burned at the stake or hacked apart with an ax, or perhaps she was just following the aristocratic custom of dying graciously. She called on Jesus Christ to "save my sovereign and master the King, the most godly, noble and gentle Prince that is, and long to reign over you."

Finishing her brief speech, Anne then knelt down as her ladies removed her outer garments, made sure her long dark hair was properly tucked away and covered the flashing black eyes that had once entranced the king. Like Katherine of Aragon, who had died just four months before, her last words were, "To Jesus Christ, I commend my soul." With that, her head was severed with one smooth stroke of the sword. The separated head and body were then gathered up and quickly buried in the adjacent chapel of St. Peter ad Vincula. Anne Boleyn had been Queen of England for nearly three and a half years. Twenty-four hours later, Henry VIII was officially betrothed to Jane Seymour.

Jane Seymour

Jane Seymour has the distinction of being the only one of Henry's six wives to be buried next to him, enshrined forever as his "true and loving wife." Lucky lady. Her exalted position came at a terrible price. While Jane was the only wife to give Henry the ultimate gift of a male heir, she died doing it—carried away twelve days after the birth of the future Edward VI by puerperal, or "child-bed" fever. Perhaps this was not the worst of it.

To become the king's "entirely beloved," she had to be not just a successful breeder, even if it killed her, but a humble, mousy one at that. After the tempestuous Anne Boleyn, Henry wanted a wife who would completely sublimate herself to him. He hit the mark with former lady-in-waiting Jane. This compliant queen's motto was "Bound to Obey and Serve," which suited the king just fine. Her pleasing disposition was exemplified by her kind treatment of Henry and Katherine's daughter Mary. While the jealous Anne Boleyn hated the girl, once threatening to give Mary "a good banging for the cursed bastard that she is," Jane was sweet and gentle to the unhappy princess, exchanging loving gifts and trying to reconcile Mary with her father.

When Queen Jane's natural submissiveness failed her, however, King Henry was prepared to put her right back in her place. God forbid she ever express an opinion or offer counsel to her mighty husband. After a series of religious uprisings in the north of England, collectively known as "The Pilgrimage of Grace," Jane ventured the unwelcome suggestion that perhaps the people were upset by the destruction of monasteries and other changes wrought by Henry's break with Rome. Big Mistake. According to one report by the French ambassador, Jane fell to her knees and "begged [Henry] to restore the Abbeys." The king demanded she get up, reminded her that "he had often told her not to meddle with his affairs," and then made a pointed allusion to the unhappy fate of her predecessor. Jane took the hint.

She would never have to worry about the executioner's ax because of her success in bearing a prince, but that's what killed her. In 1537, after less than eighteen months as queen, Jane Seymour was dead at the age of twenty-eight. Though Henry was genuinely moved by her passing, she wasn't cold in her grave before the search for a fourth wife began.

Anne of Cleves

England, at the time of Jane Seymour's death, was becoming increasingly isolated next to the Catholic powers of France and Spain, so a new wife was needed not only to give the king comfort and produce more sons, but to help shore up European relations. To this end, a foreign bride was pursued. Though Henry had known and loved his first three queens before he married them, the fourth would be a total stranger. As was generally the case with diplomatic marriages at the time, he would not even meet her first.

The famed artist Hans Holbein was sent to the royal courts of Europe to capture the images of all potential brides so at least his patron would have some idea of what they looked like. Henry was smitten by the portrait of young Duchess Christina of Milan, a niece of Emperor Charles V, but she was somewhat less enthusiastic about the English king's colorful marital history. Christina is reported to have said that she would be happy to wed Henry—if only she had an extra neck to spare. For various reasons, other attempted political matches failed as well. Then the name of Anne of Cleves came up. Her portrait was pleasant enough. She was from a German Duchy that might make a good Protestant alliance with England, and Henry's Lord Chancellor Thomas Cromwell recommended her. Anne got the job.

While there is nothing in Holbein's portrait to suggest she was a dog, the artist must have missed some intangible quality that absolutely revolted Henry. When the heretofore lusty king finally met her face to face, the daughter of Cleves came as a withering surprise. "I like her not" was his brutally frank appraisal of the mate Cromwell had selected for him. The unfortunate minister would pay with his head for engaging his royal master in this "unendurable bargain," but not before having to listen to Henry endlessly squawk about it. Anne of Cleves was "nothing so fair as she had been reported," the king liked to remind Cromwell, and if he had known any better she "would never have come within the kingdom."

But Anne *had* come to England, and there was nothing even this willful monarch could do about it without upsetting the carefully constructed alliance with Cleves. The wedding would have to go on. The reluctant groom was feeling a bit cranky on the morning of the ceremony. "My Lord," he said to Cromwell, "if it were not to satisfy the world, and my Realm, I would not do that I must this day for none earthly thing." Henry's mood had not improved after the wedding night. "How liked you the Queen?" Cromwell, no doubt desperate, inquired the next morning. "I liked her before not well, but now I like her much worse," was the devastating reply. Henry had not been able to consummate the marriage, announcing that he "could never in her company be provoked and steered to know her carnally." To his doctors the disappointed king reported that her "body [was] in such a sort disordered and indisposed" that it did not "excite and provoke any lust" in him. Although she was only twenty-three, he said her breasts sagged.

Poor Anne wasn't getting any bargain either. The once strapping and romantic king, universally praised for his good looks and charm, was becoming a bloated old tyrant with foul-smelling leg ulcers and eyes that had all but disappeared into his fat face. The wedding night couldn't have been too much fun for the bride. Fortunately, the exceedingly sheltered virgin had no idea what the evening was supposed to entail, and Henry was not inclined to show her. Night after night they just lay there, with the impotent king reporting to Cromwell that Anne "was still as good a Maid . . . as ever her Mother bare her."

Shriveled in her presence, he could manage only a few glancing kisses before he gave up completely. His wife thought this was what making love was all about. "When he comes to bed," she confided to her ladies, "he kisses me and taketh me by the hand, and biddeth me, 'good night sweetheart' and in the morning, kisses me, and biddeth me, 'Farewell, darling.' Is not this enough?" The tentative groping rapidly became intolerable, particularly since Henry had spotted a cute little lady-in-waiting attending his unpalatable queen. Her name was Catherine Howard and the king, thirty years her senior, desperately wanted to make her wife number five.

Wisely Anne, ever amiable, stepped aside. Six months after the sexless marriage began, it was over. Grateful for her cooperation in setting him free without complications, Henry treated Anne generously. She was granted a large settlement of manors and estates, and given social prominence as the king's adopted "good sister." Not bad considering the fates of other displeasing queens. Relations were so friendly after the divorce that "sister" Anne was frequently a guest at court, even dancing with the new Queen Catherine who had once served her.

Catherine Howard

With his dormant passions aroused once again, Henry married the thoroughly English Catherine Howard on July 28, 1540. Ironically, it was the same day Cromwell lost his head for, among other things, getting his king entangled in such a sorry foreign marriage with Anne of Cleves. The new queen, as a matter of fact, was the niece of Cromwell's political enemy, the Duke of Norfolk.

Besotted with his teenage bride, the king publicly caressed her, showered her with jewels, and called her his "blushing rose without a thorn." He was "so enamoured," reported the French ambassador, that he could not "treat her well enough." Catherine, however, would break Henry's heart, and pay dearly for it. It seemed the "blushing rose" had been around the garden path a few times before her royal marriage. This was not good, especially since she had been passed off as a virgin by her family eager to advance themselves. Worse still, she carried on after the wedding as well.

In retrospect, it's somewhat understandable that a young girl might stray when her husband, three decades older, was so obese that he could barely walk on his ulcerous legs, let alone do much in bed. Still, considering his increasingly savage reputation, cheating on him might be considered just a tad reckless. The object of Catherine's affections was Thomas Culpeper, a gentleman of the king's Privy Chamber and one of his favored companions.

In the one letter of hers that survives, the adulterous queen lovingly writes Culpeper, "It makes my heart die to think I cannot be always in your company," concluding, "Yours as long as life endures." It would not last long for either of them.

Henry was devastated when he heard about the affair, and the premarital shenanigans that had gone on with other men. Mouldering in self-pity, he lamented his misfortune in having a succession of such "ill-conditioned" wives. His mood then turned to bitter anger as he called for a sword to slay himself her "that I loved so much." The betrayed monarch vowed that all the pleasure "that wicked woman" had derived from her wantonness should not equal the pain she should feel from torture. Finally he broke down and cried.

A huge round-up of all the players began. Members of the Howard family who may have had knowledge of the affairs were sent to the Tower of London, including Catherine's elderly step-grandmother, the Dowager Duchess of Norfolk. Culpeper was beheaded, while another former lover was hanged but cut down while still breathing, disemboweled, and castrated before being carved into quarters. Then it was Catherine's turn. After being formally demoted from the title of Queen, she was indicted for having led "an abominable, base, carnal, voluptuous and vicious life" before her marriage, "like a common harlot with divers persons . . . maintaining, however, the outward appearance of chastity and honesty"—not to mention that she had cuckolded the king after he married her.

On the morning of February 13, 1542, Catherine Howard lost her head at the Tower of London. She had been queen a little over eighteen months and had just entered her twenties. Fearing she wouldn't know what to do at her execution, the terrified girl had requested a block be brought to her so she could practice laying her head upon it. She was the second niece of the Duke of Norfolk to have her head chopped off. The first was Anne Boleyn almost six years earlier. While both women were dispatched at the same site, with both their headless bodies buried a few feet away, one was clearly guilty of her crimes and one was not. "I die a Queen," Catherine announced from the scaffold, according to legend, "but I would rather die the wife of Culpeper."

Katherine Parr

With two wives beheaded and two others cast aside, the ladies were not exactly lining up to become the latest spouse of England's most eligible bachelor. It was way too dangerous. Prominent English families thought it prudent to find ways to advance themselves other than offering up their daughters, while foreign courts indicated they had no extra princesses to spare.

There was one lady, however, who seemed quite willing to become wife number six: wife number four, Anne of Cleves. The woman who Henry had once called "The Flanders Mare" apparently had no hard feelings. The king's "good sister" wanted to be queen again. There were some actually pushing for a remarriage, including, of all people, her own brother, the Duke of Cleves. Putting a quick end to any such talk, King Henry made it abundantly clear that he wasn't *that* lonely.

No longer the lusty rake, and severely burned by Catherine Howard, the aging king was now looking for a comforting nurse rather than a nubile lover. He turned to a lady of the court named Katherine Parr. While she was no voluptuous beauty, there was no question about her virginity. Katherine had been twice widowed before catching Henry's eye. "Gentlemen," he announced to his Council, "I desire company, but I have had more than enough of taking young wives, and I am now resolved to marry a widow." Mature, wise, and caring, in addition to sharing Henry's passion for music and art, Katherine was the perfect companion for the king and his three motherless children. Yet while Henry would eventually make her a widow for the third time, Katherine Parr barely survived the marriage with her head.

Unlike her decapitated predecessor, the new queen was not an uneducated, flighty teenager, but an intelligent and informed woman who took an active interest in theology. A religious scholar of sorts, she wrote a series of popular devotional books during her tenure as Henry's sixth wife, making her one of only eight women to be published during the first half of the sixteenth century. Queen Katherine was writing in dangerous times, however, on subjects very close to the king's heart. While Henry VIII had broken away from the power of the pope, his English Church was still essentially Roman Catholic in ritual and doctrine. It was the religion he had known all his life. Katherine, on the other hand, was part of a growing Prostestant reformist movement, organizing theological seminars and encouraging radical preachers.

What she failed to do was heed the advice she gave in one of her books. "Women married," she had instructed, should learn from St. Paul "to be obedient to their husbands, and to keep silence in the congregation, and to learn from their husbands at home." Instead, Katherine developed the dangerous habit of arguing religion with a sick and irritable king who already thought himself quite a theologian. At times, the queen seemed unwilling to back down from her fiercely held beliefs—never a good idea with Henry VIII—and "in the heat of discourse [went] very far," according to the Protestant writer John Foxe, who chronicled the nearly fatal consequences of such hubris.

Although Henry wasn't showing any outward signs of his anger at his wife's presumptuous behavior, Katherine secretly got word that she was in deep trouble and that charges had been drawn up against her. Facing the very real possibility that her head would soon roll, the queen wisely decided to humble herself completely. Rushing to Henry, she found him in the mood to discourse on religion. He was actually testing her, and Katherine's life literally depended upon passing.

She knew what she had to do. Instead of engaging Henry in his proposed discussion, she demurred, saying that "women by their first creation were made subject to men." It was a good opening move. She then continued: "Being made after the image of God, as women were after their image, men ought to instruct their wives, who would do all their learning from them."

Appealing to Henry's sense of intellectual superiority, Katherine continued to score points when she indicated that she wanted "to be taught by his Majesty, who is a prince of such learning and wisdom." She was doing well, but the crucial test was not over. Henry had more up his bejeweled sleeve. Referring to their previous heated discussions, he seemed to undermine the humility she was now attempting to project. "You are become a doctor [of the Church]," he reminded her, "able to instruct us and not be instructed by us."

Fortunately, Katherine was no fool and knew exactly what to say next. The king, she said, "had much mistaken the freedom [she] had taken to argue with him," which she did only to distract him from his pains and, as an added benefit, to learn from him herself. Bingo! "And is it even so?" responded her now placated husband. "Then Kate, we are friends again." Katherine Parr lived to marry husband number four, who happened to be Jane Seymour's brother, after King Henry finally breathed his last on January 28, 1547.

3

Head Over a Heel

Years before she lost her head in a hideously botched execution,[1] Mary Queen of Scots lost her heart to an equally hideous choice of husband. The young queen, a great-niece of Henry VIII, was already a widow of twenty-two when she fell madly for her cousin Henry Stuart, Lord Darnley, in 1565.

Her first husband had been Francis II of France,[2] and that had been a fine marriage, in its own way. Sure Francis was stunted, bloated, and sickly, with an ineffective pair of undescended testicles, but Mary loved him and he loved her. Chastely. The young couple were, in fact, more like brother and sister, having been raised together since 1548, when the five-year-old queen of Scotland was sent to France to live with the family of her four-year-old fiance. Owing to his frail health and unfortunate deformity, the marriage was most likely never consummated and Francis was dead before he turned seventeen.

No longer Queen of France, Mary went back to Scotland in 1561 to reclaim the throne that had been hers since she was six days old. Only a few years later, she came to discover a little something that had been missing from her first marriage: primal, pulsating lust. Mary had the hots for cousin Henry. Darn-

---

[1]Recounted in Part IX, Chapter 4.
[2]The first of Catherine de Medici's three sons to rule France (see Part I, Chapter 2).

ley, unfortunately, was a boastful, grasping nincompoop who just happened to look good in a pair of tights. But Mary liked what she saw. Failing to notice any of his less pleasant characteristics, the queen determined to marry him. Thomas Randolph, the ambassador to England, lamented that his "poor Queen whom ever before I esteemed so worthy, so wise, so honorable in all her doings" was now acting like a giddy teenager in love.

Good sex only goes so far, and it took only a couple months—and a nauseating pregnancy—for Mary to realize that she had saddled herself with a loser simply because he scratched her lusty itch. Darnley was a spoiled lightweight who, when he wasn't frequenting the bordellos of Edinburgh, or passing out drunk, persistently harassed his wife to grant him all the powers of a king—not just the title. He would prove himself a terrible liability to Mary's throne, which was barely secure to begin with.

Though she had been pampered and indulged in France, Scotland was a different story entirely. The cold, wet country of her birth was dominated by clannish, swaggering nobles who showed little reverence for royalty—especially a female, Catholic monarch who had been raised as a foreigner. The Protestant Reformation had swept Scotland while Mary was away in France, and her return was greeted with cool suspicion by certain nobles, including her own half-brother, and outright hostility by the new Protestant establishment. John Knox, the vicar of the Scottish Reformation, was a particularly vocal critic who railed against the "monstrous" rule of women. Permitting these "weak, frail, impatient, feeble, and foolish creatures" to sit on a throne, he declared, was the "subversion of good order, of all equity and justice" as well as being contrary to God and repugnant to nature.

Knox's bold verbal lashings were enough to drive his queen to tears of frustration, particularly since she had determined to maintain a moderate approach to matters of religion. But he wasn't her only problem. While Mary's Protestant cousin to the south, Elizabeth I of England (daughter of Henry VIII and Anne Boleyn), certainly took great exception to Knox's assessment of female monarchs, she too was wary of the Scottish queen. The two women shared the same royal blood and Mary had established a claim to the English crown because of it. This didn't sit well with Elizabeth, who was a zealous guardian of her power and position.

It was into this atmosphere of hostility and suspicion that Darnley strutted. Unlike the infatuated Mary, Queen Elizabeth and the Scottish establishment were less than enthusiastic about his presence. Besides being insufferable, Darnley was also Catholic. And he had the same royal blood that flowed through Mary Stuart and Elizabeth Tudor, which in the eyes of the English queen only made the Scottish queen's claim to her crown more of a threat. The Scottish nobles, however, soon determined that they could use Darnley's weak and vacillating nature to their advantage in undermining Mary. They appealed to his petty ego, dangling the prospect of making him sole ruler of Scotland if he would come over to their side. Darnley snatched the bait like a greedy bottom-dweller. After all, his wife was growing to hate him more and more every day and wasn't about to grant him the kingly power he craved.

Darnley and the nobles agreed on a murderous scheme designed to break the queen. Mary had an Italian secretary, David Riccio, whose company she enjoyed. She listened raptly to his advice and spent hours of quality time with him as her marriage deteriorated. Of course Darnley hated Riccio. The nobles loathed him, too, mostly because he was a Catholic and a foreigner and he had the queen's ear. They determined to destroy him. It was a March evening in 1566 when the plan was carried out. Six months pregnant (with the future King James I of England), Mary was in her private chambers at the palace of Holyrood dining with Riccio and some other companions when the conspirators suddenly burst in. "Let it please your Majesty," one of them sneered, "that yonder man David come forth of your privy chamber where he hath been overlong." Naturally, the queen protested that Riccio was there by her royal invitation and would stay right where he was. The gang informed her otherwise as they moved to snatch the terrified secretary, now clinging desperately to the queen's skirts.

As Riccio was dragged away from her kicking and screaming for his life, Mary spun on her husband and violently cursed him. The helpless secretary was then viciously slaughtered, stabbed more than fifty times before his bloody and lacerated corpse was tossed down a flight of steps. Needless to say, this savage murder didn't exactly enhance the marital relations between Mary and Darnley. Now held prisoner in her own palace, the queen choked on the hatred she felt for her husband. She was sure her own life was in danger because of him, either through the violence of the attack on Riccio or by its potential trauma to her pregnancy.

Mary knew she had to swallow her seething contempt if she wanted to help herself. While it was contrary to everything she felt, she had to play nice with Darnley if she wanted to escape her captors. The weakling would-be king, terrified by what he had done, was coaxed back to his wife's side as easily as he had been won to the murderers'. With Darnley's help, Mary was able to escape the palace and rally support from her loyalist forces. She regained her position, but domestic harmony was hardly restored. Darnley reverted back to his lazy life of debauchery, while resuming his schemes to glorify himself. "He misuses himself so far towards [Mary] that it is a heartbreak for her to think that he should be her husband," one courtier wrote. The queen would never get over her husband's complicity in Riccio's murder. "I have forgiven, but never will forget!" she angrily blasted him after their son was born several months later.

Mary wasn't Darnley's only enemy. He ruffled more than a few tartans when he betrayed his merry band of coconspirators and soon found himself their next target. In the early morning hours of February 10, 1567, an enormous explosion destroyed a house on the outskirts of Edinburgh known as Kirk o'Field. Darnley had been lodged there, recovering from a syphilitic illness. Perhaps noticing the cache of gunpowder being hauled in, Darnley managed to escape the blast. It was only a brief reprieve, though, as he was found strangled to death in the courtyard of the ruined home the next morning.

Mary's involvement in the murder, if any, remains one of history's greatest mysteries and leaves her legacy shrouded in controversy. Her cause was certainly not aided much by the fact that she ran off and married the Earl of Bothwell, who happened to be the suspected ringleader of the plot to kill Darnley. With her reputation ruined, Mary's countrymen turned against her, hounded her off the throne and held her captive. After escaping, the disgraced queen fled to England and into the waiting arms of cousin Elizabeth. She was held prisoner there for nineteen years before she was convicted in 1587 of conspiracy to kill the English queen and executed.

In the minds of many the deposed queen remained a shameless harlot, but to others Mary became a holy martyr, her past sins cleanly wiped away by the circumstances of her death. Whatever the case, no doubt Mary Queen of Scots would have been far better off if she had taken a cue from her cousin Queen Elizabeth and simply stayed single.

4

A Wedding! Let's Celibate!

Catherine the Great of Russia, whose indiscriminate sexual adventures would later become legendary,[1] came to her wedding bed a blushing virgin and, thanks to her husband, stayed that way for nearly a decade.

She arrived in Russia from Germany in 1744 with vague royal connections and soon became engaged to Peter, designated by the Empress Elizabeth to succeed her as Peter III. What she found was a frighteningly alien culture, only superficially civilized, and a massively disappointing fiance. Peter was an ugly, mean-spirited simpleton who showed no interest in his future bride. He much preferred putting his toy soldiers through endless military maneuvers. "I understood perfectly how little he wanted to see me and how little affection he bore me," she wrote in her memoirs. "My self-esteem and vanity were wounded, but I was too proud to complain."

Her wedding night was disastrous. Dressed in a pink nightie specially ordered from Paris, the naive Catherine waited anxiously in bed for her new husband, who was off carousing with his valets. The groom finally arrived after midnight, declaring

---

[1]As seen in Part I, Chapter 1.

that "it would amuse the servants to see us in bed together." With that he fell into the sack and passed out.

Night after night he ignored her, concentrating instead on his own diversions. Sometimes he would bring his huge collection of toys to bed, forcing Catherine to play army with him. Once she walked into their room to find a rat hanging by a rope. Peter explained that it had committed treason and was paying the penalty.

The future tsar also had a tendency to chatter incessantly, bombarding his bride with whatever bit of trivia happened to have captured his limited imagination. "Often I was very bored by his visits, which would last for hours," she wrote, "and even exhausted by them, for he never sat down, and I always had to walk up and down the room with him." The droning chitchat, however, never led to bed, no doubt frustrating the woman who once recalled vigorously riding her pillow as an adolescent, trying to satisfy physical yearnings not yet defined. As the unconsummated marriage progressed, Peter became increasingly tedious. During one period he decided to become a dog trainer, filling their bedroom with barking animals. "It was amid this stench," she wrote, "that we slept."

Despite her loathsome marriage, Catherine knew her future was bound to Russia and was determined to absorb its culture totally. She learned the language, read voraciously, adopted the Russian Orthodox faith and carefully cultivated alliances in the debauched court of Empress Elizabeth. She also took to physical activity to relieve the marital strains, riding her horse for hours. "The more violent this exercise was the more I loved it," she wrote.

Peter, for his part, would not have been able to satisfy his wife even if he wanted to. In the words of French agent Champeaux, he was "unable to have children because of an obstacle, which the Oriental peoples remedy by circumcision, but for which he thought there was no cure." He had phimosis, a deformation of the foreskin that made erections excruciatingly painful. Even after he consented to the operation that liberated him, he still refused to sleep with his wife. Instead, he took on a series of mistresses, keeping Catherine apprised of every dalliance.

Catherine, meanwhile, was becoming wiser to the ways of the world. Engaging in innocent court flirtations, she gradually discovered that she was indeed desirable. Her confidence and passions aroused, the long-deprived princess finally lost her virginity to a young officer—eight years after her wedding. A succession of lovers and several illegitimate children followed; then Catherine really got her revenge. The Empress Elizabeth died in 1762, and Peter became ruler over subjects who hated him. He made peace with Frederick the Great of Prussia, just as the Russian army was at the point of defeating Frederick's armies, and compounded the outrage by making his troops wear Prussian-style uniforms.

Peter III also made the foolish mistake of humiliating his now formidable wife in public, forcing her at one point to stand up with the rest of his subjects when the royal family was toasted. Her dignified behavior in the face of all her husband's insults gained Catherine sympathy and respect, and soon a plot to overthrow the tsar centered around her. With the Russian army and establishment firmly behind her, Catherine forced Peter's abdication. She was proclaimed empress, while her husband was discreetly murdered a few days later. He was a far more effective general, it seems, with tin soldiers on a loveless bed.

5

Wails From the Vienna Wood

Austrian Empress Maria Theresa should not be judged too harshly for the series of miserable marriages she arranged for her large brood of children in the late eighteenth century. Sure, dynastic and diplomatic considerations took precedence over any potential happiness they might have enjoyed in the arrangements, but, in her defense, the empress probably had no notion of what wedded bliss meant. She was, after all, married to a shameless philanderer who humiliated her with his numerous and less than discreet affairs.

From his frequent flirtations with young dancers and opera singers of the Vienna stage to long-term liaisons with ladies of the court, Emperor Francis was the ultimate adulterer. He was particularly enamoured of Princess Auersperg, a paramour thirty years his junior. "The emperor makes no secret of his passion for her," one visitor to the Austrian court noted. Indeed, Francis and his mistress enjoyed frequent trysts in his hunting lodges, his theater box in Vienna, and the cozy home he purchased for her. Even his somewhat sheltered children knew what was going on. "The emperor is a very good-hearted father," wrote his daughter Christina, "one can always rely upon him as a friend, and we must do what we can to protect him from his weakness.

I am referring to his conduct with Princess Auersperg." Her mother, Christina continued, was "very jealous of this devotion."

Despite her displeasure, and the fact that she held all the power as the sovereign of both Austria and Hungary, the empress could do nothing to rein in her wayward husband. Instead, she became obsessed with controlling the moral conduct of her subjects. With its opulent theaters, grand opera houses, and an up-and-coming talent by the name of Mozart, the glittering city of Vienna was a cosmopolitan mecca in the midst of a cultural wasteland. It was "a city of free adultery," as one visitor put it. And it was here that Emperor Francis's lifestyle thrived.

Transferring her anger at her husband's betrayals, Maria Theresa established her Chastity Commission, a special department of the police charged with suppressing vice. The purity patrols were everywhere, infiltrating theaters, social gatherings, and even private homes. Anyone suspected of being less than upright was arrested, while foreigners accused of corrupting the local citizenry were banished from the kingdom. Some said the betrayed empress herself played a part in the commission, disguising herself and roaming Vienna in search of her wayward man.

The usual punishment for those convicted of moral violations was harsh, meant to serve as an example to others. The violators were chained to stone pillars at the city gates where they sat in their own filth, sometimes for weeks or months, completely dependent on the kindness of strangers for food and drink. The punishments, however, backfired. Instead of being ridiculed and scorned, the chained souls became heroes of sorts. The citizens of Vienna fed and catered to them while laughing at the prudish empress with the unfaithful husband.

When she wasn't storming the bedrooms of her people,

Maria Theresa busied herself inflicting marriage on her helpless children. Like many royal offspring, they were to be used as political capital, helping to strengthen their parents' position through arranged matrimony. This was a particularly rich and ancient tradition in the empress's Habsburg family line.[1]

Crown Prince Joseph, as heir to the throne, was given top priority in the marriage market. Luckily for him, he actually fell in love with the mate chosen for him, Princess Isabella of Parma. Unfortunately, Isabella's affections were directed elsewhere. She had a major crush on Joseph's sister, Christina. "I am told that the day begins with God," Isabella gushed to Christina in a letter. "I, however, begin the day by thinking of the object of my love, for I think of her incessantly."

Empress Maria Theresa would never have tolerated a lesbian relationship between daughter and daughter-in-law, but the issue became moot when Isabella died suddenly from smallpox at age twenty-one. The prince was devastated by his loss, but his mother, ever conscious of dynastic priorities, quickly married him off again. Joseph was given a choice of two brides, neither of whom stirred much desire in him. "I prefer not to marry either," he announced to his mother, "but since you are holding a knife to my throat, I will take [Princess Josepha of Bavaria], because, from what I hear, she at least has fine breasts."

Josepha's breasts, alas, were a disappointment, along with the rest of her. She was short, thickset, and painfully ugly, with festering sores all over her body and bad teeth. Joseph was repulsed by his bride and avoided her at all costs. "They want me to have children," he wrote despondently. "How can we have them? If I could put the tip of my finger on the tiniest part of her body,

---

[1]With devastating results that are recounted in Part VI, Chapter 2.

which was not covered with pimples, I would try to have children." Poor Josepha, abandoned and humiliated, suddenly died of smallpox like her predecessor, though this time her husband was not particularly moved by grief.

The smallpox epidemic also saved several of Joseph's siblings from horrible marriages. His brother Charles died of it before a match could be arranged for him, while his sister Elizabeth, once the great beauty of the family, was so scarred by the disease that no suitor would have her and she was forced into a bitter spinsterhood. Another daughter, Josepha, died just in the nick of time. She had been betrothed to Ferdinand, the child-king of Naples, renowned for his stupidity. He was so dumb, in fact, that his father decided he should be spared the rigors of an education. Needless to say, Josepha was not pleased with the match and made it abundantly clear. Her mother, however, was determined. "I consider Josepha a sacrifice to politics," the empress wrote firmly to her daughter's governess, "and if she fulfills her duty to her husband and her God, I shall be content . . . I hope my daughter will not be selfish; she has a tendency in that direction."

Mercifully, on the day she was to leave Austria to become Queen of Naples, Josepha also succumbed to smallpox. Young King Ferdinand was not terribly upset over the death of his intended. An English ambassador reported seeing him playing funeral, amid much hilarity, with a pal dressed up like the dead Josepha—complete with chocolate dotted all over his face to resemble smallpox. Besides, what was the loss of one sister when another was waiting in the wings to take her place?

That sister, Caroline, was equally displeased with the arrangement. Bitterly homesick, she called her life in Naples "a martyrdom," and wrote: "I now know what marriage is, and I have a deep pity for [youngest sister] Antoinette who has yet to experience marriage. I admit frankly that I would rather die than be forced to live again what I have gone through. If I had not been taught by my religion to think of God, I should have killed myself, for it was hell to live like that for a week. I shall weep bitterly if ever my sister is in the same situation."

Sadly, young Antoinette found herself in a very similar situation. She was pawned off to the dauphin of France, the future King Louis XVI, in what her mother considered the ultimate diplomatic coup with Austria's ancient enemy. Louis was hardly the prince young girls dream about. He was, quite frankly, a rude, pudgy, seemingly asexual loser, with filthy hygiene to boot. The Neopolitan ambassador remarked that the dauphin seemed to have been "born and raised in a forest," while Madame Du Barry, mistress of his grandfather, Louis XV, called him a "fat, ill-bred boy."

Young Louis had another problem, one shared by Catherine the Great's husband, Peter III. He had phimosis. This, combined with his almost phobic shyness and his desperate fear of the surgery necessary to correct his deformity, made Louis less than a great lover. And Marie Antoinette a very lonely bride. Louis studiously avoided her and their marriage bed, leaving the poor girl all alone in the strange, debauched court of Louis XV at Versailles. Though they would eventually reach an accommodation after Louis inherited the French throne, the ill-fated couple would have little time to enjoy it. Their frivolous new lifestyle was disrupted by a pesky revolution that would claim both their heads.

6

A Marriage Made in Hell

Among the legendary fiascoes that were so many royal marriages, few stand out as more discordant than the one between George IV of Britain and Caroline of Brunswick. This miserably mismatched pair made a royal sideshow out of a union that was doomed before it ever began. George, Prince of Wales at the time, already had a favorite mistress and a secret wife. But he had married the widow Mrs. Fitzherbert on the sly, without the king's consent, which violated one law, plus she was Catholic, which violated another. Prince George was facing the prospect of losing his place at the head of the line for the throne.

Lured by the promise of having Parliament pay off his massive debts, George was persuaded to dump his illegal wife and marry his German cousin, Caroline. It was a steep price to pay for a clean credit report. Among other qualities, Caroline was a crude, foul-smelling exhibitionist with an enormous sexual appetite. Harris, Lord Malmesbury, the diplomat given the task of bringing Caroline from Brunswick to marry the prince, described her as having "no acquired morality, and no strong innate notions of its value and necessity"—a reputation she enjoyed all over Germany. She was short and stocky, described by

Malmesbury as having "a head always too large for her body, and her neck too short."

She also apparently shared the same royal malady—porphyria—that is thought to have driven her future father-in-law and uncle, George III, into babbling fits of insanity. While Prince George's mother, Queen Charlotte, had serious reservations about Caroline's suitability, his father was delighted. Demonstrating all the shrewd judgment he had earlier used in assessing the mood of the American colonists, George III roundly endorsed his niece. "Undoubtedly she is the person who naturally must be most agreeable to me," he wrote Prime Minister William Pitt. "I expressed my approbation of the idea."

The Prince of Wales was introduced to his betrothed for the first time on April 5, 1795. Malmesbury was there to relate the scene at St. James's Palace. "He turned around, retired to a distant part of the apartment, and, calling me to him, said, 'Harris, I am not well; pray get me a glass of brandy.'" Three days, and many brandies later, the happy couple were married. George spent the wedding night passed out drunk on the floor, with his mistress Lady Jersey in close attendance during the entire honeymoon.

Several weeks later, they were no longer living as man and wife, although Caroline did manage to get pregnant. Having satisfied the dual purposes of his marriage—siring a legitimate heir and settling his debts—George announced to Caroline a formal separation. "Our inclinations are not in our power," he wrote her, "nor should either of us be held answerable to the other, because nature had not made us suitable to each other. Tranquil and comfortable society is, however, in our power; let our intercourse, therefore, be restricted to that."

Caroline took her estranged husband's letter as a license to let loose, which she did on a spectacular scale. She took to indecorous public displays of flesh. Basically, she became a flasher. "Oh! what an impudent woman was that Princess of Wales," cried Lady Hester Stanhope. "How many sea-captains used to color up when she danced about, exposing herself like an opera-girl." Lord Holland called her "utterly destitute of all female delicacy," while the Rev. William Mason wrote to Bishop Hurd and declared himself "a perfect convert to Your Lordship's Hypothesis of Insanity."

All the tongue-wagging eventually landed Caroline in court. A Lady Douglas was spreading tales that the wayward princess had gotten pregnant in an adulterous affair and had given birth to a bastard boy. Caroline's indignant husband called for an inquiry and the king agreed. What became known as "The Delicate Investigation" convened in July 1806. Several months later, Caroline was acquitted of the charges, but a thorough review of her sex life left her reputation in ruins.

The Princess of Wales became a social pariah. Eight years later, tired of the relentless persecution, she fled Britain right into the arms of King Joachim of Naples. This was a stinging slap at George, now serving as Regent of his father's kingdom, because Joachim was the brother-in-law of the Prince Regent's archenemy, Napoleon of France. While the Naples revel ended when Napoleon escaped his exile on Elba in 1815, Caroline's adventures abroad were just beginning. Soon she had a new beau. "I have Napoleon's courier with me," she announced, "which is quite a treasure to me, faithful and prudent. I shall keep him." The courier and the queen-to-be marauded all over Europe, flaunting their treasonous affair everywhere they went. She showered him with honors, having him named a Knight of Malta and a Knight of the Holy Sepulchre, for example, as well as Grand Master of her own Order of St. Caroline.

Never intending to return to England, Caroline found she had changed her mind upon the death of her husband's father, George III. Since she was not officially divorced, she was now the Queen of England and fully intended to serve. But the new King George IV thought otherwise and set out pursuing a divorce through Parliament. A problem arose, however, as it was determined that the public sentiment was firmly with Caroline—not so much out of loyalty to her, but due to deep disdain for him.

The people reminded George just how unpopular he was with them when they turned out in droves to support Caroline as she faced the "Bill of Pains and Penalties" to "deprive Her Majesty Caroline Amelia Elizabeth of the Title, Prerogatives, Rights, Privileges and Pretensions of Queen Consort of the Realm, and to dissolve the Marriage between His Majesty and the said Queen." Guards had to be stationed all over the area of Westminster to control the crowds as a parade of witnesses testified inside about the queen's outrageous conduct abroad. But without the support of the people, the bill, after some debate, was abandoned in Parliament.

George was stuck, but not defeated. When Caroline, looking like a caricature of a queen, arrived at his coronation and demanded entry, the doors to Westminster Abbey were slammed shut right in her face. Several weeks later she was dead, suffering from acute porphyria, or maybe poison, as some suggested. The inscription on her coffin, which she wrote herself, read: "Deposited, Caroline of Brunswick, the Injured Queen of England."

George IV never remarried.

PART IV

Mom Was a Monster, Pop Was a Weasel

The tree shrew is one species of animal known for eating its young. Royalty is another. Consumed as they were with kingdoms and crowns, many blue-blooded parents willingly sacrificed the well-being of their children to their own agendas. And, in some cases, they made growing up at the palace downright dangerous.

The execution of Lady Jane Grey. Where was Mom?

1

How to Make a Bloody Mary

When it came right down to it, Henry VIII was no better a father than he was a husband. Each of the king's children was bruised to some degree by his overwhelming personality, but Mary, his eldest daughter by Katherine of Aragon, was absolutely battered by it. For more than three decades the sad princess endured being alternately doted upon, terrorized, and regarded with devastating indifference by her father until he finally died and left her alone.

Mary Tudor's birth in 1516 was greeted with little enthusiasm by her dad, other than his belief that it boded well for the eventual arrival of vastly preferable male children. "If it was a daughter this time, by the grace of God sons will follow," the disappointed but hopeful monarch remarked soon after Mary was delivered. The little princess was raised amidst all the trappings of royalty, but away from her parents, as was customary at the time. When he did see her, Henry occasionally showed delight in his daughter's developing musical skills and obvious intelligence. Though he called her his "chieftest pearl," this was not so much out of any abounding love; rather it was his recognition that Mary was a valuable commodity in the European marriage market. Before she turned twelve, in fact, she had been variously betrothed to the dauphin of France, his younger brother, and her Habsburg cousin, the Holy Roman Emperor Charles V.

Despite her father's appreciation of her worth, Mary nevertheless remained an only child—and a girl. For the king who determined to secure the Tudor dynasty with sons, this was simply unacceptable. She was not yet twelve when Henry revealed his conviction that his marriage to Katherine had been invalid from the beginning. The princess was in store for a hideous adolescence as her parents' marriage unraveled before her.

Queen Katherine's stubborn insistence that she was the king's true and lawful wife enraged Henry, and Mary was forced to watch as her mother was degraded a hundred different ways in her father's effort to shed her. One of his cruelest weapons was setting Katherine up in a household close to Mary's, but only allowing mother and daughter to meet for the briefest of moments. And though Henry still occasionally showed Mary some affection, there was no disguising the fact that his split with Katherine and the invalidation of their marriage would automatically make her a bastard.

When King Henry eventually defied Rome and married Anne Boleyn, Mary acquired one of history's meanest stepmothers. That in addition to an increasingly remote and hostile father. The new queen loathed the girl, mostly because Mary represented a threat to any children she might have with the king. Anne was incensed when the loyal people affectionately cheered for Mary at her coronation. "As much rejoicing went on as if God Almighty had come down from heaven," Anne bitterly complained. She later threatened to install Mary as one of her servile maids and then use the opportunity to perhaps "give her too much dinner on some occasion"—that is, poison her—or "marry her to some valet."

The exiled Katherine heard of Anne's threats and sent Mary a letter of warning when she heard the new queen was pregnant. "Daughter," she wrote, "I heard such tidings this day that I do perceive (if it be true) the time is very near when Almighty God will provide for you." Having seen firsthand how cruel her former husband and his new wife could be, Katherine was convinced that Henry would acquiesce to any demand Anne might make for Mary's death. Believing this could be the last letter her daughter might ever receive from her, Katherine encouraged bravery in the face of possible murder and concluded with an outpouring of maternal love. "I would to God, good daughter, that you did know with how good a heart I write this letter unto you. I never did write one with a better."

As it turned out, Mary did survive the birth of her half sister, the future Queen Elizabeth I, but her troubles were far from over. The Act of Succession passed by Parliament in 1534 gave all rights to the throne to Anne Boleyn's children, excluding Mary entirely. Now she was no longer a princess, but an official bastard. Just before the Act was passed, and in anticipation of it, Mary was ordered to move into baby Elizabeth's household and act as her servant. The command from the king, addressed to "the lady Mary, the king's daughter," provoked a brave response to the diminished title. "I could not a little marvel" at the letter, Mary wrote her father, "trusting verily that Your Grace does take me for your lawful daughter, born in true matrimony." She signed it, "Your most humble daughter, Mary, *Princess.*"

The young woman, now almost eighteen, had learned much from her mother's situation and her courage. Though she avowed herself to be obedient to her father in anything he might demand of her, she would never betray her conscience or compromise her rights by acknowledging that she was not the king's legitimate heir. Henry, on the other hand, resented his daughter's defiance as much as he did Katherine's, and went out of his way to make Mary's life miserable as long as she refused to bend to his will and accept her reduced status.

After all the people who had cared for her growing up were sent away, Mary was given one of the smallest rooms in Elizabeth's household. There was only one princess now, and she was Anne Boleyn's daughter. Whenever the baby traveled in her velvet litter, Mary was forced to walk beside her in the mud. At dinner, Elizabeth was given the chair of honor while Mary had to sit with the lower ranks. Any servant who showed her the slightest bit of compassion was sent away. Those suspected of encouraging her pretenses as the true princess were locked away in the Tower. And, perhaps worst of all, Anne Boleyn's aunt was put in charge of Mary and given license to persecute her any way she liked.

Because Mary had been advised to always assert her rights as Henry's true heir lest they be compromised by neglect or acquiescence, she had to object every time she was called simply "Lady Mary," or Elizabeth was called Princess. This brought constant punishment upon her. First her jewels and fine clothes were taken away, in time followed by nearly everything else she owned. When she sent a message to her father advising him of her destitution, Mary ordered the messenger to accept any money or clothing that was offered, but not to accept any writing in which she was not titled princess.

Henry VIII did occasionally visit the household, but it was always to see Elizabeth. Mary was locked away in her room every time he came. There was one occasion, however, when the king did give his first daughter a small taste of the affection he once had for her. She had sent word to the king, begging for permission to see him and kiss his hand. She was refused, but slipped away to the roof terrace to watch him leave. Looking up, Henry noticed her. She was kneeling with her hands clasped together in supplication. Nodding, he touched his hat to her and rode away. The simple but tantalizing gesture would be the last Mary would receive in a long time. A campaign of terror was about to begin.

King Henry began enforcing the Act of Succession with a rigor not yet seen. The law not only declared the king's marriage to Katherine of Aragon invalid and their daughter illegitimate, it also explicitly denied the authority of the pope in England. Those who refused to swear by it were now subject to the terrible death of traitors. Scores of people were killed. Monks and nuns were hanged, still clad in their religious garb, while the head of the king's once close friend and chancellor, Thomas More, sat rotting atop Tower Bridge.

Mary's obstinate refusal to acknowledge the Act was now putting her life in serious peril. Henry began talking openly about killing his daughter, accusing her of conspiring with her mother to thwart his will and encourage rebellion. When Mary fell desperately ill, the king initially kept doctors from treating her, and refused Katherine's plea to let Mary be with her during her recuperation. His "chieftest pearl" was now his "worst enemy."

As Mary came close to dying from her mysterious illness, thoughts of Anne Boleyn's poisoning threats became all the more immediate. The queen, gradually losing her own power struggle, accused Mary of "waging war" against the king and the new order, dramatically pronouncing, "She will be the cause of my death unless I get rid of her first." With all the malice and tyranny closing in on her, Mary was desperate to escape England. Fearing for her life, she sent word to the Spanish ambassador, "begging him most urgently to think over the matter [of her escape], otherwise she considered herself lost, knowing that they wanted only to kill her," noted Spanish records of the time.

Meanwhile, Mary's beloved mother finally expired from grief and illness in 1536. Katherine bequeathed a golden cross to the daughter she had not been allowed to see for more than five years, but Henry confiscated it. Queen Anne also went rummaging through Katherine's possessions, taking anything of worth and leaving Mary nothing. Soon after, however, Anne Boleyn herself was dead, beheaded on a trumped-up charge of adultery.

Mary's fortunes now began to improve just a bit. Henry's new wife, Jane Seymour, encouraged the king to reconcile with his daughter and bring her to court, while Mary wrote her father loving letters of humility and obedience. The king's counselor, Thomas Cromwell, dictated the words that she hoped would save her life and restore her to some level of favor. "In as humble and lowly a manner as is possible for a child to use to her father and sovereign lord," one letter began, Mary acknowledged all her faults and offenses, sought forgiveness and professed herself to be "as sorry as any creature living" for defying him. She asked for his "fatherly pity" on her frail sex, noting that "I am but a woman and your child." Another letter begged Henry to envision her "most humbly prostrate before your noble feet, your most obedient subject and humble child."

With the letters, Mary bowed as low as she possibly could without explicitly acknowledging the Act of Succession. It wasn't far enough. The king sent his counselors to her, insisting she elaborate on her claim of obedience by openly accepting that she was a bastard and that the pope had no place in the kingdom. In response, Mary repeated to them what she had already told Cromwell when she wrote the humiliating letters of submission he had dictated: That she would rather die than displease her father, but as for embracing the Act, "my conscience will in no ways suffer me to consent thereto."

Henry was white with rage when word of Mary's refusal got back to him. Contemptuously ignoring Jane Seymour's entreaties for mercy, he ordered his daughter tried for treason. This time, he was determined to be rid of her once and for all. It was only the reluctance of the judges to try the king's daughter that spared her life. As a delay tactic, the court suggested that she be given a paper to sign, officially documenting her acceptance of the Act.

Trusted advisers warned Mary that this would be the last chance she had to save her life. Failure to sign would surely lead to the block and, to further encourage her, they persuaded her that a greater good was at stake. She must live as Catholicism's hope for the future, they argued. She would be no good to anyone dead. With this idealistic entreaty, Mary was convinced. Though she signed the document, she did so without reading it to protect her conscience. She also wrote a secret protest against the paper, stating that she had signed it only under duress. From then on, an uneasy truce between father and daughter emerged. Though she was restored to some measure of favor, Mary remained an official bastard with no hopes of a decent marriage or a place in the succession. She rued her hopeless existence. While her father lived, she lamented, "I shall only be Lady Mary, the unhappiest lady in Christendom."

When Henry VIII died in 1547, she was finally free of his tyranny and was restored in his will as an heir to the crown. Still, she had to endure the six-year reign of her half brother Edward VI during which her faith was under constant assault and the aborted attempt to place her cousin Lady Jane Grey on the throne. She finally came into her inheritance in 1553, embarking on a campaign against heresy that would brand her forever as "Bloody" Mary.

2

Jane Grey's Blues

One of the more tragic figures in English history was Lady Jane Grey, "The Nine Days Queen." This abused pawn of Tudor-era intrigue owed her misery almost entirely to her grasping and malicious mother, Frances Grey, Henry VIII's niece. Even at a time when children of the aristocracy knew little of parental love, Jane had an especially brutal mother bent on using her to the best advantage (her father was every bit as bad, just a little more passive). Jane had had the poor circumstance to have been born a girl, an undervalued commodity in the power market, and Frances delighted in reminding her daughter of her mistake by regularly thrashing her silly.

The quiet, studious girl, raised at a time when the failure to honor and obey one's parents was considered a sure path to damnation, did once allow herself the luxury of revealing her horrendous situation to her tutor: "I will tell you, and tell you a truth which, perchance, you will marvel at . . . whether I speak, keep silence, sit, stand or go, eat, drink, be merry or sad, be sewing, playing, dancing or doing anything else, I must do it, as it were, in such weigh, measure and number, even as perfectly as God made the world, or else I am so sharply taunted, so cruelly threatened, yea, presented sometimes with pinches, nips and bobs, and other ways (which I will not name for the honor I bear them) so without measure misordered, that I think myself in Hell. . . ."

The "nips and bobs" she suffered were mere nips and bobs compared with the lethal end to which her parents' greed and ambition consigned her. Henry VIII's successor, the boy-king Edward VI, was dying and with him the hopes of John Dudley, Duke of Northumberland.[1] As a sort of regent during King Edward's minority, Dudley had set England on a course of extreme Protestantism. He and his plans would be doomed, however, if Edward was succeeded by his half sister, the staunchly Catholic Mary Tudor.

Desperate, Dudley conspired with the Greys to have his son Guilford marry their daughter Jane. He then persuaded the dying king to exclude both his sisters, Mary and Elizabeth, from succession and name his Protestant cousin Jane instead. With this arrangement, Dudley believed he could maintain his power after Edward's death by manipulating his royal daughter-in-law when she became queen. The self-effacing girl, all of fifteen, was horrified at the prospect of marrying Guilford Dudley, whom she considered an arrogant bully. For the first time in her life, Jane actually stood up to her parents and refused to consider the union. Her mother eventually beat the girl into submission.

When Edward VI died in 1553, Dudley immediately declared Jane to be queen, forcing the Council to go along with him. The terrified teen, who had had no idea Edward was even sick—let alone that she had been tapped to replace him—was sickened at the prospect of ruling, particularly at the expense of her cousins Mary and Elizabeth. Fainting at the news, she was slapped awake by her mother. When the crown was brought to her, Jane

---

[1] John Dudley also was the father of Elizabeth I's great love, Robert (see Part I, Chapter 3).

refused to try it on, protesting that she had no right to it. She was also unnerved to see everyone—including her heretofore brutal parents—now bowing in deference before her.

Jane Grey was Queen of England for only nine days before "Bloody" Mary Tudor claimed her rightful throne. The nine-day queen's father delivered the news by shredding the cloth of estate that hung behind her throne. While she had been staying at the Tower of London in preparation for her coronation, Jane was now kept prisoner there. Her mother completely abandoned her, absorbed as she was with saving her own skin. Frances Grey did find time to plead successfully with her cousin Queen Mary to pardon her husband for his part in the usurpation attempt, but didn't bother putting in a good word for her daughter.

Jane was left to defend herself. Writing a humble letter to Mary, she swore that she had never wanted the throne, insisting that it had been forced on her, not only by Dudley and her parents, but under King Edward's will. "Although my fault be such that but for the goodness and clemency of the queen, I can have no hope of finding pardon," she wrote, "having given ear to those who at that time appeared, not only to myself, but to a great part of this realm to be wise, and now have manifested themselves to the contrary, not only to my and their great detriment, but with common disgrace and blame of all, they having with shameful boldness made so blameable and dishonorable an attempt to give to other that which was not theirs." She continued the letter, lamenting her "want of prudence" in accepting the crown, "for which I deserve heavy punishment," but asked for Mary's understanding, "it being known that the error imputed to me has not been altogether caused by myself."

Jane's plea to the queen may very well have been successful under ordinary circumstances. Despite the bloody reputation she earned later in her reign for her ruthless persecution of heretics, Mary Tudor was naturally inclined to mercy. She had known and loved Jane since her cousin was a little girl and knew she had nothing to do with the plot to steal her throne. But then Jane's father, who had already been pardoned once, involved himself in another failed rebellion against Mary. He did this knowing full well that his daughter was still vulnerable in the Tower. Now the queen's hand was forced. She wanted to marry her cousin King Philip II of Spain, but was told by the Spanish that it would be impossible if she continued to be so casual about treason in her midst.

The hapless girl was not yet seventeen when she was beheaded at the Tower in February 1554. In her final hours, the "Nine Days Queen" wrote in a prayer book three small verses— each in a different language:

In Latin: "If justice is done with my body, my soul will find mercy with God."

In Greek: "Death will give pain to my body for its sins, but the soul will be justified before God."

In English: "If my faults deserve punishment, my youth at least and my imprudence were worthy of excuse. God and posterity will show me favor."

She died on the block without ever hearing from her mother, who by some accounts was at that moment romping with a servant fifteen years her junior.

3

Hun, I Shrunk the Kid

Kings have always needed their sons to propagate their dynasties but have often hated them for the same reason. Rising sons have represented grating reminders of the king's mortality, and were frequently suspected of wishing to hasten it. So it was with Frederick William I, the crude, obese, bigoted eighteenth-century ruler of Prussia, who seems to have had a particularly virulent loathing of his eldest son, Frederick.

It didn't take the prince long after his birth to begin aggravating the bully king. A frail and sickly child, young Frederick was a gross insult to his father's vision of what constituted a future monarch. Frederick William would storm into the boy's nursery, mercilessly poking and prodding him as if he were some odious specimen. As the boy grew older, the treatment grew worse.

Holding that "all learned men are fools," the blustering king hated the arts, literature, and science. Indeed he went out of his way to insult members of the esteemed Academy of Sciences, founded by his own father. Young Frederick had the misfortune of naturally embracing the very pursuits his father so despised. He was regularly beaten and tormented by the king, left tearful, and trembling in his presence. Prince Frederick's sister and soulmate, Wilhelmina, often witnessed the ruthless treatment. "The king could not bear my brother," she once recalled. "He abused

him whenever he laid eyes on him, so that Frederick became obsessed with a fear of him which persisted even after he reached
the age of reason."

Determined to eradicate all the cultured interests his son
pursued, King Frederick William ordered a Spartan regimen intended to mold the boy into a miniature version of himself—a
cruel and hostile tyrant. As for music, plays, and other "dissipa-
tions," young Frederick's tutors were ordered, on pain of death,
to "inspire him with a disgust of them." The father would flip at
any perceived foppish behavior on the part of his son, once beating him senseless for using a three-pronged silver fork instead of
the standard two-pronged steel one.

Most everything the prince did invoked his father's violent
wrath, and the relationship deteriorated to such a level of spite
that Frederick once wrote the king begging for understanding.
The reply was written in the glowing warmth of the third person: "The prince," wrote the king, "has a willful and wicked disposition; he does not love his father. A son who loves his father
does the will of that father, not only in his presence, but also
when he is not there to see. He knows perfectly well that I cannot endure an effeminate boy, who is without a single manly inclination, who cannot ride, nor shoot. . . . He has no pleasure
but to follow his own head. That is my answer."

King Frederick William was growing increasingly paranoid
of a plot to kill him, imagining his son at the center of it. He
once accused the prince in the presence of half a dozen Prussian
officers of intending to murder him, not in a direct attack, "since
you are too cowardly," but by stabbing him in the back. Another
encounter led the king to strike his cringing son repeatedly, saying contemptuously, "Had I been treated so by my father, I
would have blown my brains out. But this fellow has no honor,
he takes all that comes."

To escape his father's relentless brutality, Frederick determined to seek refuge at the court of his cousin George II in England. But his plan was discovered, and the prince was arrested and sent to a hellish prison. The king then ordered Frederick and his friend, Lt. Hans von Katte, court-martialed. The military tribunal refused to try Frederick, however, calling it a family matter, but it sentenced von Katte to life imprisonment. Waving aside their verdict, the king sought his own revenge. Von Katte was beheaded, while Frederick was forced to watch.

Eventually humbling himself before his father, Prince Frederick was able to effect a tenuous peace. He then had only to wait quietly for the king's demise. His patience paid off and he assumed the throne in 1740 at age twenty-eight. He would be known to the world as Frederick the Great—famed poet, musician, and military giant who set the stage for the emergence of the German Empire.

4

Peter the Not-So-Hot

Peter the Great was what might be best described as a super-tsar. Standing nearly seven feet tall, this swaggering colossus revolutionized Russia at the turn of the eighteenth century. He founded St. Petersburg, one of the world's most elegant cities. He introduced Western culture to his insular nation and gave it a modern navy. He also tortured his son to death.

The towering tsar was never particularly fond of his heir, Alexis. The mere fact that the tsarevitch was the product of Peter's first marriage to Empress Eudoxia—whom the emperor had cruelly discarded and sent to a nunnery—was one strike against him. Alexis also was lazy, bookish, and disinclined toward anything military—in short, everything his aggressive and domineering father was not. But what really irked Peter was that his son showed no interest in developing the skills necessary to inherit the great Russian throne. Instead, Alexis preferred boozing with members of the old Russian order that the tsar was trying to reform, and romping with his mistress, a Finnish serf named Afrosina.

Tsar Peter was so determined to rouse Alexis to his responsibilities that the heir lived in pathological fear of disappointing him. Once, dreading an appointment with his dad to demonstrate the military maneuvers he was supposed to be learning, Alexis contrived to create a diversion. It was quite a diversion.

He tried to shoot himself in the hand, but flinched and succeeded only in sustaining a severe gunpowder burn.

Growing tired of his son's gross evasion of duty, Peter sent Alexis a blistering letter, outlining all his failures. "Remember your obstinacy and ill-nature," the tsar wrote, "how often I reproached you for it and for how many years I almost have not spoken to you. But all this has availed nothing, has effected nothing. I was but losing my time, it was striking the air. You do not make the least endeavors, and all your pleasure seems to consist in staying idle and lazy at home. Things of which you ought to be ashamed (forasmuch as they make you miserable) seem to make up your dearest delight, nor do you see the dangerous consequences of it for yourself and for the whole state."

Peter concluded his missive with a threat to disinherit his son if he didn't shape up. To his great surprise, Alexis told him to go ahead and do it. "If Your Majesty will deprive me of the succession to the crown of Russia by reason of my incapacity, your will be done," he wrote. "I even most urgently beg it of you because I do not think myself fit for government." Suspicious of the tsarevitch's easy capitulation, Peter issued a more ominous ultimatum: Either buckle down and prepare to one day rule, or join a monastery. In a blind panic, Alexis opted for something entirely different. He fled Russia.

Dressed as an anonymous Russian officer, accompanied by Afrosina, who was disguised as a male page, and several servants, the terrified Alexis made his way to the Viennese court of his Habsburg brother-in-law, the Emperor Charles VI. Just before Alexis left his homeland, one of his supporters offered a bit of advice: "Remember, if your father sends somebody to persuade you to return, do not do it. He will have you publicly beheaded." If only Alexis had listened.

Peter was livid when he discovered his son was missing. It

was bad enough that Alexis would defy him, but the flight would also encourage all the dissenters who hoped one day to overturn the tsar's sweeping reforms. It didn't take him long to track down the wayward heir, first in Austria, then Naples. Alexis broke into a fit of uncontrollable sobs when he was discovered. He soon received a letter from pop:

My Son:

Your disobedience and the contempt you have shown for my orders are known to all the world. Neither my words nor my corrections have been able to bring you to follow my instructions, and last of all, having deceived me when I bade farewell and in defiance of the oaths you made, you have carried your disobedience to the highest pitch by your flight and by putting yourself like a traitor under foreign protection. This is a thing hitherto unheard of, not only in our family, but among our subjects of any consideration. What wrong and what grief you have thereby occasioned to your father, and what shame you have drawn upon your country!

I write to you for the last time to tell you that you are to do what Messrs. Tolstoy and Rumyantsov [who had been sent to fetch Alexis] will tell you and declare to be my will. If you are afraid of me, I assure you and I promise to God and His judgment that I will not punish you. If you submit to my will by obeying me and if you return, I will love you better than ever. But if you refuse, then I as a father, by virtue of the power I have received from God, give you my everlasting curse; and as your sovereign, I declare you a traitor and I assure you I will find the means to use you as such, in which I hope God will assist me and take my just cause into His hands.

As for what remains, remember I forced you to do nothing. What need had I to give you a free choice? If I had wished to force you, was it not in my power to do it? I had but to command and I would have been obeyed.

Peter

Not only was the prodigal son being lured home with the promise of amnesty, he was further enticed by the guarantee that he could give up the throne, marry Afrosina, and retire to the country. Poor Alexis swallowed it whole. In a public ceremony at the Kremlin, the returning tsarevitch renounced his claim to the throne in favor of his infant half-brother, while prostrating himself before his father, admitting his sins and pleading for forgiveness. Now he could disappear with Afrosina and wait for better times—or so he thought.

While Peter had publicly pardoned Alexis, he was consumed with gnawing doubts about the escape. Had there been a larger conspiracy behind it? Had his life or crown been in danger? Retracting his earlier promise of unconditional immunity, the tsar demanded from his son the names of every person who had been involved with the ignominious flight, or even knew of it. A huge round-up followed. Some of the people Alexis named were executed immediately in a vast public spectacle. Others had their noses and tongues cut off, or their bones broken with a hammer. Some were stretched on a wheel until they died. Some were burned with red-hot irons and glowing coals, or impaled rectally.

Alexis felt lucky to avoid the carnage, but his relief was premature. Peter was convinced his son hadn't told the whole truth regarding any conspiracy to dethrone him. He wanted Alexis to spill all and, to help him along, subjected him to a uniquely Russian torture: the knout, a thick, hard leather whip about three and a half feet long that tore the skin off a victim's back. Fifteen to twenty-five lashes were considered standard; any more than that often led to death.

Alexis received twenty-five strokes the first day of interrogation, but revealed no more than he had already admitted (that he had spoken disparagingly of the tsar to the Austrian emperor). Fifteen more strokes several days later elicited the admission that he had once confessed to a priest that he wished his father were dead. Several days after that Alexis was himself dead, sparing his dad from having to sign his death warrant. It was possibly the greatest price anyone ever paid for running away from home.[1]

---

[1]Peter the Great wasn't the only Russian monarch to murder his child. In 1581, Ivan the Terrible grew so enraged at his son and namesake that he clobbered him with his iron staff, killing young Ivan instantly.

5

We Are Not Abused.
We Are Abusive

Queen Victoria reigned longer than any British monarch before or since, and considering her vigilance in keeping him politically and socially impotent while she lived, her longevity was perhaps her final and greatest disservice to her eldest son and heir, the future King Edward VII.

The rigid, repressed Victoria was never a particularly cozy mum, candidly acknowledging early on that she derived "no especial pleasure or compensation" from her large brood of children. Even when they were tiny babies, Victoria regarded them as distasteful little creatures. "I have no tendre for them," she once remarked, "til they have become a little human; an ugly baby is a very nasty object . . . and the prettiest is frightful when undressed . . . as long as they have their big body and little limbs and that terrible frog-like action."

Victoria displayed a particular enmity toward Prince Edward almost from the beginning. "The hereditary and unfailing antipathy of our Sovereigns to their Heirs Apparent seems thus early to be taking root," Lord Grenville noted, while Lord Clarendon later said that the queen's dislike of the Prince of Wales was "a positive monomania with her. She got quite excited while speaking of him, and it quite irritated her to see him in the room."

The young prince was gregarious and fun-loving—everything his mother forced herself not to be, and with her driving fear that he would grow up to be like her debauched Hanoverian uncles,[1] the queen prescribed a torturously rigid upbringing that stifled the boy's natural inclinations for enjoyment. His rebellion from the constraints imposed did little to endear him to his mama, who bombarded him with criticism and rarely missed an opportunity to register her disappointment in him. "I am in utter despair!" the queen wrote her daughter Vicky in 1858. "The systematic idleness, laziness—disregard of everything is enough to break one's heart, and fills me with indignation!"

On another occasion, Victoria spoke of "the sorrow and bitter disappointment and the awful anxiety for the future this causes us." Even her son's appearance seemed to annoy her. "Handsome I cannot think him," she sniffed, "with that painfully small and narrow head, those immense features and total want of a chin." It was an ironic critique coming from a woman who could very well have been describing herself and who at least admitted of Edward: "He is my caricature."

The chasm between mother and son widened considerably upon the death of Victoria's husband, Prince Albert, to whom she was fanatically devoted and for whose death she loudly blamed Edward. It was enough to make any son feel special. The prince had been caught in a youthful indiscretion with an actress, and the morally sensitive Albert was devastated by the scandal surrounding his son. Coincidentally, he died a short time later. Victoria could not be convinced that it was typhoid,

---

[1]George IV and William IV, among a number of her other licentious uncles.

not grief, that carried her beloved away. In her gloom, the queen declared that she could never look at Edward again "without a shudder." With his typical good nature and kindness, however, the prince overlooked his mother's cruel accusations and remained solicitous and devoted to her.

During Victoria's morbid, self-imposed seclusion that would last for decades, the crepe-draped queen remained determined to keep the Prince of Wales away from anything even remotely resembling responsibility. She was convinced, unjustly, of Edward's inherent unworthiness. "What would happen if I were to die next winter!" she wrote her daughter. "One shudders to think of it: it is too awful a contemplation. . . . The greatest improvement I fear will never make him fit for his position." On another occasion she confided, "I often pray he may never survive me, for I know not what would happen." All important state papers were kept from the prince, providing zero training for his future role. Removing a key from his pocket, Edward's little brother, Leopold, once said: "It is the Queen's Cabinet key, which opens all the secret despatch boxes. . . . The Prince of Wales is not allowed to have one."

Warm-hearted as he was, Edward couldn't help but resent how insignificant his mother made him feel. "I am not of the slightest use to the Queen," he once complained. "Everything I say or suggest is pooh-poohed and my brothers and sisters are more listened to than I am." The more the queen kept him away from responsibility, the more Edward turned to other idle distractions like gambling and womanizing. This only confirmed in Victoria's mind how unworthy he really was.

Never trusting his judgment, the queen even tried to control Edward's private life long after he was married. Lord Stanley noted in 1863 that all London was gossiping about the "extraordinary way" in which the queen insisted on directing "the Prince and Princess of Wales in every detail of their lives. They may not dine out, except with previous approval. . . . In addition, a daily and minute report of what passes at Marlborough House [their London residence] has to be sent to Windsor."

Throughout it all, the prince handled the mistrust and disapproval with dignity and good humor, always remaining a respectful and dutiful son. After he inherited the throne in 1901 at age fifty-nine, King Edward VII would reign with distinction for nine years, proving his mother's attitude toward him totally unfounded. He lent his name to a genteel era, and was nicknamed Edward the Peacemaker for his adroit efforts to keep Europe from war. He was a good king, his mother be damned.

PART V

Royal Family Feud

Bear, like the Turk, no brother near the throne," wrote Alexander Pope in *An Essay on Man*, recalling the days when Eastern kings would secure their thrones by gouging out the hearts and livers of their brethren. Royal relationships were no warmer in Western Europe. The crown meant power, and monarchs spent their days either defending it from predatory relatives, or lording it over the more compliant of their kinsmen. Family ties tended to suffer as a result, rendered as fragile as antique lace.

Richard III: History's most evil uncle?

1

The Royal Raptors

*F*euding royal families have been a part of Britain's heritage from the very beginning. William the Conqueror had barely staked his claim to the island in 1066 before his snarly clan started bickering among themselves. His son, Henry I, imprisoned another son, Robert, Duke of Normandy, for twenty-eight years and is suspected of having orchestrated the tragic hunting "accident" that killed a third son, William II, in 1100. Vying for the crown years later, two of the Conqueror's grandchildren, Stephen and Matilda, plunged the kingdom into a fierce civil war that was only settled when Matilda's son became Henry II in 1154. Poor Henry was subjected to no fewer than four rebellions by his grasping sons, all urged on by their mother, Eleanor of Aquitaine, whose bitter estrangement from Henry resulted in her lengthy imprisonment. This loving family would hound its patriarch to death.

Ruler of vast domains that included all of England and much of France, Henry II decided to divide up his territory among his sons while he was still alive. He even had his eldest son, Henry the Younger, crowned king of England while he, too, retained the title. If Henry was hoping this would make the boys happy and ensure a peaceful transition after his death, he was tragically mistaken. The children wanted the power as well as the titles, and rebelled when Henry indicated he wasn't ready to relinquish that. In various combinations, and with stunning treachery, they rose up against their father—and each other.

There was, at the time, a tapestry hanging in the royal chamber at Westminster. It featured four eaglets preying upon the parent bird, the fourth poised at the parent's neck prepared to gouge out the eyes. "The four eaglets are my four sons who cease not to persecute me even unto death," King Henry reportedly said. "The youngest of them, who I now embrace with so much affection, will some time in the end insult me more grievously than any of the others." And so it came to be.

The fourth eaglet ready to rip out the father's eyes turned out to be Henry's beloved youngest son, the infamous future King John of Magna Carta fame. King Henry had striven to advance John's fortunes, especially since he didn't inherit all the land his brothers did (hence the "Lackland" that is often attached to his name). Showing just how grateful he was, John joined older brother Richard (the Lion Hearted) in his final rebellion against their father.

At least Richard had some legitimate gripes with dad, not the least of which was the recurring rumor that Henry was sleeping with Richard's fiancée. But John's betrayal was too much for his father to bear. When he saw his beloved son had covertly switched allegiance, and that his name now headed the list of conspirators, Henry was finally defeated and broken. The once proud monarch lay back in his bed, closed his eyes in despair, and died. John subsequently kept himself busy during the next reign—that of Richard I—trying to steal his brother's throne while the new king was off fighting in the Crusades. It was against this background of fraternal disloyalty that the legendary Robin Hood played his part.

Royal family relations had hardly improved several generations later when Queen Isabella, estranged wife of Edward II, raided her husband's kingdom with her lover in 1326 and had the king put to a ghastly death.[1] Their son Edward III then sired a family whose descendents engaged in a bloody feud that lasted for more than three decades and became famous as "The Wars of the Roses."

---

[1] One of a number of undignified royal demises explored in Part IX.

2

Crown of Thorns

*T*he Wars of the Roses was a fancy name, coined years later, for a nasty feud in the late fifteenth century between the royal houses of York, represented by the white rose, and Lancaster, represented by the red, over which branch of the Plantagenet dynasty should rule England. Three kings, a prince of Wales, and numerous royal dukes were murdered, executed, or killed in battle during this dark era of inbred intrigue.

The extended royal drama, which so intrigued Shakespeare that he devoted half his history plays to it, originated late in the fourteenth century when Edward III's grandson, who became Henry IV and started the Lancastrian line of kings, usurped the throne of his cousin, Richard II, and had him murdered. While regicide wasn't any way to promote kinship, things nevertheless went fairly smoothly for the Lancastrian kings—at least for a time. Though Henry IV faced a series of rebellions, his son peacefully inherited his throne and went down in history as the heroic Henry V who defeated the French at Agincourt and other great battles during the Hundred Years War while reasserting English power on the continent. The triumphant king died young, however, and was succeeded by his far less inspiring son.

Henry VI, who was not yet a year old when he became king in 1422, grew up to be a kind, pious man, if a bit of a simpleton. Plain and unassuming, he much preferred wearing a hair shirt to a crown and abhorred war and bloodshed. He is still revered to-day as the founder of the famed boys' school Eton and of King's College, Cambridge. Good guy though he was, Henry proved to be a dazzlingly incompetent monarch.

In the medieval world, when mighty rulers were needed to subdue sometimes overwhelming chaos, Henry VI was a tooth-less lion on a savage plain. He was, as Pope Pius II described him, "a man more timorous than a woman, utterly devoid of wit or spirit." Blushing at the very mention of sex, and sincerely be-lieving his son was sired by the Holy Spirit, Henry was hardly the type meant to dominate the feudal food chain.

Surrounding himself with greedy and inept advisors who picked his coffers clean, Henry allowed England to slide into disorder, debt and decay. Crowned ruler of France as well, he stood by as the once vast English possessions there were gradu-ally snatched away by the likes of Joan of Arc until almost noth-ing was left. And further undermining his effectiveness were his debilitating bouts of insanity.

As England fell into ruin and France leaked away under Henry's timid rule, the king's powerful cousin Richard, Duke of York, watched with increasing agitation. Descended from two of Edward III's sons on both his parents' sides, York had a claim to the throne that was arguably superior to Henry's. In time, out of sheer frustration, he would move to assert it. An ugly family clash was looming.

The Duke of York was put in charge of the kingdom while cousin Henry suffered through one of his early bouts with mad-ness, but his influence quickly waned after the king recovered his senses. Seeking to gain more control—and especially to oust Henry's greedy favorite, their mutual cousin, the Duke of Somerset—York confronted Henry by force at St. Albans in 1455. Somerset was killed and the king wounded in the neck by a passing arrow. It was the first battle of the Wars of the Roses, yet while the Yorkists were now ahead by one, the removal of King Henry VI, was not yet part of their plan. That would come later.

The meek monarch sought peace and reconciliation more than anything else, but his ferocious French queen, Margaret of Anjou, was eager to quash York once and for all. Since she was the partner in the marriage with all the mettle, Margaret usually got her way. London at this time was swarming with agitated supporters of both the Duke of York and the Lancastrian King Henry as the government tried to mediate their differences. Ever the dependable sap, the king staged a "loveday" ceremony to encourage and display family unity. Although Queen Margaret went along with the idea—even walking hand in hand with her sworn enemy York in a procession to St. Paul's Cathedral—she did so with clenched teeth.

Margaret was convinced York was out to steal Henry's throne, a suspicion that became all the more gnawing after St. Albans, when Henry suffered through another one of his "episodes" and the royal duke once again assumed control of the kingdom. Raising an army, the angry queen defeated her husband's cousin at the Battle of Ludlow in 1459 and sent him scurrying away to Ireland. She then introduced legislation declaring him a traitor. The act, which not very subtly deplored York's "most diabolic unkindness and wretched envy" and his "execrable and most detestable" deed at St. Albans, was passed by the group of English peers who subsequently became known as "The Parliament of Devils."

Bill or no bill, the now-outlawed Duke of York was far from finished. He returned from Ireland, his forces routed the king's at Northumberland, and Henry was brought back to London a prisoner. When York himself entered the city, he formally submitted his claim to the throne. For once, Henry VI stood up for himself. In defiance of his cousin York's claim, he proclaimed to a gathering of peers, "My father was king [Henry V]; his father was also king [Henry IV]; I have worn the crown for forty years, from my cradle. You have all sworn fealty to me as your sovereign, and your fathers did the like to my fathers. How then can my right be disputed?"

While no one was prepared to unseat an anointed king, York now held the power. Parliament came to a compromise of sorts, reluctantly declaring that the duke would be first in line to inherit the crown, displacing Henry's only son, Edward of Lancaster. Now Queen Margaret was *really* mad. Raising another army in 1460, she had her forces attack York's at the Battle of Wakefield and the duke was killed. His severed head was displayed on the gates of York city with a paper crown stuck to it— a fun, kind of medieval way of mocking his kingly pretensions.

Heading south, the king's victorious Lancastrian forces then attacked the remnants of York's in the second Battle of St. Albans. King Henry was reunited with his family after reportedly spending the entire skirmish laughing and singing to himself. Margaret, meanwhile, treated their son to a little post-battle entertainment; she allowed the seven-year-old Prince of Wales to condemn the Yorkist leaders and then watch their executions. The queen, however, would have little time to gloat. The Duke of York was dead, but his formidable seventeen-year-old son and heir, Edward, was gathering strength. Certainly he didn't find the stunt with his father's head one bit funny.

The people of London also were unamused by all the looting and pillaging King Henry's forces had done while heading south. They slammed the city's gates shut on the royal family and their Lancastrian army and instead welcomed in York's son, who immediately declared himself King Edward IV. Issuing a rather windy proclamation, Edward lamented that in the time of "our adversary, he that calleth himself King Henry the Sixth" there existed "not plenty, peace, justice, good governance, policy and virtuous conversation, but unrest, inward war and trouble, unrightwiseness, shedding and effusion of innocent blood, abusion of the laws, partiality, riot, extortion, murder, rape and vicious living, have been the guiders and leaders of the noble realm of England." It was an elaborate justification for the second usurpation of the throne by a family member in less than a century. And this one would not be the last.

Edward IV was now sovereign, but Henry VI still lived. England's new monarch chased the old to the north, where he met and defeated the ex-king's forces at Towton in the most savage encounter of the long, dreadful family feud. "This battle was sore fought," one chronicler wrote of the cold winter clash, "for hope of life was set [a]side on every part and taking of prisoners was proclaimed a great offence." The snow shimmered with the blood of thousands hacked apart or pierced by arrows, including that of forty-two Lancastrian knights whom Edward ordered immediately beheaded on the battlefield after their capture.

The new king had proved a victorious warrior at Towton. With his hulking frame covered in gilded armor and his helmet adorned with a jeweled coronet, he inspired his forces whenever he appeared among them in the thick of battle. Cousin Henry, on the other hand, characteristically spent the night praying. After the devastating loss, the deposed royal family made a midnight escape to Scotland, carrying whatever possessions they could.

The former King Henry VI became an elusive shadow, hovering forlornly around his lost kingdom for years to come. In 1465, after wandering from refuge to refuge, he was finally captured, betrayed by a monk who had been sheltering him. "He fell into the bloody hands of his deadly enemies, his own subjects," as one contemporary put it. To compound the indignity, the former king of England—his feet tied to the stirrups beneath the belly of his horse and wearing a straw hat—was paraded through several towns on his way to imprisonment in the Tower of London. Parliament, meanwhile, had declared "the said Henry, usurper" a traitor, while enthusiastically confirming Edward's claim to the throne after his formal coronation.

Despite pockets of Lancastrian resistance, often led by the indefatigable former Queen Margaret, Edward IV's Yorkist regime seemed secure. The Wars of the Roses, however, were far from over. King Edward wore the crown, but he had another close relative, the Earl of Warwick, to thank for it. Known to history as "The Kingmaker," Warwick was the second most powerful man in England. Problem was, he wanted to be the first. The eventual confrontation between the king and his "over mighty subject" would result in the stunning restoration of Henry VI. Given the family history, Edward should not have been surprised by the turn of events.

The king's relationship with Warwick started to deteriorate gradually as the earl attempted to control his royal kinsman in exchange for all the help he provided in gaining Edward the crown. But when the king married Elizabeth Woodville, a former lady-in-waiting to ex-Queen Margaret, relations between the two collapsed entirely. Warwick loathed the new queen, primarily because she had a load of upstart relatives whom she sought to advance. With King Edward's support, they married well, reaped huge financial rewards, and were given influential positions in government. The mighty earl felt threatened by all these arrivistes and lashed out.

His first move was to encourage a popular revolt in Kent in 1469, seeding widespread discontent over Queen Elizabeth Woodville's relatives. Her father and brother were early victims of the rebellion, beheaded without trial on Warwick's orders. It was a none too subtle message from the earl to cousin Edward IV that he was not happy. Warwick's cohorts, including Edward's own brother, the Duke of Clarence, continued to sow rebellion, even capturing the king at one point. Edward was forced to abandon any pretense of friendship with his treacherous relatives and declare war. Though he issued a proclamation in the spring of 1470 denouncing Warwick and brother Clarence as "rebels and traitors," he would lose his crown that fall.

Warwick was convinced that he could never control Edward the way he wanted. He also realized the English people would never accept his ally, the Duke of Clarence, as their sovereign. If he wanted to wield power, his only option was to restore the simple-minded and malleable Henry VI. Sailing to France, Warwick made an uneasy peace with his former enemy, Queen Margaret, and swore fealty to Henry. Then he invaded England. Edward barely had time to escape before the earl's forces swarmed London, and the kingmaker moved to put back on the throne the same monarch he had helped knock off it nine years earlier.

A dazed and bewildered Henry VI was released from the Tower of London, where it was noted that he looked and smelt like a prisoner who had definitely not been given the royal treatment. According to a chronicler, they "new arrayed him, and did to him great reverence, and brought him to the palace of Westminster." Meek and simple as ever, "mute as a crowned calf," as one put it, Henry got his old job back. This time he would be Warwick's puppet.

King Henry barely had time to readjust the seat of his newly restored throne before King Edward returned to England with an army in 1471. Warwick was killed in the Battle of Barnet, and Queen Margaret was defeated several weeks later at the Battle of Tewkesbury. Her seventeen-year-old son, Edward of Lancaster, heir to the throne and last hope of the Lancastrians, was killed. Lodged once again in the Tower, Henry VI was quietly murdered there as his cousin, once again, became Edward IV. The dead king's corpse was openly displayed in London to show anyone who may have doubted it that the house of Lancaster was finished.

Thus, the Wars of the Roses were temporarily suspended. With no one left to fight, the house of York simply turned on one another. Besides the Duke of Clarence, whom Edward eventually had executed, the king had another brother, Richard, Duke of Gloucester, who had served him well during the clashes with his Lancastrian foes. Richard, however, proved himself a far better brother than an uncle.

&

After Edward IV died in 1483, his eldest son by all rights should have succeeded him as King Edward V. Thanks to his dear uncle Richard, though, he was never crowned. Richard, who had been named Protector in Edward IV's will, snatched away the thirteen-year-old boy-king as he traveled to London for his coronation and immediately lodged him in the Tower of London. Edward was soon joined there by his younger brother, the duke of York, whom Uncle Richard had lured out of sanctuary at Westminster. The "Protector" then proceeded to have both his nephews declared bastards and took the crown for himself as King Richard III.

The two young boys in the Tower were never seen or heard

from again. Although certain partisans of Richard III dispute it,[2] most historians believe the usurping king had them murdered— smothered to death as they slept, by some accounts. It was a crime that even in the darkest of ages the English people could not stomach. "The hatred which Richard's crime had roused against him throughout the land remained sullen and quenchless," wrote Winston Churchill in his *History of the English Speaking Peoples*, "and no benefits bestowed, no sagacious measures adopted, no administrative successes achieved, could avail the guilty monarch."

Two years after the wicked uncle managed to become King Richard III, the Wars of the Roses briefly resumed. In 1485, the last remaining Lancastrian heir, who became Henry VII, defeated Richard III at Bosworth Field, where he was killed. With the last Yorkist king dead, Henry united the battling houses of York and Lancaster when he married Edward IV's daughter, Elizabeth, and established the house of Tudor. After one final Yorkist uprising at Stoke in 1487, the Wars of the Roses were officially over. The bloody legacy of the great family clash, however, would spill over well into the next century.

Henry VII efficiently executed any Yorkist relatives who got too close to his throne, but he was plagued nevertheless by

---

[2]Among his most ardent supporters is a group called The Richard III Society, which believes the king has been maligned by history, especially by Shakespeare and by one of the sources for his unflattering play about Richard, Sir Thomas More. Far from the demonic "bottled spider" conjured by the Bard, many Ricardians see a cuddly medieval teddy bear. "I just know that if I were alive in the fifteenth century I could borrow a cup of sugar from Richard," one Ricardian gushed in a society newsletter. Thomas More, partisans say, was nothing but a Tudor-era lackey, writing his history of Richard III during the reign of Henry VIII (the son of Richard's vanquisher), and loath to offend his monarch—never mind that More eventually lost his head for his willingness to defy royalty. While it is true that Richard was not deformed—that was a literary device to indicate raw evil—the evidence of his treachery is compelling indeed. There is, among so much else, the well-documented heap of bodies and reputations that Richard climbed over to achieve power, and the inescapable fact that it was during his reign that his young nephews disappeared forever.

people claiming to be dead relatives. One of them, Perkin Warbeck, was the son of a boatman who claimed to be the younger of Edward IV's sons murdered in the Tower of London by their uncle Richard III. Warbeck went from a pesky imposter to a serious threat when his bold impersonation received the backing of various European monarchs and surviving Yorkists, including the dead boy's own aunt. Proclaimed "Richard IV," Warbeck launched an invasion of England before he was finally captured and eventually hanged.

During the next reign, Henry VIII's multiple marriages were prompted in part by his desire to avert the chaos of the previous century by siring a son to succeed him peacefully. Even after he achieved this goal, though, Henry still faced an extremely dangerous Yorkist foe: his sixty-nine-year-old kinswoman Margaret, Countess of Salisbury. Although the king had once revered this daughter of the Duke of Clarence almost as a mother, late in his reign he suddenly decided that she was an intolerable threat. Henry ordered the old lady beheaded in 1541, but she didn't go quietly. Attempting to escape the headsman's ax, the countess ran around the scaffold trying to elude him. With the executioner in hot pursuit, she was hacked to death. The Tudor dynasty was now safe for its last monarchs, all half-siblings, to make each other's lives miserable.

3

Trouble in the House of Tudor

The children of Henry VIII were never particularly close. Three different mothers and appalling emotional deprivation made it a bit tough for the kids to bond. Instead, they became dangerous rivals. The youngest, Henry's longed-for son by third wife Jane Seymour, succeeded him as Edward VI in 1547. Though he was only nine at the time, Edward was a precocious lad, well-versed in the classics and a master of languages. He was also a cold-hearted prig who actively sought to have his two half sisters, Mary and Elizabeth, disinherited from the crown.

Despite his youth, the boy king was a seasoned fanatic on matters of religion. While Henry VIII had broken away from the Church of Rome after disagreeing with the pope over the validity of his first marriage, his English Church remained essentially Catholic in doctrine and ritual. The rigidly Protestant Edward and his like-minded advisers, however, sought to strip away all vestiges of the old religion in a revolution of reform. Only problem was the young king got sick.

Edward knew that when he died, his staunchly Catholic sister Mary—every bit the fanatic he was—would inherit and immediately destroy his reform efforts by returning the Church to Rome. No amount of threats, and there had been plenty, ever persuaded her to join the Protestant cause. In retaliation for his sister's stubbornness, the king moved to bar her from ever sitting on the throne.

Dying of tuberculosis, Edward ordered a new "Devise for Succession" that declared Mary, and their sister Elizabeth, "illegitimate and not lawfully begotten." The loving little brother was officially calling his older sisters bastards unfit to rule. In direct defiance of Henry VIII's will, which provided that Mary, then Elizabeth should succeed, Edward left the crown to their cousin, Lady Jane Grey. He expected the two women stripped of their birthright to accept their fate politely and "live in quiet order, according to our appointment."

Fat chance of that.

After Edward VI died in 1553 at age sixteen, cousin Jane ruled for only nine days before Mary reclaimed the throne that was rightfully hers. Poor Jane was eventually beheaded, but Queen Mary I spared most of her wrath for sister Elizabeth. Although the new queen, England's first undisputed female monarch, had invited Elizabeth to ride with her in a triumphant parade into London, it didn't take long for unresolved issues that had been festering for years to resurface. Mary had never forgotten the cruel treatment she and her mother, Katherine of Aragon, had endured at the vindictive whim of Elizabeth's mother, Anne Boleyn.

Though Elizabeth was too young to have had anything to do with her mother's behavior after she supplanted Katherine and became Henry VIII's second wife, Mary saw flashes of Anne Boleyn in her half sister that deeply annoyed her. She would frequently remark that Elizabeth had "the face and countenance of Mark Smeaton, who was a very handsome man." It was not a compliment. Smeaton had been executed as one of Anne Boleyn's alleged lovers, and Mary's clear implication was that she and Elizabeth—who actually looked a lot more like Henry VIII than did Mary—weren't even related.

Beyond the bitchy paternity references, Mary mistrusted and feared Elizabeth's magnetic popularity with the English people and, even more seriously, her avowed Protestantism. Her innate suspicions about her sister were deliberately stoked by the Spanish ambassador, who also feared Elizabeth because of her potential threat to Catholic Spain if she came to the throne. He warned the queen that her sister "might, out of ambition or being persuaded thereto, conceive some dangerous design and put it to execution by means which would be difficult to prevent." Mary hardly needed to be reminded.

Elizabeth was shrewd enough to know that Mary's fanatic Catholicism, which guided her entire public policy, could make her a fearsome adversary. The queen, after all, didn't earn the name "Bloody" Mary for nothing. Hundreds of Protestants were burned at the stake during her reign. With her piercing eyes, manly voice, and uncompromising outlook, this was one scary lady. Wisely, Elizabeth decided to play the game and get herself to church.

Thrilled with the conversion—having no clue just how expedient it really was—Mary showered her sister with jewels of favor. But she wasn't fooled for long. Elizabeth seemed unable or unwilling to play the pious churchgoer to the full, acting more like a fidgety four-year-old. At her first Mass, Elizabeth "complained loudly all the way to church that her stomach ached, wearing a suffering air," according to one report. Mary's animosity, compounded by her shock that someone could be so insincere in matters of salvation, soon came rushing back.

Because Elizabeth appeared to conform, however, the queen was unable to move against her sister. She did raise before Parliament an act invalidating Henry VIII's marriage to Anne Boleyn, which would make Elizabeth illegitimate, but this was nothing new. Most of England, including her father and brother, had at one point or another called Anne Boleyn's daughter a bastard. Mary needed something else to bring down her sister. She would spend the rest of her life trying to find it.

Around this time the queen made one of the most disastrous decisions of a five-year reign filled with them. She became engaged to the heir to the Spanish throne, her cousin, the future Philip II. Never crazy about foreigners to begin with, the notoriously isolated English balked at the idea of being ruled by one. Oblivious to the sensibilities of her xenophobic subjects, Mary was determined to return England to the pope, with Philip ruling right by her side. As agitation over the impending marriage spread, Mary was convinced her sister was at the center of it all. She sent an ominous message to Elizabeth, warning that her "present unwise conduct was known," and if she continued to misbehave she "might have reason to regret it." When national discontent turned to active rebellion, Mary made good on her threat.

Elizabeth, who had earlier received permission to leave Mary's court and move to the country, was ordered back to London after a revolt led by Thomas Wyatt reached the capital. Though she was vigorously questioned about the rebellion, which had as its aim to place her on the throne, no evidence against Elizabeth could be found. But Mary wasn't about to let something as trivial as apparent innocence get in her way. Elizabeth was ordered to the Tower of London, where her mother had lost her head years before.

Terrified by what might happen to her, Elizabeth begged for permission to write her sister before being sent away. The princess opened the letter on which she believed her life depended by affirming her innocence in any plot against the queen, swearing that she had "never practiced, counseled, nor consented to anything that might be prejudicial to your person in any way, or dangerous to the state by any means."

Elizabeth knew these assurances would mean little to Mary, who was convinced her sister was a dissembling heretic filled with malice, so she appealed to the queen on another level. After reminding Mary of a promise she had made before Elizabeth left for the countryside never to punish her "without answer and due proof," she alluded to an earlier tragedy to which they had both been witness.

During the reign of their brother Edward VI, the king's uncle, Thomas Seymour, was beheaded without ever being allowed to plead in person to his brother, the Lord Protector, who was running the country in the young king's name. "I have heard in my time of many cast away for want of coming to their prince," Elizabeth wrote Mary, believing that the queen's actions were in part being prompted by her ultraconservative Catholic counselors eager to see her forced out of the way. "I pray God that evil persuasions persuade not one sister against the other, and all for that they have heard false report." Mary was unmoved by her sister's plea. Instead, she was angry that Elizabeth had been given time to write the desperate letter rather than being conveyed immediately to the Tower as she had commanded.

The queen's wishes were carried out the very next day when Elizabeth was taken away by barge in the pouring rain. At the entrance to the forbidding structure that had been witness to centuries of torture, murder, and execution, Elizabeth mustered the dramatic flair that would serve her so well when she became queen herself. She at first refused to leave the barge that carried her to the Tower, but then relented and proclaimed, "Here landeth as true a subject, being prisoner, as ever landed at these stairs." With that, she plopped herself down on the steps and refused to budge. With the rain pelting her, she rebuffed pleas to move inside. "It is better sitting here than in a worse place," she huffed.

The scene so moved some of those present that they wept for the proud Tudor princess rendered so vulnerable, but Elizabeth immediately made it clear that her actions were a protest against injustice, not symptoms of despair. "She knew her truth to be such that no man would have cause to weep for her," a witness recorded. With that, Elizabeth, head raised high, swept grandly into the prison.

Much to Queen Mary's chagrin, it became clear that Elizabeth could not be held forever without charges being brought against her. And the evidence just wasn't there. Undeterred, the queen went out of her way to make her sister's stay at the Tower as unpleasant as possible before reluctantly releasing her. When Mary heard that a five-year-old boy was in the habit of bringing Elizabeth flowers during her brief walks, she forbade the kindness, harmless though it was. "I can bring you no more flowers, Lady," the boy sadly told the princess.

After her release, Elizabeth was put under house arrest at one of the queen's manor houses. In some ways it was worse than the Tower. A zealous guard ensured Elizabeth would enjoy very little freedom and have her routine meticulously regimented. Exasperated, she wrote an angry letter to Mary, addressing her throughout as "You," rather than the appropriate qualifier of Highness or Majesty. The letter did not enhance Elizabeth's standing with her sister, who angrily responded by reiterating her reasons for suspecting Elizabeth of treason and reminding her that she had been treated with "more clemency and favor . . . than [those] in like matters had been accustomed." The insulted queen concluded by stating that in the future she did not wish to be "molested" by such her "disguise and colorable letters."

Despite her greatest efforts to bring Elizabeth down, though, Mary was losing the struggle. Her popularity was plummeting as she persecuted hundreds of Protestants by burning them at the stake. She had also been persuaded by her husband King Philip to join his fruitless war against France. In the process Calais, England's last possession on the continent, was lost. It was a stunning psychological blow to the nation and to Mary, who also suffered the humiliation of a false pregnancy she had hoped would solve the problem of her sister ever succeeding to the throne.

Elizabeth, on the other hand, only gained more esteem among the people through her persecution. The queen was forced into the terrible realization that she could do nothing to stop her. Brokenhearted over her many failures, Queen Mary I grew increasingly ill, but she did live long enough to see all eyes turn to Elizabeth as it became obvious that her succession was inevitable. It was a cruel blow. The unhappy queen finally died in 1558 at age forty-two. Upon hearing the news, the new Queen Elizabeth I was overcome by emotion. Falling to her knees, she exclaimed in Latin, "This is the doing of the Lord, and it is marvelous in our eyes." No tears at that funeral.

A century later, another set of sister queens were at each other's throats.

4

Shattered Sorority

Although the feud between Mary II and her sister, the future Queen Anne, lacked the potential deadliness of the one between Mary I and Elizabeth I, it was every bit as bitter. Oddly enough, Mary and Anne got along famously as they sought to overthrow their father James II. In what became known as The Glorious Revolution, King James was forced to abandon his kingdom and flee to France in 1688. Neither his subjects nor his Protestant daughters would tolerate his autocratic Catholic tendencies. With the throne still warm, Mary and her invading Dutch husband William settled right in as coregents. This was fine with Anne, who even gave up her right to succeed immediately if Mary died before William.

But then things started to get nasty. Mary began bossing her sister around, acting like she was, well, queen of England. Anne was having none of it. The first fight of many was over Anne's allowance. Mary was annoyed that her sister's friends, led by Sarah Churchill, the Duchess of Marlborough, had brought the matter of Anne's finances to the attention of Parliament without ever telling the king and queen. When Mary approached her sister about it, Anne replied nonchalantly that she believed some of her friends simply wanted her to have a decent settlement. "Pray, what friends have you but the king and me?" the queen demanded imperiously.

With that, the claws emerged and a feud was born. Mary started by arbitrarily denying Anne her choice of residence, and at one point took away her guards. Anne ended up getting mugged. King William III joined in, too. Next to his lovely and complacent wife, the king found his hefty sister-in-law willful and obnoxious, and he treated her lazy husband, Prince George of Denmark, little better than a piss boy. In retaliation, and urged on by Sarah Churchill, Anne deliberately snubbed William and Mary. Among her friends she referred to the king as "the Dutch abortion" and slighted her sister at every available opportunity. It was all petty and ridiculous, but it would get much worse.

At the center of the growing breach was Anne's friend Sarah, the Duchess of Marlborough. While Sarah had already made a habit of stirring things up between the royal sisters, as in the finance matter, her presence in Anne's inner circle became intolerable to Queen Mary for another reason. Sarah's husband, the Duke of Marlborough, (the couple were Winston Churchill's ancestors) had been a leader in the Glorious Revolution that drove James II from the throne. There were indications, however, that the duke's loyalty was turning back to the deposed king. Certainly he had corresponded with James in exile. For this reason, Marlborough was a threat to William and Mary, and the queen viewed Anne's friendship with the wife of such a man as insulting, if not treasonous. She demanded her sister send Sarah away, but Anne, stubborn as always, refused.

"This year began with family troubles of mine," wrote Mary at the beginning of 1692. "Where they will end God only knows." With the help of Sarah, the rift was growing wider and wider. The night before the Duke of Marlborough was dismissed from court as a suspected traitor, Mary and Anne had a terrible fight. The queen flew into a rage over the fact that Anne was sharing with Sarah some of the money she had received from Parliament, making it clear that she felt public money should not be spent on the wife of the man strongly suspected of treachery. Again she demanded Sarah's removal—and again Anne refused.

Several weeks later Anne brazenly showed up at court with Sarah in tow. While Queen Mary kept her cool publicly, the next day she fired off a scathing letter of rebuke to her sister. In it, she reiterated her position that Sarah had to go, adding "that I have all the reason imaginable to look upon your bringing her [to court], as the strangest thing that ever was done."

Anne was not pleased with the lofty attitude of the letter and showed it to Sarah, who later noted that it seemed to be Mary's intention "to remind her sister of the distance between them and of what was due from the Princess of Denmark to the Queen of England." Anne agreed and sat down to write her own angry letter. "Your care of my present condition is extremely obliging," she wrote sarcastically. "And if you would be pleased to add to it so far, as upon my account to recall your severe command [to send away Sarah], I should ever acknowledge it as a very agreeable mark of your kindness to me. And I must freely own, that as I think this proceeding can be for no other intent than to give me a very sensible mortification, so there is no misery that I cannot readily resolve to suffer, rather than the thoughts of parting with her."

Given Mary's passion for her own friend Frances Apsley,[1] it would seem that she might at least understand Anne's devotion to Sarah, but that was not the case. She responded to Anne's letter with a curt message informing her that Sarah was forbidden to stay at her house. The duchess, always right in the thick of it,

---

[1] Details of Mary's crush on Frances are found in Part I, Chapter 3.

noted that her friend was being denied the right every subject had "of being mistress in her own house." The relationship grew even frostier. "In all this," wrote Mary, "I see the hand of God, and look upon our disagreeing as a punishment upon us for the irregularity by us commited upon the Revolution" against their father.

While the mutual animosity never mellowed between them, Mary did visit her sister one last time. Anne had just given birth to one of her many dead babies, but instead of consoling the devastated woman, Mary took the opportunity to once again harp about Sarah. Anne was left white with anger, and the sisters would never see each other again.

Some time later, when Mary II was dying of smallpox at only thirty-two years of age, there would be a reconciliation of sorts between the sisters, but not face to face. Their father James, on the other hand, was apparently still so bitter over his forced retirement from the throne that he refused to allow his court in exile to mourn for his dead daughter.

Anne became queen in 1702 after the death of her brother-in-law William III. Plagued by gout, obesity, and all manner of other maladies, she was never the picture of vigorous good health. Seventeen pregnancies didn't help matters, either. Unfortunately, most of her children were born dead, or did not live very long. None survived her. So when the last monarch of the Stuart dynasty mercifully passed away in 1714, a foreigner came to the throne.

5

Dislike Father, Dislike Son

A vaguely ridiculous princeling from the German duchy of Hanover, a distant cousin, was the royal family's closest legal relative after the death of Queen Anne.[1] Although he barely spoke a word of English, he was promptly imported from Germany to rule Britain as King George I. Thus, the House of Hanover was established. It would be distinguished by five generations of fathers and sons who absolutely despised one another.[2]

The animosity that existed between George I and his son, also named George, went back years to when the father was sovereign of only his miniature German kingdom of Hanover, the son was just a boy, and a messy affair alienated them forever. The elder George's beautiful but reckless wife, Sophia Dorothea, was found to be sleeping with a Swedish officer by the name of Philip von Konigsmark. After the affair was discovered, Konigs-

---

[1] Queen Anne did have a half brother, James Edward Stuart, known as "The Old Pretender." He was James II's son by his second wife Mary of Modena, but was declared ineligible to inherit the British crown because he was an avowed Catholic. Nevertheless, he did have supporters, including Louis XIV of France, and they declared him King James III upon his father's death in exile. The Old Pretender made several abortive attempts to gain the throne, as did his son, Charles Edward Stuart, known as both "The Young Pretender" and "Bonnie Prince Charlie." The Stuart cause was a lost one, however, and the foreign Hanoverian line continues to rule to this day.
[2] And who, as seen in Part I, Chapter 3, raised lechery to new heights.

mark mysteriously disappeared. It was rumored that George had him hacked to pieces and buried beneath the floorboards of his palace at Hanover. Sophia Dorothea's fate was arguably worse. After divorcing her, George ordered his ex-wife locked away for the rest of her life. She would live another thirty-two years, forbidden from ever seeing her children again.

Young George was so despondent over the fate of his mother that he once reportedly swam the moat of her castle prison in a vain attempt to rescue her. He never forgave his father for the mistreatment of his mother and grew up hating him. The feeling was mutual. When George I became king of Britain, his son, now Prince of Wales, sought to undermine him at every opportunity by courting political opponents to the king's party. He even formed his own opposition party in both houses of Parliament. This did not endear son to father.

Simmering tensions between the two evolved into all-out war when King George booted Prince George out of the palace. He was forbidden from seeing his own children, who remained in the king's care, and was declared persona non grata to anyone who wished to retain the king's favor. Undeterred, the Prince of Wales established a rival court at his new home, Leicester House. Among the favorite activities of the dissidents who gathered there was making fun of the king and all his blundering ways—especially his penchant for ugly mistresses.

Whenever father and son did meet, fearful scenes tended to erupt. King George even ordered the prince arrested at one point, but nothing came of it except even more hostility. It was said that Prince George could not wait for his father to die so he could finally free his mother, but this was not to be. Sophia Dorothea died in 1726, a year before her ex-husband. When the prince heard the news that the king had finally expired, he could hardly believe it. "Dat is one big lie," he exclaimed in his thick German accent, incredulous that he was at last free from his paternal enemy.

❧

Relations between the new King George II and his own son, Frederick, Prince of Wales, were even less tender. "Our first-born is the greatest ass, the greatest liar, the greatest canaille and the greatest beast in the whole world and we heartily wish he was out of it," the proud papa once said. George I had wanted his grandson to marry Princess Wilhelmina of Prussia, but as soon as George II ascended to the throne he immediately nixed the match. "I did not think that ingrafting my half-witted coxcomb upon a mad woman would improve the breed," he later explained.

Prince Frederick held his father in equal esteem, describing him as "an obstinate self-indulgent miserly martinet with an insatiable sexual appetite." He had a point. Like his father before him, the king became the object of ridicule within his son's social circles. Hearing such insightful declarations as "I hate all boets and bainters," who could resist? Thanks to King George's increasing obsession with order and punctuality, his court became rigid and dull. "No mill horse ever went on a more constant track on a more unchanging circle," Lord Hervey once remarked. All the fun was to be had at Prince Frederick's alternative court.

Hoping to undermine his son's ability to entertain, and thus his social standing, King George slashed the prince's allowance. He also made it clear, just as his own father had done to him before, that any contact with Frederick or his wife would be considered a gross insult to the king. But the Prince of Wales thrived nevertheless, and constantly eclipsed his father among London's glittering elite. "My Got," gasped the outraged king, "popularity always makes me sick, but [Frederick's] makes me vomit."[3] King George could barely muster even a facade of mourning when Prince Frederick died in 1751.

⬥

Because of Frederick's early death, George II was succeeded by his grandson, George III, in 1760. With a large brood of debauched sons, the king who lost the American colonies had plenty of opportunity to continue the great Hanoverian tradition of father-son feuding. When he wasn't exhibiting symptoms of madness, King George was rather prudish in his moral outlook. His sons' wild behavior, therefore, upset him tremendously, and he never failed to scold them whenever the opportunity arose.

He was particularly disturbed by his eldest son and heir, the future George IV. During his rational moments the king berated the Prince of Wales for his compulsive drinking, gambling, and womanizing, but it was during his lapses into insanity that King George really let loose on his son. During one episode, the royal family was dining at Windsor Castle when the king exploded in a mad fit. Interrupting the conversation, George suddenly rose up from the table, grabbed the prince by the collar, yanked him out of his chair and flung him against a wall. Prince George broke into tears after the scene, but recovered sufficiently to use his father's mental illness to his advantage.

The loyal son delighted audiences all over London with his wicked imitations of his dad's foaming-at-the-mouth bouts of insanity. And he made no secret of his desire to see the king locked away forever so he could rule in his stead. When it looked like the king's illness was becoming permanent, the younger George joyfully swept into action and prepared for his Regency.

---

[3]Some sources attribute this sentiment to Frederick's equally unloving mother, Queen Caroline.

George III disappointed him, however. The king seemed to rally after each episode, leaving the prince to wait like a buzzard for a permanent descent into insanity. He was finally rewarded in 1810, when his father left reason behind for good.

With no son of his own to carry on the father-son feuding for which the Hanoverians had become so famous, George IV simply turned on his daughter, Charlotte. He was repelled by the spirited girl, detecting in his heir elements of her crude, licentious mother, Caroline, from whom he was bitterly estranged.[4] When Princess Charlotte had the grace to die in labor, there were no other children among George III's sons, so a mad scramble began among them to settle down and sire an heir. Edward, Duke of Kent, was the lucky one, fathering the future Queen Victoria in 1819.

---

[4]See Part III, Chapter 6.

6

In-Laws on the Outs

After George IV died in 1830, he was succeeded by his brother William IV. Victoria was next in line right after him. The girl's mother couldn't stand the king her daughter was destined to replace, finding him to be an oversexed oaf, and she was fiercely determined to keep her precious Victoria away from him. King William did not appreciate the effort. In front of a large group of guests gathered one night at Windsor Castle, he lacerated his sister-in-law for her rudeness:

"I should . . . have the satisfaction of leaving the royal authority to the personal exercise of that young lady (pointing to Victoria), the heiress presumptive of the crown, and not in the hands of a person now near me [Victoria's mother], who is surrounded by evil advisors and who is herself incompetent to act with propriety in the station in which she would be placed.

"I have no hesitation in saying that I have been insulted—grossly and continually insulted—by that person, but I am determined to endure no longer a course of behavior so disrespectful to me. Amongst many other things I have particularly to complain of the manner in which that young lady has been kept away from my court; she has been repeatedly kept from my drawing-rooms, at which she ought always to have been present, but I am fully resolved that this shall not happen again.

"I would have her know that I am king, and that I am determined to make my authority respected, and for the future I shall insist and command that the Princess do upon all occasions appear at my Court, as it is her duty to do so."

Recalling the terrible scene some twenty years later, Queen Victoria told her eldest daughter how she remembered always being "on pins and needles, with the whole family hardly on speaking terms. I (a mere child) between two fires—trying to be civil and then scolded at home! Oh! it was dreadful, and that has given me such a horror of Windsor, which I can't get over." If that family tension upset her, imagine how the queen would have felt had she lived to see her grandsons—Kaiser Wilhelm II of Germany and King George V of Britain—face off in a little conflict that became known as World War I.

7

The Battling Bonapartes

While the royal families of Britain spent centuries squabbling among themselves, their ancient enemies across the channel were engaged in similar pursuits. In France it had always been Valois versus Valois or Bourbon versus Bourbon. Then came the Bonapartes—perhaps the most dysfunctional bunch of them all.

Things were going fairly well for Napoleon after a series of dubious military victories made him a star in post–Revolutionary France. But then the diminutive Corsican with the gargantuan ego had to go and make himself royal. As soon as he crowned himself emperor in 1804, his already fractious family started acting royal as well. Judging by the way they treated one another, the Bonapartes all played their new roles magnificently.

When the clan wasn't maneuvering for more power and wealth, they were rebelling against their brother's imperious rule and making his life miserable. "The Emperor is truly rendered unhappy by his family," Madame Desvaisnes said at the time of Napoleon's coronation. "They are all acting like a pack of devils deliberately bent on tormenting him." The emperor, for his part, indulged his siblings' greed with kingdoms, titles, and lots and lots of cash, but only because it suited him. When it did not, he never hesitated to snatch his gifts away. And in return for the generous bounty, his brothers and sisters were subjects of his unbending will.

Napoleon's rapid rise to glory was particularly hard on his older brother, Joseph, who had grown accustomed to being the respected leader of the fatherless family. It was to him they always turned in times of trouble, and his word was law. Even Napoleon—who bowed to no man—handed over his salary to Joseph for investment and dispersal. "Whatever circumstances fate reserves for you," Napoleon wrote his older brother in an uncharacteristically mushy letter in the years before his fame surged and his heart closed, "you certainly know, my friend, you can have no better friend than I, who holds you most dear and who desires most sincerely your happiness. . . . We have lived together for so many years, and have been so closely united, that our hearts are one, and you know better than anyone how fond I am of you. I find in writing these words an emotion I have rarely felt in my life."

The warm feelings between the Bonaparte brothers would soon evaporate. Joseph was left seething with jealousy as his younger brother eclipsed him and came to dominate not only the family, but Europe as well. He was losing his treasured place of honor, and though Napoleon tossed him lucrative positions and other consolation prizes along the way, it still rankled.

The emperor wanted his family to participate in his new dynasty, but he made a decision that would forever alienate him from Joseph. Childless at the time, Napoleon named his nephew heir to the throne—a position Joseph naturally assumed would be his. "If my brother cannot entrust this to me," Joseph fumed after firing a pistol at a portrait of Napoleon, "if he does not do for me what is expected of him [then] . . . to sacrifice one's tastes, one's ambitions, for nothing, for the mere possibility of an eventual position of power, to endure all that, and then possibly in vain, one must be either insane or a born intriguer."

A fearful scene between the brothers erupted a few months

before Napoleon's coronation, with Joseph screeching about his rights as the eldest member of the family and Napoleon becoming infuriated at his presumption. "How dare he speak to me of *his* rights and of *his* interests!" Napoleon raged. "To do this before me, his brother, to arouse his jealousy and pretensions, is to wound me at my most sensitive point. I shall not forget that . . . It is as if he had said to an impassioned lover that he had fucked his mistress. Well . . . my mistress is the power I have created. I have done far too much to achieve this conquest to permit someone else to ravish or even covet her."

When one of his counselors attempted to speak up for Joseph, Napoleon lashed out again: "You forget therefore that my brothers are nothing without me, that they are great now because I have made them so . . . there are thousands of men in France who have rendered far greater services to the state. But let's face the hard facts. Joseph is not destined to reign. He is older than I: I will live longer than he, and in addition, I am in good health. Moreover, he was not born in a high enough social position to have warranted such an illusion on his part . . . He, like myself, was born in a common position. But I raised myself by my own abilities. He, on the other hand, has remained exactly the same since birth. To rule in France, one must either be born in grandeur . . . or else be capable of distinguishing oneself above all the others . . . For the succession to the throne to succeed, it must therefore be passed on to our children born in that grandeur."

The spat between Joseph and Napoleon continued unabated as the coronation approached and Joseph threatened to boycott the entire ceremony. This did nothing to ease the tension. "If you refuse to come to the Coronation," Napoleon warned, "from that very moment you may consider yourself my enemy. In such a situation how do you propose to fight me? Where is

your army with which to carry out your attack? You lack everything and I will annihilate you." Joseph did show up, in a huff,
glowering at Napoleon as he sat across from him in the royal carriage taking them to Notre Dame Cathedral. He was hardly
mollified when he was given the throne of Naples after Napoleon
conquered it, and the relationship would deteriorate even further when the emperor later propped him up on the Spanish
throne.

Believing Napoleon's campaign to conquer Spain ill-
conceived and a horrendous waste of lives and money, Joseph
never wanted the crown. But after his other three brothers rejected it for their own reasons, Joseph reluctantly agreed to trade
in his relatively peaceful realm of Naples for the agitated penin-
sula bristling under French domination. He did so under the
condition that the emperor promise not to give Naples to anyone outside the immediate family. Yet no sooner had he crossed
the border into Spain than Napoleon went back on his word—
as he so often did—and handed Naples over to a brother-in-law,
Joachim Murat.

Joseph was incensed by the betrayal, but he had more to
worry about when he reached Madrid. The city was in revolt
against the brutal French occupation and the new king was
forced to flee almost immediately upon arriving. "You make war
like a postal inspector, not a general!" Napoleon scolded him after the flight. Although Joseph was restored to the throne by the
emperor and his army, he was never given a chance to rule.
Napoleon waved aside his plea for benevolence toward Spain
which Joseph argued was essential to quelling the intense hatred
for France and in restoring order. "Joseph still believes himself to
be my elder," the emperor snorted, "he still has pretensions to
head the family. Is there anything more absurd!"

Instead of heeding his brother's advice, Napoleon stepped

up his effort to crush Spain. And by putting his forces in charge of the government, he rendered Joseph a virtual puppet king. "If his . . . purpose is to make me feel disgusted with Spain," Joseph wrote his wife, "he has achieved his end. . . . The vexing position in which he wishes to leave me as ruler of a great country is quite unacceptable. I want to know precisely what he wants of me, and if that position includes humiliating me, then I wish to retire from here. I do not want to be under tutelage of those beneath me [French officers and other officials]. I do not want to see my provinces administered by men I do not trust. I do not want to be merely a crowned child-king, because I do not need a crown to prove myself a man, and I feel myself quite great enough on my own merits without having to put up with such charades."

Joseph traveled to Paris and confronted his brother, demanding more political and military independence for himself and more financial help for Spain. Napoleon appeared to acquiesce and Joseph returned to his "kingdom" somewhat placated. But only four days later the emperor announced that all Bonapartes ruling as monarchs within his European empire (there were three) were thereby reduced from kings to mere French princes. This did not enhance Joseph's standing in the country he was supposed to be ruling and the Spanish Cortez immediately pounced on Napoleon's decree. "Joseph is more than ever a marionette in the power of the French, a man without authority," it was proclaimed, "[and] can be considered only an object of profound contempt by all Spaniards who love the independence and honor of their country."

With a simultaneous campaign to conquer Russia going as disastrously as the one to subdue Spain, Napoleon decided to withdraw from the latter. He just never bothered to tell Joseph of his plans. Instead, he finally gave his older brother some responsibility by putting him in charge of the military assault against Spanish rebels—a sham that cost hundreds of thousands of lives and accomplished nothing in light of the predetermined French withdrawal. Though Napoleon had betrayed him time and again—and even had the audacity to blame him for the failures in Spain—Joseph remained loyal to his brother to the bitter end.

Not so, the other Bonaparte siblings.

Sitting beside Joseph on that tense carriage ride to the coronation was his brother Louis. If Joseph was feeling resentment toward the emperor, Louis was churning with a hatred only the deranged can muster. And Louis was indeed deranged, possibly due to an advanced case of gonorrhea. Like Joseph, Louis had been bypassed from the succession in favor of his son because of his deteriorating mental condition.

"No, I shall never consent to it!" Louis had burst out upon hearing Napoleon's plan to disinherit him and personally raise his son as heir. "Rather than renounce my right to the throne, rather than agree to bow my head before my own son, I will leave France. . . . Then we will see if you will dare to kidnap the son from his father in broad daylight!"

Louis, who had married Napoleon's stepdaughter Hortense, by his wife Josephine, was convinced Hortense was part of the plot to shunt him aside and took all his wrath out on her. He refused to let her see her mother, confined her to the house, and put spies on her twenty-four hours a day. "If you support your mother's interests at the expense of mine," he threatened, "I swear I will make you regret it. I will separate you from your son. I will have you locked up behind high walls in some utterly unknown place from which no human power can ever extricate you, and you will spend the rest of your life paying for your condescending view of me and my family. And just you take special care that none of my threats reaches my brother's ears! All his power cannot protect you from my wrath."

Napoleon made Louis king of Holland in 1806, leaving the country nominally autonomous rather than annexing it outright. The effectiveness of King Louis's reign would closely mirror Joseph's in Spain—only with the added handicap of mental illness. He fancied himself a Dutchman and insisted on speaking the language, no matter how badly he butchered it. He dismissed most of the French advisers Napoleon had sent and ordered the remainder to renounce their French citizenship and speak Dutch, too.

When Hortense—seeking refuge from her erratic husband in Paris—gave birth to another son in 1808, she refused to hand the child over to Louis. Napoleon ignored his brother's demand that he force Hortense's cooperation and announced instead that he was adopting the boy himself. The fraternal breach was growing ever wider. It would be completed two years later when Napoleon swept Louis off his throne and took Holland for himself.

The emperor had funneled all the country's resources to fight his wars all over Europe and blamed Louis for its instability. A British attack on Holland gave the emperor a convenient excuse to take the crown away from his brother. The younger Bonaparte did not want to abdicate, but Napoleon's will was implacable. "There is only one way I will agree to do this if Your Majesty absolutely wants this," Louis wrote, as if he had a choice, "and that is by replacing me with my son."

Desiring Holland for himself, the emperor swiftly rejected the idea. "If the king abdicates," he responded, "in no case do I intend to replace him by the prince royal. . . . His throne has been destroyed as a result of the English expedition. When the king demonstrated his total inability to defend himself and therefore Holland can no longer exist."

So much for that relationship.

&

Joseph and Louis were the only brothers of Napoleon to show up at his coronation. Lucien Bonaparte wasn't there because he happened to be in exile after having displeased big brother Napoleon. The two had been allies during the emperor's rapid ascent and as a reward for his services, Lucien was given the plum position of interior minister when Napoleon achieved power as First Counsel.

Charming, affable, and as greedy as any Bonaparte could be, Lucien plundered the French treasury, to which he had full access, and spent wildly on himself and his mistresses. With most of France living in poverty at the time, Napoleon preferred to see the family accumulate wealth quietly. But this wasn't the real problem, nor was the fact that Lucien was utterly incompetent as interior minister and left the department in shambles. The real problem was the younger brother's ambition for power, which rivaled Napoleon's in its intensity. Unfortunately, it also came at the elder's expense.

Lucien presented himself as a moderate version of Napoleon, who was then trying to solidify his new autocratic government. He even went as far as to publish a pamphlet, at government expense, called *Parallels Between Caesar, Cromwell, Monck, and Bonaparte.* This was too much. Napoleon, who came off looking like a fanatic in the tract, which in fact he was, quickly edged his brother out of his post and assigned him the far less rewarding job of ambassador to Spain.

This turned out to be a disaster as well. After receiving enormous bribes from King Carlos IV to ensure a peace treaty with France, Lucien fled the country with all the loot the king had given him. He was afraid he would be forced to give it back when Napoleon refused to ratify the treaty delivered to him as a done deal without his prior approval and consultation. "Lucien's complete lack of judgment, and of any moral sense, pushed ambition to the point of utter frenzy, and the thirst for riches, to sheer robbery," wrote historian Louis Madelin. But what was worse in Napoleon's eyes, was that he got his mistress Alexandrine Jouberthon pregnant and married her. It was this single event that severed the relationship between Lucien and Napoleon forever.

The older brother had big dynastic plans for his siblings, and the tart Lucien had married most definitely did not fit into them. "Betrayal!" he fumed. "Sheer betrayal." The couple was forced to leave Paris for an Italian exile from which they never returned. Over the years that followed, Napoleon, now emperor, was relentless in his attempts to break up the marriage, but Lucien always stubbornly refused to leave his wife. "I cannot, without dishonoring myself, divorce a woman who has given me four children," he wrote in response to one of Napoleon's final demands. "In the Imperial Administration I could perhaps usefully serve my brother. Why can I not be allowed to prove my devotion to him by holding a nonhereditary post, where the position of my wife and children would not matter?"

"So be it!" the emperor responded. "Let him live and die as he pleases. I know what I must do, what politics dictate. Lucien implored my clemency. That clemency would include my recognition of his children, provided that he rids himself of that wife of a bankrupt [Alexandrine's first husband]. . . . What he has proposed, however, is quite absurd. Lucien can assume a proper role in my empire only by assuming the role of a dynastic prince, nothing less, and his children can serve me properly only as princes of my house. Lucien cannot accept this. All right! It is all over! I charge you with instructing my family never again to speak to me about this matter."

&

Youngest brother Jerome was far more amenable to dumping his wife at Napoleon's demand than Lucien ever was. He had too much to lose. The hell-raising nineteen year old had married an American girl by the name of Elizabeth Patterson during a trip to Baltimore in 1803. Receiving the news, Napoleon issued an order barring his brother from returning to France with his new bride. "If he brings her with him, she will not set foot on French territory," he decreed. "If he comes alone, I will overlook his error."

Here was yet another brother interfering with his plans for a Bonaparte dynasty that was to be formed by marrying his siblings into the finest families of Europe. Napoleon wasn't about to tolerate another nobody marrying into his family. Jerome, on the other hand, believed his older brother would soften upon meeting his new wife and planned to set sail with her in time to make the coronation. But their ship sank in a storm and they missed the ceremony.

Napoleon, meanwhile, was busy trying to nullify the union. When Jerome and his wife finally arrived in Europe, they were informed that Elizabeth, now pregnant, would not be allowed on European soil—Emperor's orders. Enraged, Jerome set off to confront his brother, leaving his wife on the coast. "Rest assured," he wrote her, "your husband will never abandon you. I would give my life for you, and for my child."

Elizabeth never saw him again.

Napoleon had appealed to Jerome's pleasure instinct, insisting that if he did not abandon his wife, his staggering debts would never be covered, and he would be stripped of all ranks and titles, lose his place in the succession, and be an outcast from the empire. Accustomed as he was to high living, Jerome got the message and was duly rewarded for his cooperation with an increased allowance and titles galore. Napoleon even created the kingdom of Westphalia for his little brother, carved out of several formerly independent German states.

The youngest Bonaparte took to his new kingdom as if it were his own personal playground, extravagantly spending on every whim while draining Westphalia in the process. This irked Napoleon, who considered it his right to plunder his brothers' domains in order to finance his grand rampage through Europe. With Jerome as king, there was rarely anything to take. The Westphalians under the strain of both Bonapartes soon rose in rebellion and Napoleon had to swoop in and save his hapless brother. "Your kingdom has no police, no finances, and no organization," the emperor berated King Jerome. "One does not found monarchies by living in the lap of luxury, by not lifting a finger. I quite expected that revolt to happen to you, and I hope it will teach you a lesson." Alas, it did not.

With the empire collapsing and the Russians closing in, Jerome abandoned his brother just when the emperor needed him most. Napoleon had counted on Westphalia as a buffer, but when the Russians entered his kingdom, Jerome bolted in fear. After Napoleon's forced abdication and attempted suicide, his youngest brother was all sympathy: "The Emperor, after causing all our troubles, has survived!"

⚜

While Napoleon's three brothers played the most active roles in his empire, his relationships with the Bonaparte women—his mother and three sisters—were every bit as rancorous. He was stunned when the matriarch of the family, Letizia Bonaparte, whom they called Madame Mere, refused to attend his coronation, preferring to spend the occasion with her exiled son Lucien in Italy. His sisters were all there, but they were as sour as Joseph and Louis that day, all three loudly complaining about having inferior titles to Napoleon's wife Josephine. *She* was to be empress, while they, mere princesses, would have to bow to her and carry her train. The outrage!

Indeed, if there was one thing that united the cantankerous clan, it was their all-consuming hatred for Josephine—or "the Whore," as Madame Mere called her. The most joyous moment in the family was not when Napoleon achieved the very pinnacle of power, benefiting them all. It was when he sadly announced his divorce from Josephine, a casualty in his quest to sire a male heir.

Napoleon had the most difficulty with his rather promiscuous sister, Caroline. "Of my entire family, it is Caroline who most resembles me," he remarked, which might explain why they didn't get along. She bucked all Napoleon's efforts to control her and against his will married Joachim Murat (who had slept with Josephine, cuckolding the emperor). Nevertheless, Napoleon made the couple king and queen of Naples. But when his fortunes were waning and he was being attacked on all sides, Caroline and Murat committed the ultimate act of treachery. They joined the allied forces against him. By this time, Napoleon's exile on Elba must have seemed a sweet relief for all concerned.

PART VI

Strange Reigns

The randomness of birth, or the strength to conquer, left the thrones of Europe open to a rich assortment of truly bizarre characters. Some were insane, others just appeared to be, yet all managed to disturb or frighten the people around them in one way or another.

Peter the Great hacks away at Russia's beard problem.

1

Temper, Temper

$\mathcal{H}$enry II was a model for the ideal monarch: strong, judicious, and fair. Many historians, in fact, credit this twelfth-century king as the father of English Common Law. But Henry had a serious flaw: a blinding temper that tended to diminish his royal dignity.

Besides his treacherous family,[1] King Henry is perhaps best remembered for his deadly dispute with Thomas Becket, Archbishop of Canterbury, over the relative rights of Church and State. Exasperated by Becket's intransigence, Henry screeched, "Will no one rid me of this turbulent priest?" Several knights, hoping to please the king, took him literally at his word and slaughtered the archbishop in his own cathedral. As a result of Henry's fit of pique, Becket was launched almost immediately into sainthood while the king was reduced to wearing sackcloth and ashes in repentance.

While this is the most famous example of the royal temper, it is by no means the most illustrative. Henry looked positively regal in his sackcloth compared to the spectacle he made of himself over a conflict with King William of Scotland. The scene is preserved in a letter written by John of Salisbury: "I heard that when the king was at Caen and was vigorously debating the mat-

---

[1]Henry's strained family relations are recounted in Part V, Chapter 1.

ter of the king of Scotland, he broke out in abusive language against Richard du Hommet for seeming to speak somewhat in the king of Scotland's favor, calling him a manifest traitor. And the king, flying into his usual temper, flung his cap from his head, pulled off his belt, threw off his cloak and clothes, grabbed the silken coverlet off the couch, and sitting as it might be on a dungheap, started chewing pieces of straw."

2

Swimming in a Shallow Gene Pool

*J*oanna the Mad brought the emerging Spanish empire into her disastrous union with Philip the Fair,[1] thus greatly expanding the power of the Habsburg royal family. She also introduced an enduring legacy of mental instability. And, handsome though he himself may have been, Philip carried the gene that would mutate into the grotesque facial deformity known as the Habsburg jaw. Together, Joanna and Philip planted the seeds from which sprung a genetic freak show—nurtured and replenished generation after generation by chronic and relentless inbreeding.

Emperor Charles V was the first beneficiary, and victim, of his parents' miserable marriage. From Philip he inherited Austria, the Low Countries, the Holy Roman Empire, and a lower jaw so grossly extended that it was almost impossible for him to keep his mouth closed. Seeing his king for the first time, a stunned Spanish peasant reportedly shouted, "Your Majesty, shut your mouth, the flies of this country are very insolent." Charles himself acknowledged his unsettling features in a letter to the king of France inviting him to a meeting. It was true that

---

[1]See Part III, Chapter 1.

his mouth often hung open, "but not to bite people," he reassured the French king. From Joanna, Charles gained the Spanish empire and, though he was spared her madness, a brooding melancholy would ultimately lead him to walk away from all his thrones and retire quietly.

Before his abdication in 1556, Charles split his vast domains in two. The Austrian possessions, including the Holy Roman Empire, went to his brother, Ferdinand, while Spain and all her territories were passed to his son, Philip II. From then on, for years to come, the Austrian and Spanish branches of the Habsburg royal family would rule side by side. They kept in touch by marrying one another.

On the Spanish side, Philip II—a religious fanatic who sent the ill-fated Armada against Elizabeth I of England—married his cousin, Maria of Portugal, and produced Don Carlos, one of the jewels of the Habsburg crown. Hunchbacked and pigeon breasted, with his entire right side less developed than his left, Don Carlos's twisted frame mirrored his unbalanced mind. Tales of his cruelty and bizarre behavior were legion.

As a child, Don Carlos enjoyed watching rabbits roasted alive and, for kicks, once blinded all the horses in the royal stable. Things got even worse when doctors removed part of his skull to drain built-up fluids after a head injury Don Carlos sustained when he was sixteen. Half-lobotomized, he took to roaming the streets of Madrid, assaulting young girls and hurling obscenities at respectable women. That conk on the head also made him even more ornery than he was before. Once, when a bootmaker delivered the wrong size, Don Carlos ordered the footwear cut into pieces, stewed, and then force-fed to the unfortunate man.

All of this became too much for King Philip, who in 1568 finally had his only son and heir locked away. "I would like to talk in all frankness about the life and conduct of the prince," Philip wrote his sister, "the degree to which he carried on with licentiousness and confusion, and the means I used to induce him to change his behavior." All was for nought, the king concluded, thus justifying his son's imprisonment.

Don Carlos eventually died raving in confinement, leaving his father without an heir. To remedy the situation, Philip married his twenty-one-year-old niece, Anna of Austria. From this, his fourth marriage,[2] came King Philip III, who married an Austrian cousin and had Philip IV, who in his turn married an Austrian niece. From that union came the last of the Spanish Habsburgs, Carlos II.[3]

Impotent, malformed, and hopelessly simple, he was called Carlos the Bewitched—as if some gathering of malevolent forces had conspired against him. No one had any idea about the poisonous effects of chronic incest. With seven of his eight great-grandparents directly descended from Joanna the Mad and Philip the Fair, Carlos was so inbred he could have been his own first cousin. No wonder he was such a mess.

"His constitution is so very weak and broken much beyond his age [thirty-five]," wrote the English ambassador to Spain in 1696. "He has a ravenous stomach, and swallows all he eats whole, for his nether jaw stands so much out, that his two rows of teeth cannot meet; to compensate which he has a prodigious wide throat, so that a gizzard or a liver of a hen passes down whole, and his weak stomach not being able to digest it, he voids in the same manner."

---

[2]In addition to his first wife, Maria of Portugal (Don Carlos's mother), Philip also was married to "Bloody" Mary I, with whom he shared the English crown until her death in 1558, and Elizabeth of Valois, daughter of Henri II and Catherine de Medici.

[3]To avoid confusion with Charles II of England, who reigned at roughly the same time, Charles II is spelled the Spanish way here.

Nothing engaged this semi-animated corpse of a king, including the administration of the crumbling Spanish Empire or the siring of an heir. Carlos preferred to spend his days among the moldering remains of his dead ancestors, occasionally having the coffins opened so he could better enjoy their company. When Carlos finally joined the deceased—mercifully childless—in 1700, the Spanish Habsburgs came to a sputtering end and the War of the Spanish Succession began.[4]

The Austrian branch of the Habsburgs, meanwhile, continued to mingle among themselves and carried on for two more centuries. But by the late nineteenth century their empire was crumbling and Emperor Francis Joseph faced a remarkable string of family tragedies. His wife Elizabeth was stabbed to death by anarchists in 1898; his brother Maximilian, sent to Mexico to rule as emperor, was shot by a firing squad there in 1867; and his nephew and heir, the Archduke Franz Ferdinand, was assassinated in Sarajevo in 1914. It was this murder that sparked the outbreak of World War I.

The tragedies faced by the "Emperor of Sorrows," as Francis Joseph was sometimes called, were attributed by some to a curse by Countess Carolyn Korolyi, whose son was put to death for participating in the Hungarian uprising of 1848. She called on "heaven and hell to blast the happiness of the emperor, to exterminate his family, to strike him through those that he loved, to wreck his life and ruin his children." It was another curse, however that contributed to the most devastating loss faced by Francis Joseph: The curse of Joanna the Mad. Her blood ran strong in the emperor's melancholy son, Rudolf, whose suicide in 1889 was one of the most devastating blows to the empire.

Chafing under the autocratic rule of his cold and aloof fa-

---

[4]The war resulted in the acension of a French Bourbon king, Philip V, to the Spanish throne.

ther, Rudolf abandoned himself to promiscuity and drug abuse, which served to deteriorate his already fragile mental state. As his erratic behavior increased over the years, so did the estrangement he felt from his father. It didn't help that the crown prince dallied with the liberalism that was slowly creeping its way into the scattered empire and undermining the monarchy that had ruled over it for centuries. It was even alleged that Rudolf was involved in the Hungarian independence movement from Austria.[5]

But there was nothing about his only son's behavior that prepared the emperor for his shocking demise. On January 30, 1889, Archduke Rudolf was found dead in the royal hunting lodge of Mayerling. He had shot himself in the head. Beside him was his eighteen-year-old mistress, Marie Vetsera, whom Rudolf had killed only a few hours before turning the gun on himself.

Although Marie had been devoted to him, she meant nothing to the deranged prince—just someone to accompany him to the grave. Her body was left in a heap for nearly two days after her death while the royal family engineered a conspiracy of misinformation about the murder-suicide. Rudolf, the official line went, died of a heart attack—alone. All information surrounding the tragedy was destroyed.

The genetically compromised line of Joanna the Mad and Philip the Fair finally came to an end with the defeat and collapse of the ancient Habsburg monarchy after World War I ended in 1918.

---

[5]The Dual Monarchy of Austria-Hungary was formed in 1867, and lasted until the collapse of the Habsburg monarchy in 1918.

3

The Belle of Versailles

*I*f Louis XIV was France's Sun King, then his brother, Philippe, Duc d'Orleans, was its Drag Queen. Monsieur, as the duke was always referred, loved putting himself on dazzling display, sashaying his way through the gilded halls of Versailles blowing kisses at all the pretty boys. "Monsieur was short and pot bellied," the court observer Saint Simon wrote, "and wore such high heels he looked as though he was on stilts. He was forever dressing like a woman, with rings, bracelets, and gems everywhere; a long, black powdered wig frilled in the front, ribbons wherever he could put them, and all kinds of perfumes." In short, he was a little light in the velvet slippers.

In Alexandre Dumas's classic tale, *The Man in the Iron Mask*, Louis XIV's identical brother is locked away with his face obscured so as to never pose a threat to the king. In truth, Louis and Philippe were not twins and looked little alike—the latter only a "flaccid reflection" of his brother, as one writer described him. Monsieur was never imprisoned, either. He was rendered impotent not by an iron mask, but by the constant encouragement he received as a young boy to engage in all his frilly interests—leaving the boy stuff to his big brother Louis.

Although the king hated homosexuals, he made an exception for his brother. Monsieur was accorded the highest prominence at court, and Louis was very affectionate toward him. He actually seemed to enjoy his brother's incessant chattering, and even tolerated his periodic snit fits. But there was always the hint of condescension. "Now we are going to work," Louis remarked when it was time to settle down to the business of the kingdom. "Go and amuse yourself, brother." And off Monsieur would flit—to a wig fitting, a gossipy soiree, or any of the other frivolous pastimes that occupied his day.

Yet despite his flamboyant appearance and feminine behavior, Monsieur proved himself a brave warrior. Leading his troops into battle wearing blush, jewels, and a perfectly coiffed wig, the duke fought without fear. "He was more afraid of the sun, or the black smoke of gunpowder, than he was of musket bullets," his wife once remarked.

4

A Great Mind Is a Terrible Thing

*D*uring the dynamic reign of Peter the Great there were occasions when the mighty Russian tsar liked to step off his throne and embark as an eager student on educational field trips across Europe. During these expeditions, which Peter preferred to make incognito so he could explore and learn without undue notice or ceremony, the tsar absorbed a wide variety of skills and knowledge that he brought back home with him and applied with great success. After learning the art of shipbuilding, for example, he personally helped build Russia's navy, and later he raised St. Petersburg from a swamp to a modern European capital.

Yet while Peter's intense curiosity about the world helped drag his backward kingdom out of its medieval malaise, many of his subjects would probably have preferred their emperor to be just an ignorant, provincial bumpkin. It would have been easier on them. Peter demanded the people around him share his lust for learning, and woe to those who demonstrated any reluctance. Once, during an anatomy lesson in Holland, the tsar heard squeamish groans coming from his comrades when a dissected corpse was produced. Infuriated by their weakness, Peter ordered each of them to approach the cadaver, bend down, and take a bite out of the body.

He loved to practice the skills he picked up on his journeys. Among them were surgery and dentistry. In the collection of the prestigious Russian Academy of Science, which Peter founded in 1724, are rows and rows of healthy-looking teeth—all neatly mounted and identified. Peter had pulled all of them out himself. He always carried with him a bag filled with surgical instruments. Any servant or courtier who fell ill went to great pains to keep his condition a secret lest the tsar appear at his bedside ready to operate.

After one trip abroad, Peter returned to Russia in 1698 determined to modernize the faces of his male subjects. Facial hair had always been a traditional symbol of Russian religious belief and self-respect. "To shave the beard is a sin that the blood of all the martyrs cannot cleanse," Peter's royal ancestor, Ivan the Terrible, once declared. "It is to deface the image of man created by God." To Peter, however, beards were uncivilized and ridiculous adornments that symbolized Russia's insular barbarity and made his kingdom a laughingstock in Europe. And so, producing a sharp razor after a welcoming party arrived at his palace, the tsar began hacking at their beards, leaving the stunned group with smooth faces for the first time since childhood.

At one party given in honor of his return, Peter sent his court jester around the room with a razor. Many faces with thick beards that had been cultivated for years were left gouged and bloody from the rough shave. No one dared complain, though, knowing the tsar would personally box their ears if they did. Soon after, he issued a decree that banned beards throughout Russia. To enforce the law, officials were given the power to cut off any they encountered, no matter how important the wearer. Peter did relent a little for those too enmeshed in tradition to shave, allowing them to pay a tax on their beards instead. They were given a little bronze medallion to wear around their necks that noted the tax had been paid. Still, it was never a good idea to come near the tsar with a beard, even with the medallion. According to one chronicler, those who did regretted it, for Peter, "in a merry humor, pulled out their beards by the roots or took it off so roughly [with a razor] that some of the skin went with it."

Bearded Russians weren't the only ones adversely affected by Peter's passion for the West. His foreign hosts often found him to be a troublesome guest. The hard-drinking tsar and his companions loved to party and, like modern-day frat boys, often trashed the place. The English writer John Evelyn discovered this when he rented his elegantly appointed home to Peter and found it utterly destroyed three months later. Windows were smashed, paintings ripped, furniture used as firewood, feather beds, sheets and canopies shredded. The lawn and garden, Evelyn's pride and joy, were trampled into mud and dust, "as if a regiment of soldiers in iron shoes had drilled on [them]." Neighbors even reported seeing the drunken tsar pushed along in a wheelbarrow—a then unknown contraption in Russia—right into the estate's carefully cultivated hedges.

Destructive as he was when traveling abroad, Peter was meticulous in maintaining his cabinet of curiosities at home. In addition to the teeth he pulled out of his subjects' mouths, the collection included a wide variety of other items that the tsar found fascinating. Among them, preserved in alcohol, was the head of Marie Hamilton, one of his wife's ladies-in-waiting who was executed for having killed her three illegitimate babies.

Intrigued by human freaks of nature, Peter also kept the preserved remains of babies born deformed, which he encouraged his subjects to send him, as well as the skeleton of a giant who stood nearly eight feet tall. Not all the genetic anomalies in Peter's collection were dead, however. Like many royals of the era, he loved midgets and dwarfs, thinking them utterly hilarious.

He kept a large stable of them for his amusement. At banquets, they were placed in huge pies, with Peter howling with laughter when he cut open a pie and a dwarf popped out. He particularly enjoyed watching them in mock ceremonies that mirrored the elaborate rituals of his court.

Two days after the marriage of his niece in 1710, a wedding of two dwarfs was held with equal pomp and ceremony. Friedrich Christian Weber, the ambassador of Hanover, described the scene: "A very little dwarf marched at the head of the procession, as being the marshall . . . conductor and master of the ceremony. He was followed by the bride and bridegroom neatly dressed. Then came the Tsar attended by his ministers, princes, boyars, officers and others; next marched all the dwarfs of both sexes in couples. They were in all seventy-two. . . .

"The Tsar, in token of his favor, was pleased to hold the garland over the bride's head according to the Russian custom. The ceremony being over, the company went . . . to the Prince Menshikov's palace. . . . Several small tables were placed in the middle of the hall for the new-married couple and the rest of the dwarfs, who were all splendidly dressed after the German fashion. . . .

"After dinner the dwarfs began to dance after the Russian way, which lasted till eleven at night. It is very easy to imagine how much the Tsar and the rest of the company were delighted at the comical capers, strange grimaces, and odd postures of that medley of pygmies, most of whom were of a size the mere sight of which was enough to produce laughter. . . . When these diversions were ended, the newly married couple were carried to the Tsar's house and bedded in his own bedchamber."

5

Drool Britannia

After conscientiously ruling Britain for nearly thirty years, George III was overcome by a disturbing change in 1788. His behavior became so bizarre that it seemed the once dull and dutiful monarch was slowly losing his mind. It started one October morning when the king woke up with a severe stomachache—like someone had socked him in the gut as he slept. His joints were so inflamed that he could barely move and a mean rash covered his arms. The king's physician, Sir George Baker, attributed the symptoms to his "having walked on the grass for several hours, and, without having changed his stockings, which were very wet, went to St. James; and that at night he ate four large pears for supper." Sir George prescribed what any good doctor of the day would—a bowel-cleansing purge.

Several days later, though, the king was no better. The whites of his eyes had turned a ghastly yellow and his urine brown. Worst of all, he was showing distinct signs of becoming mentally unbalanced. For three nonstop hours the king railed at his doctor, repeating himself frequently, and displaying what Sir George called "an agitation of spirit bordering on delirium."

The staff started noticing a change in the king's behavior as well. Fanny Burney, Queen Charlotte's Keeper of the Robes, unexpectedly encountered him one evening at Windsor Castle. There she recorded that George spoke in "a manner so uncommon that a high fever alone could not account for it; a rapidity, a hoarseness of voice, a volubility, an earnestness . . . a vehemence, rather . . . it startled me inexpressibly."

Weeks after the onset of the symptoms, King George attended a concert at Windsor. He barely heard the music as he chatted throughout the entire performance, frequently changing topics and continuously sitting, then standing, and then sitting again. The day before, while worshiping at chapel, George suddenly stood up in the middle of the sermon, threw his arms around his wife and daughters and exclaimed loudly, "You know what it is to be nervous. But was you ever as bad as this?"

At this point the king still had the presence of mind to know he was losing it. "They would make me believe I have the gout," he complained, kicking one foot against the other, "but if it was gout, how could I kick the part without any pain?" Aware of his babbling, yet unable to control it, King George ordered his attendants to read aloud to him—yet still he kept chattering away. Bursting into tears on the shoulders of his son, the Duke of York, the king anguished over his condition. "I wish to God I may die," he wept, "for I am going to be mad."

The self-diagnosis seemed sadly prescient as King George's behavior became increasingly erratic over the weeks that followed. This period was highlighted by the king's sudden and violent attack on his eldest son during dinner one night at Windsor Castle—when he grabbed the Prince of Wales by the collar, pulled him out of his chair, and hurled him against a wall. Upon examining the king after this unpleasant domestic scene, Sir George Baker decided that he was now "under an entire alienation of mind and much more agitated than he had ever been." Queen Charlotte noted that his eyes were like "blackcurrant jelly, the veins in his face were swelled, the sound of his voice was dreadful; he often spoke till he was exhausted . . .

while the foam ran out of his mouth." The king himself was heard to mutter in a hoarse, barely audible voice, "I am nervous. I am not ill, but I am nervous. If you would know what is the matter with me, I am nervous."

Bad nerves, however, were the least of George III's problems. After the violent dinner incident, his mental condition deteriorated even further. He still talked incessantly and incoherently, at one point rambling on for nineteen hours with barely a pause. But his chatter was increasingly peppered with obscene language the normally prudish monarch would otherwise have been mortified to hear, let alone speak.

He gave orders to people who did not exist. On one occasion he became convinced that London was flooded and ordered his yacht there. Looking through a telescope, he claimed he could see his ancestral German homeland of Hanover. He composed letters to foreign courts on imaginary causes and lavished honors on all who approached him, even the lowliest servant. After refusing to be shaved for weeks, he relented by allowing only one side of his face to be clipped.

King George clearly was not well, but his doctor was at a loss over just what to do. A succession of other physicians were summoned, but all left equally mystified. Then came Francis Willis, an elderly clergyman who had been granted a medical degree by Oxford University. His treatment of the king was nothing short of torture. Doctor and patient were introduced in December 1788, two months after the onset of the king's mysterious illness. George disliked him from the start. When Willis acknowledged that he had been a clergyman before becoming a doctor, the king grew angry.

"I am sorry for it," he said with rising agitation. "You have quitted a profession I have always loved, and you have embraced one I most heartily detest."

"Sir," Willis protested, "Our Savior Himself went about healing the sick."

"Yes, yes," the king answered irritably, "but He had not £700 [a year] for it."

Willis immediately concluded the king was "in a decided state of insanity" and set about breaking him, like a horse—his preferred method of treatment. The goal was complete and total submission. When the king refused his food or became too restless, he was put into a straitjacket or tied to his bed. Later, a specially made chair was used to keep him confined—what the king came to call with bitter irony his "coronation chair." At one point, while George was strapped to the terrible contraption, Willis stuffed a handkerchief into his mouth to keep him quiet during a lecture admonishing him for his crude and inappropriate remarks about a lady of the court. Hoping "to divert the morbid humors" from King George's head, Willis applied poultices all over his body that made him blister. A formidable array of medicines was forced down his throat—some making him so sick that the king prayed he would die.

In spite of Willis's treatment, the king began to recover. And on April 23, 1789, a service of thanksgiving was held at St. Paul's Cathedral. Public buildings were decorated in the king's honor and shouts of "God Save the King" echoed on the streets. A Regency by his eldest son, whom the people despised, had been averted, making King George III all the more popular.

It might have been the devastating loss of the American colonies that sent the king over the edge, or the Revolution raging in France that threatened the very institution of monarchy. Most historians believe, however, that something else caused George III's strange behavior: A rare hereditary blood disorder known as porphyria. In addition to severe abdominal pain, weakness of the limbs, and discolored urine—all symptoms exhibited by the king—the disease causes mental derangement leading to rambling speech, hallucinations, and symptoms of hysteria, paranoia, and schizophrenia.

Whatever the cause of his illness, the king suffered through two more brief episodes in 1801 and 1804. Then in 1810, when King George was a little over seventy years old, permanent insanity settled upon him. His eldest son finally obtained the long coveted Regency of the kingdom while the old king was confined to a meager set of rooms at Windsor Castle for the rest of his life. It was a sad spectacle, the nearly blind old man with a long white beard shambling around his isolated rooms. Only the badge of the Star of the Order of the Garter, which he kept pinned to his chest, offered any reminder that this deranged man was king of Britain. Neglected and forgotten, he finally died in 1820 at the age of eighty-one.

6

The Law Is an Ass

As her long and lusty reign neared its close, only two things seemed to frighten Catherine the Great—an empty bed and the ascension of her half-mad son Paul to the Russian throne. The empress soothed the first fear with nights of passion right up to the very end. Her second, and far deeper concern, wasn't so easy to exorcise.

Though in all probability Paul was not sired by Catherine's despised husband Peter III (more likely he was the son of Serge Saltykov, whom Catherine bedded during her lonely nights as a neglected wife),[1] he showed all the most unattractive traits of the murdered tsar he considered to be his father. "This young Prince gives evidence of sinister and dangerous inclinations," the French charge d'affaires noted when Paul was still a boy. "A few days ago, he was asking why they had killed his father and why they had given his mother the throne that rightfully belonged to him. He added that when he grew up, he would get to the bottom of all that."

But while Catherine reigned, her nasty, pug-faced son would have to stew in his own resentment. As he grew older, Paul started showing signs of the unbalanced cruelty for which his nominal father, Peter III, had been known. Frederick the Great

---

[1]See Part III, Chapter 4.

of Prussia, whom Paul greatly admired, found him to be "haughty, arrogant, and violent, which makes those who know Russia fear that he will have difficulty maintaining himself on the throne."

To ensure that he never got there, Catherine secretly drew up a document bypassing Paul in the succession in favor of his son, the future Alexander I. Unfortunately, while rifling through his mother's desk as she took her last gasps of breath, Paul discovered the document and immediately burned it. He was proclaimed tsar at age forty-two, right after Catherine died in 1796.

With four decades of impotent rage behind him, Paul took to his new throne with a vengeance. All the late empress's fears about her son were confirmed almost immediately. In a macabre effort to honor the man he believed to be his father, Paul had the remains of Peter III disinterred and placed in a coffin to lie in state next to his mother. Thus, thirty-four years after Peter's murder, the couple who loathed one another in life were reunited in death. Paul delighted in the irony. To further right the wrongs of the past, Paul ordered the men responsible for the late tsar's death to serve as pallbearers at the joint funeral. And, while he was at it, he had the bones of his mother's one-eyed lover Potemkin dug out of his grave and scattered.

Having settled these scores, Paul turned his unsteady gaze onto his new subjects. He was determined to control every aspect of their lives, down to the smallest detail. In a flurry of decrees, Paul established the rules of living for all Russians. He was particularly concerned about dress and appearance. He ordered that everyone should powder their hair and brush it up and away from their foreheads. Round hats, low collars, and tailcoats were all banned, and tailors, hatters, and shoemakers had to apply to the tsar's enforcers for approved patterns. Fashion offenders were subject to arrest, fines, and jail.

The social lives of the Russian people were similarly regimented, with Paul issuing strict guidelines on what people could read, where they could travel, and even how they were to entertain. Rules were posted for behavior at funerals, weddings, concerts, and other social gatherings. If someone wanted to have a party, they had to apply for a permit. A police officer was always present at the approved event to ensure that proper standards of "loyalty, propriety, and sobriety" were observed.

"My father has declared war on common sense," said Paul's son during the height of his legislomania, "with the firm resolve of never concluding a truce." It was a sentiment echoed by many Russians. In 1801, after four years of Paul's insane rule, the tsar was assassinated, and peace finally came to a grateful nation.

The Eyes Have It

On the surface, Gregory Rasputin didn't seem to have much recommending him to Russia's royal family. A greasy, drunken peasant, with the manners of a barnyard pig, and a staggering case of b.o. to boot, he was also kind of creepy. Some said the "mad monk's" strange allure was in his eyes. "They were pale blue," recalled the French ambassador Maurice Paleologue, "of exceptional brilliance, depth and attraction. His gaze was at once piercing and caressing, naive and cunning, far-off and intense. When he was in earnest conversation, his pupils seemed to radiate magnetism." Prime Minister Vladimir Kokovtsov was less impressed. "When Rasputin came into my study and sat down in an armchair, I was struck by the repulsive expression of his eyes," Kokovtsov wrote. "Deep seated and close set, they glued on me, and for a long time, Rasputin would not turn them away as though trying to exercise some hypnotic influence. When tea was served, Rasputin seized a handful of biscuits, threw them into his tea, and again fixed his lynx eyes on me. I was getting tired of his attempts at hypnotism and told him in as many words that it was useless to stare at me so hard because his eyes had not the slightest effect on me."

While Kokovtsov was apparently immune to Rasputin's se-ductive glare, Tsar Nicholas II and especially his wife, Alexandra, were enthralled by this bizarre character from the far reaches of

Siberia. He passed himself off as a *starets*, a man of God living in poverty and solitude, offering comfort to distressed souls. Empress Alexandra believed his act and was convinced he was a holy man blessed with the gift of healing. She had seen for herself the mysterious effect he had on her ailing son, Alexis, who inherited the life-threatening, often excruciating disease hemophilia from his maternal great-grandmother, Queen Victoria of Britain. "God has seen your tears and heard your prayers," the fraudulent monk had written the empress in response to her first agonized plea for his intervention in saving the life of the young tsarevich, who was in a dire state at the time because of a fall. "Do not grieve," Rasputin continued in his note to Alexandra. "The little one will not die. Do not allow the doctors to bother him too much." When Alexis's hemorrhaging stopped the next day, the empress became Rasputin's devoted disciple. He became a royal family intimate, continuing to minister to Alexis while gradually wielding more and more influence on the imperial government. Empress Alexandra, whom he called "Mama," was his champion, and often bombarded her husband with Rasputin's ideas and suggestions. She refused to see her savior's dark side.

Rasputin had always had an enormous appetite for women, which, despite his ascetic persona, he never hesitated to satisfy— by force, if necessary. His name, in fact, means "dissolute" in Russian. He earned it as a young man in his native village and never sought to change it. As his power and influence at court expanded, so did his sex life. And plenty of women in the higher social circles were willing to entertain him, attracted not only by his mysterious aura and access to the throne, but also by the novelty of sleeping with a brutish, unwashed peasant. "He had too many offers," noted his secretary Simanovich. Flushed with success, Rasputin even tried to bed Tsar Nicholas's own sister and bragged (falsely) of deflowering the tsar's daughters.

Despite his unsavory reputation, the empress refused to believe anything bad about him. "Saints are always calumniated," she said. "He is hated because we love him." Nothing could convince her that the man in whom she put all her trust, who seemed to control her son's deadly hemophilia, was a fraud whose influence was feeding the widespread and dangerous resentment that would eventually culminate in revolution.

"Rasputin was a Janus," Basil Shulgin, a member of the Duma, later wrote. "To the Imperial family he had turned his face as a humble *starets* and, looking at it, the Empress cannot but be convinced that the spirit of God rests upon this man. And to the country he has turned the beastly, drunken unclean face of a bald satyr from Tobolsk. Here we have the key to it all. The country is indignant that such a man should be received under the Tsar's roof. And under the roof there is bewilderment and a sense of bitter hurt. Why should they all be enraged? That a saintly man came to pray over the unhappy Heir, a desperately sick child whose least imprudent movement may end in death? So the Tsar and the Empress are hurt and indignant. Why should there be such a storm? The man has done nothing but good. Thus a messenger of death has placed himself between the throne and the nation. . . . And because of the man's fateful duality, understood by neither [Tsar nor people], neither side can understand the other. So the Tsar and his people, however apart, are leading each other to the edge of the abyss."

Ignoring the mounting discontent, Alexandra kept Rasputin by her side, heeding his advice and passing along "Our Friend's" ministrations to the tsar. Prime ministers rose and fell at Rasputin's whim, and when Russia entered the war in 1914, he was instrumental in the fall of Grand Duke Nicholas, the Commander-in-Chief of the Russian armies, who hated him. "The Grand Duke is deliberately currying favor in the army and overshadowing the

Tsar so that one day he can claim the throne," Rasputin told the empress, poisoning her against his enemy. "The Grand Duke cannot possibly succeed on the battlefield because God will not bless him. How can God bless a man who has turned his back on me, the Man of God? In all probability, if the Grand Duke is allowed to keep his power, he will kill me, and then what will happen to the Tsarevich, the Tsar, and Russia?"

Fearing the spreading hatred and discontent Rasputin was generating, members of the extended royal family begged the empress to part with him. She refused, even in the face of numerous reports that she had taken Rasputin as her lover. When her sister Elizabeth, the wife of the tsar's assassinated Uncle Serge, tried to intervene, Alexandra cut her off coldly. "Perhaps it would have been better if I had not come," Elizabeth said sadly as she prepared to depart. "Yes," was all the empress replied. The sisters never saw one another again. There was, however, one member of the nobility who was not so easily dismissed. Prince Felix Yussoupov, the richest man in Russia and the tsar's nephew by marriage, wanted Rasputin dead. His efforts to that end resulted in a macabre comedy of errors.

After luring Rasputin to the basement of his palace, Yussoupov plied him with poisoned cakes which were supposed to kill him instantly. They didn't. Instead, Rasputin asked for some wine to wash down the cakes. The wine was also poisoned. After gulping two glasses, Rasputin was still standing, asking Yussoupov to play his guitar and sing for him. "My head swam," the frustrated killer would later say of this unexpected twist, as he played one song after the other while Rasputin merrily clapped along. After two hours of entertaining his quarry, Yussoupov was desperate. Excusing himself, he rushed upstairs to consult with his fellow conspirators. One handed him a revolver to finish off Rasputin, who was downstairs calling for more wine. When his host returned, the death-defying monk suggested a visit to the Gypsies for sex—"With God in thought, but mankind in the flesh," he said with a wink. Yussoupov instead led him to a cabinet containing an ornate crucifix. Rasputin remarked that he liked the cabinet better than the cross, to which Yussoupov replied, "You'd far better look at the crucifix and say a prayer." With that, he pulled out the revolver and shot him in the back. Rasputin fell onto the white bearskin rug with a scream, while the other conspirators rushed into the room. One of them, a doctor (the same doctor who had assured Yussoupov that there was enough poison in the cakes to kill an army), felt for Rasputin's pulse and declared him dead.

Not long after, Rasputin's face began twitching and his eyes fluttered open. "I then saw both eyes—the green eyes of a viper—staring at me with an expression of diabolical hatred," Yussoupov wrote. Foaming at the mouth, Rasputin suddenly leaped to his feet and grabbed his murderer by the throat. Terrified, Yussoupov broke away and ran upstairs, chased by Rasputin and hollering to his companions to shoot him. One of the other killers, Vladimir Purishkevich, was stunned by what came next. "Rasputin, who half an hour before lay dying in the cellar, was running quickly across the snow-covered courtyard towards the iron gate," Purishkevich recalled. "I couldn't believe my eyes. But a harsh cry which broke the silence of the night persuaded me. 'Felix! Felix! I will tell everything to the empress!' It was him all right, Rasputin. In a few seconds, he would reach the iron gate. . . . I fired. The night echoed with the shot. I missed. I fired again. Again I missed. I raged at myself. Rasputin neared the gate. I bit with all my force the end of my left hand to force myself to concentrate and I fired a third time. The bullet hit him in the shoulder. He stopped. I fired a fourth time and hit him probably in the head. I ran up and kicked him as hard as I could with my boot in the temple. He fell into the snow, tried to rise, but he could only grind his teeth."

Yussoupov then returned, and seeing Rasputin prostrate on the ground but still alive, started beating him with a club. At last the body lay still. The killers bound it up, cut a hole in the frozen Neva River, and dumped it in. When the corpse was found three days later, its lungs were full of water. Rasputin had actually drowned. As unseemly as his death was, his royal patron and her entire family would soon meet a far grislier demise.[1]

---

[1]See Part IX, Chapter 11.

PART VII

When in Rome

The Roman emperors of the first century were Europe's first true monarchs—mega-kings ruling vast tracts of the continent in the years before the emergence of independent kingdoms. The roiling stream of royal scandal that runs through all of European history goes right back to them. These wicked icons elevated murder, lust, and all manner of vice to a highly corrupted art, leaving a lavish blueprint for all future royal misbehavior. Fortunately, ancient historians like Suetonius, who had a healthy taste for the tawdry, recorded it all for posterity.

*Nero takes in a little
gladiatorial entertainment.*

1

The Rage of Tiberius

Sex and violence could never be tweezed apart when it came to Tiberius Caesar, during whose reign Jesus was crucified. His rule, which began in A.D. 14, was somewhat wise and temperate in its early years, but something snapped as the emperor grew older and left Rome to settle for the rest of his life on the island of Capri. It was there that he became infamous for his voracious sexual appetite and murderous rampages.

If animal lust were to be further categorized, reptilian would probably best describe the slimy and dangerous tendencies exhibited by Tiberius. Never particularly handsome as a young man, he grew grotesque as he aged, covered with pus-filled eruptions that emitted a revolting stench as they festered. His personality came to mirror his appearance and aroma.

Suetonius reports that Tiberius built pleasure palaces for himself on Capri, importing boys and girls from all over the vast empire to serve as his sexual playthings. He loved to watch them copulate in groups under his pornographic artwork, or in hidden groves he had carved out for the purpose. A group of boys, whom Tiberius called "minnows," were made to follow him as he swam, and to dart between the legs of the imperial pedophile, nibbling on the "bait" he left dangling for them.

Once, when he was sacrificing to the gods, the emperor took a fancy to one of the altar boys. After racing through the ceremony, he assaulted the boy and his brother behind the temple. When they protested, Tiberius did what any scorned suitor would do. He had their legs broken. Another young victim, this time a girl, was so revolted after being forced to bed with the dirty old emperor that she ran home, reportedly cursing "that filthy-mouthed, hairy, stinking old man," and stabbed herself to death.

Sex with Tiberius was probably worse than death at his command, but not by much. Along with his pleasure palaces, he built elaborate torture chambers, dungeons, and execution sites on Capri. Even the gods couldn't help anyone invited to these hellish places. Though he lived in self-imposed exile, no one was safe from his frequent and random execution orders. Everyone from senators in Rome to children on Capri trembled at the very thought of incurring the almost whimsical wrath of the all powerful emperor.

Bodies of his victims were left to rot on the Gemonian Steps in Rome, which descended from the Capitol to the Forum, or were dragged by hooks and tossed into the Tiber River. On Capri, Tiberius enjoyed sitting atop a cliff and watching as condemned souls, already hideously tortured, were hurled off. A contingent of soldiers was stationed below to whack them with oars and boat hooks just in case the fall failed to do the trick.

To Tiberius, death was a relatively light punishment. What he really enjoyed was the slow process of getting there. When a man named Carnulus drank poison rather than endure what Tiberius had in store for him, the emperor was heard to exclaim, "Carnulus has got away!" Another prisoner under torture begged to be put out of his misery, but Tiberius wouldn't hear of it. "No," he sneered. "We are not yet friends again." There was one torture the emperor found particularly amusing. After tricking an intended victim into drinking vast quantities of wine,

Tiberius would suddenly order a cord tied so tightly around the man's genitals that it would cut into his flesh and made urination virtually impossible.

A good deal of this emperor's monstrous cruelty was reserved for members of his own family. It is almost certain that he ordered the secret poisoning of his adopted son Germanicus, who had been a beloved military hero. The citizens were outraged by this murder and their suspicions that Tiberius was behind it were strengthened by the way he treated Germanicus's widow, Agrippina the Elder, and her children.

Like a sadistic cat, he toyed with Agrippina, leaving her utterly paranoid as to what he might do to her. At one meal he offered her an apple, which believing it was poisoned, she refused. Tiberius then used her lack of trust as an excuse to have her flogged and exiled. The beating was so bad she lost an eye. Agrippina then tried to starve herself as a means of ending her misery, but Tiberius had her force-fed. Though she eventually succeeded in killing herself, the emperor wasn't quite through with her. He slandered Agrippina's memory, going so far as forcing the Senate to declare her birthday an official day of ill omen. He then bragged about his own benevolence, saying he could have had her strangled and thrown down the Gemonian Steps. He even caused a bill to be passed that praised him for his clemency.

Two of Tiberius's grandsons fared no better than their mother. The emperor was miffed when prayers for their safety were included with his own during one New Year's celebration. He turned on the boys with a vengeance, encouraging false reports against them and using their resulting indignation as evidence of their treachery. The two boys were declared public enemies and ordered starved to death. One committed suicide. The other, as Tacitus and Suetonius both report, grew so hungry that he tried to eat the stuffing out of his prison mattress. Both were then chopped into so many pieces that it was difficult to gather them all up for burial.

A third grandson somehow survived the cruel reign of Tiberius to inherit his throne. It is widely believed that Gaius, or Caligula as he is better known today, hastened his inheritance by arranging the old emperor's murder in A.D. 37. News of Tiberius's death brought joyful relief among the Roman citizens who had grown disgusted by his relentless depravity. "To the Tiber with Tiberius!" they shouted. The unwary populace might not have been so quick to celebrate had they even an inkling as to just how bad the new emperor would be. Tiberius himself had a pretty good idea. "I am nursing a viper in Rome's bosom," he once said of his successor.

2

Oh, God!

While Tiberius correctly saw a snake, the people believed Caligula to be just a teddy bear in a toga. He was, after all, the son of the noble and heroic Germanicus, the revered martyr and military master who had subdued Germany. They treated Caligula as a national treasure, remembering him fondly as a young lad when they gave him cute little names like "Star," "Baby," and "Pet." Even the name Caligula was adorable, Latin for "Bootikins" or "Little Boots." His father's soldiers gave him that one when he was a little boy left in their company.

The people were overjoyed at his ascension in A.D. 37, but "Bootikins" would soon show them just how wrong first impressions can be. He transcended Tiberius in depravity, making the dead emperor seem like a harmless island hermit by comparison. They both enjoyed large-scale torture and execution, but Caligula became a true connoisseur. His favorite method of killing was to have numerous small wounds inflicted on a victim until the sum became lethal. "Make him feel like he is dying," the mad emperor said.

A good torture session often provided mealtime entertainment for Caligula, who kept a headsman always on hand in case he felt the need for his services. At one meal, some fellow diners became a bit disconcerted when Caligula suddenly burst into fits of laughter. Politely inquiring as to whether they might share the joke, they almost choked on their grapes at the menacing response. "What do you think?" the emperor sneered. "It occurred to me that I have only to give one nod and both your throats will be cut on the spot!"

Caligula liked to have parents forced to watch the executions of their children. When a father asked to be excused on one occasion due to illness, the emperor generously provided a litter to pick him up so he wouldn't miss out on all the fun. "Bear in mind that I can treat anyone exactly as I please," he once offered as a gentle reminder of his power.

Violent entertainment always gave Caligula a buzz and he proved himself to be a great patron of gladiatorial matches and wild beast shows. He organized many of them himself and sometimes even participated. When a gladiator once dropped to his knees to end a fight, Caligula raced onto the field and stabbed him to death. Then he proudly claimed the victory laurels for himself. On another occasion, a man about to be thrown to the wild beasts screamed his innocence of any crime. Caligula had the man brought before him as if to hear him out, but instead of listening to his case, he had the man's tongue cut out and then tossed him to the beasts as planned.

Conventional cruelty sometimes bored him at these events, and he delighted in presenting alternative matches—pitting old people against old animals, for example, or setting up matches between the handicapped. He was, however, frugal when it came to his entertainment. Finding butcher's meat too expensive to feed to the wild animals, he decided chopped-up criminals would do just as well.

All this is not to imply that Caligula wasn't a religious man. Indeed he was. So much so that he declared himself a god. While other Roman emperors had to wait until they were dead to be deified, Caligula bypassed that technicality and declared his divinity while he was still alive. He had the heads knocked off the statues of the other gods and replaced with his own image. At his command, a temple was raised in his honor, featuring a life-size, golden statue of himself that he ordered dressed daily in the same clothes he happened to be wearing. Caligula's temple became *the* place to worship in Rome, with rich sacrifices and fierce competition among citizens to serve as priests.

With his delusions of divinity, the emperor was often found in dialogue with his fellow gods, inviting the moon goddess to join him in the sack, for example, or whispering secret communications to a statue of the mighty god Jupiter. Once he was overheard threatening him. "If you don't raise me to heaven," he warned, "I will cast you down to hell." Having put Jupiter in his place, Caligula announced the god wanted them to share a home and ordered his palace connected with Jupiter's temple at the Capitol so they could be closer.

To his credit, Caligula wasn't a jealous deity. He shared the glory with his sister, Drusilla, ordering her name be included with his whenever an oath was taken or a prayer was spoken. His generosity to his sister may have had something to do with the fact that he was sleeping with her. Having stolen Drusilla from her husband, he treated her as his own wife. When Caligula grew dangerously sick at one point, he willed her all his property and named her heir to the throne. Fate, alas, spared Caligula but took Drusilla instead. Crazed with grief—if it was possible for him to get much crazier—he ordered the empire into mourning. It became a capital offense to laugh, bathe, or even eat with one's family during this period, and he came to swear by Drusilla's divinity. For some reason, his other two sisters didn't hold the same appeal. Sure he bedded them, but he let his friends do the same and then publicly denounced them as adulteresses.

When he wasn't ravaging his sisters, other men's wives served just as well, including one on her wedding day. "Hands off my wife," Caligula warned the groom sitting across from him at the reception feast. He then had the bride carried off to his palace and married her himself. Within a week he tired of her and they were divorced. Caligula had his eyes set on another woman, but that relationship didn't last long, either. After they split, the emperor forbade her from ever sleeping with another man.

It must have been difficult for any of Caligula's lovers to feel completely comfortable in his arms. "And this beautiful throat will be cut whenever I please," he would coo whenever he kissed the neck of his mistresses. Still, his love for a woman named Caesonia was almost touching. Though she was neither young nor beautiful, and something of a tramp, Caligula was smitten. So much so that he paraded her naked in front of his friends. Happy as he was, though, he refused to dignify Caesonia with the title of wife until she bore him a child. She obliged him with a baby girl.

Despite the brief period of domestic harmony, the little family was doomed. The people who had once adored "Little Boots" had discovered what a bastard he could be. Fed up, they turned on him. Less than four years after being joyfully hailed as the new emperor, Caligula was assassinated in A.D. 41. Caesonia also was murdered, along with her baby daughter, whose brains were reportedly bashed out against a brick wall. No one was interested in seeing that family line propagated.

3

I Claudius, Aren't I?

*I*f you believe Suetonius, Caligula's uncle and successor, Claudius, was every bit as stupid as his nephew was nuts—and almost as cruel. An ugly, uncouth clod, he was called "a monster: A man whom Nature had not finished but had merely begun," by his own mother. Antonia's maternal pride was such that when she wanted to emphasize someone else's stupidity she would exclaim, "He is a bigger fool even than my son Claudius!"

Other family members held similar opinions. When his sister Livilla heard someone predict that Claudius would one day inherit the imperial throne, she dropped to her knees and prayed aloud that Rome would be spared such a horrible fate. He was such a buffoon that, even in the midst of the bloodbath of other family members, Caligula kept him alive just for laughs.

Claudius, in fact, had a tough time commanding respect from anyone before he came to the throne. When he fell asleep after dinner, as was his tendency, the gathered guests would pelt him with dates and olive pits. He later tried to explain away his stupidity, saying it was merely an act that served him well during the reign of his vicious nephew. Few were convinced, however, including the author of a contemporary book called *A Fool's Rise to Power*.

Claudius certainly seemed to justify the book's title when he heard himself proclaimed emperor at the age of fifty. A glorious occasion it was not. He was hiding behind a curtain at the time, cowering in fear, having just heard of the assassination of Caligula. When a guard saw his feet poking out and drew aside the curtain to see who it was, Claudius dropped to the floor and clung to the soldier's knees pleading for mercy. He was far from reassured by the proclamation that he now ruled, whimpering that he would be destroyed by the same forces that had done in his nephew. It was only when he heard the crowd chanting for monarchy that he began to relax and eventually flex his muscles.

After a brief honeymoon, with Claudius making a great show of benevolence and amiability, things started to get ugly. The new emperor was basically a simpleton with a bad attitude, and his vicious inner-child soon emerged with a vengeance. Like his predecessors, he loved presiding over tortures, executions, and fights to the death. Gladiatorial contests enjoyed the addition of some whimsical new rules introduced by the emperor. He decreed, for example, that any fighter who fell accidentally should have his throat slit—in full view, so Claudius could observe the death throes. At one scheduled mass execution, Claudius became violently annoyed when an executioner could not be found to kill the group of condemned that were tied up to stakes and ready to be dispatched. Determined not to miss an opportunity to satisfy his lust for blood, Claudius summoned an executioner from outside the region and, with nothing better to do, sat around all day waiting for his arrival.

His cruelty was by no means diminished by his stupidity, however. After executing one of his wives, Messalina, for adultery, bigamy, and treason, he apparently forgot what he had done and asked where she was at dinner one night. Another time, he sent for some men to play dice with him. Irate when they failed to appear at his command, he fired off an angry missive calling them lazy—completely oblivious to the fact that he had already ordered them executed.

Despite his ruthlessness, or perhaps because of it, Claudius never sat comfortably on his throne. He was convinced that he would be killed and, as a result, showed himself to be a monumental coward as well as savagely paranoid. Anyone perceived as a threat he would have killed, including members of his own family. Claudius's paranoia became an effective tool for the scores of people who wielded influence over him in getting rid of people they didn't like.

When his treacherous wife, Messalina, and his secretary, Narcissus, decided to remove one enemy, Appius Silanus, they settled on a plan that had worked for others before. They agreed that Narcissus would alert Claudius to horrible dreams he was having about the emperor's murder by Appius. With that cue, Messalina would awaken from a fake sleep and pretend to be astonished, saying she had been having the very same dream. The couple had already arranged to have Appius summoned to the emperor, so that when he arrived they could say he was forcing himself in, just as their dreams had foretold. Not surprisingly, the ruse worked, and Appius was dragged away and killed.

Claudius so feared for his life that he bravely tried to abdicate on several occasions. After one man was arrested carrying a knife Claudius believed was meant to kill him, he summoned the Senate in a panic. The emperor broke down in tears and protested loudly that he wasn't safe anywhere. He then disappeared from the public eye for several days to nurse his fears. After hearing of another plot, this time to kill him and put Messalina's lover on the throne, Claudius fled in terror to his guards' camp while repeating over and over, "Am I still Emperor?"

In the end, all his fears were justified. He had executed one dangerous spouse, Messalina, but another soon took her place. Her name was Agrippina the Younger, one of Caligula's sisters and Claudius's own niece. She spent years grasping for power, and once having achieved it, completely dominated the emperor. Her influence was such that she was able to persuade Claudius to adopt her son Nero and disinherit his natural son by Messalina, Brittanicus. Then, in A.D. 54, she had Claudius poisoned.

4

A Son Should Love His Mother, But . . .

Claudius's porcine successor, Nero, had a series of singularly unpleasant experiences with women. This may have had something to do with the fact that he was a feral, sadistic, sexually depraved lunatic—even if he never actually fiddled while Rome burned. Still, you would think he might have found some respect and affection in his heart for Agrippina the Younger, if not because she gave him life from her loins, then because she arranged the murder of his predecessor to make him Caesar.

But Agrippina crossed the line. She was his mom but she also reportedly became his lover, and, in that dual role, she developed into something of a nag. Nero did not take nagging well. According to Suetonius, Nero deprived his mother–lover of all honors and power before booting her out of the palace. After she moved, he sent people to her house to torment her with lawsuits and scream insults into her windows.

Then he set out to kill her.

Three times he tried poison, but she always seemed to have the antidote. He rigged her bedroom ceiling so it would collapse while she was sleeping, but someone warned her in advance. One time he had a boat sabotaged so it would fall to pieces and sink while Agrippina was sailing on it. Sure this plan would work, Nero happily accompanied his unsuspecting mother down the gangplank—kissing her breasts as she stepped aboard. She swam away from the wreck. Finally, he had her stabbed to death and exulted over her corpse.

Nero's other relationships fared no better than the one with mom. He tried strangling his first wife, Octavia, on several occasions because she bored him. Finally he simply divorced her and later had her executed. Twelve days after the divorce he married Poppaea Salina, the wealthy wife of a Roman knight whom Nero had to kill to make room for himself. Though he doted on her, Poppaea also proved to be a pest. When she had the temerity to complain when he returned home late from the races, the emperor kicked her to death. She was pregnant. Considering his track record, Claudius's daughter Antonia refused an invitation to become the next Mrs. Nero. She was charged with attempted rebellion and summarily executed.

Women! Who needed them anyway, especially when young men could fill the void quite nicely. Nero at one point had an adolescent boy castrated so he could take him as his wife. There was a wedding ceremony, complete with dowry and bridal veil. Then the emperor began squiring the unfortunate lad around Rome in the late empress's clothes. Both men and women were lucky enough to participate in a novel game Nero invented. According to the rules, the frisky emperor would dress up in the skin of a wild animal and pace around in his cage. When the cage door was opened, he would bound out, run up to his playmates, who were tied up to stakes, and attack their private parts.

Eventually, even Rome's notoriously licentious citizenry had enough of Nero's nonsense. He was hounded into suicide. Savage and nutty as he was, though, this emperor deserves a little credit. He did banish all mimes from Rome.

5

The Year of Living Dangerously

The death of Nero in A.D. 68 was followed by civil wars and the brief and insignificant reigns of Galba, Otho, and Vitellius. All three came and went within about a year.

Galba's biggest claim to fame during his seven months in power was his grossly undignified demise. After being murdered, as was the established pattern among Roman emperors, Galba was decapitated by a private soldier. Being completely bald, the dead emperor's severed head was difficult to grasp, so the soldier improvised and carried it to Otho, the new emperor, with his thumb stuffed into its mouth.

Otho then handed off the head to the gathered crowd, who carried it away on a spike. They made wicked fun of the gruesome trophy, chanting insults. Galba had once made a bit of an ass out of himself by quoting Homer in response to a passing compliment on his robust appearance. "So far my vigor undiminished is," he said at the time. The mob now gleefully responded: "Galba, Galba, Cupid Galba, Please enjoy your vigor still!"

Otho, who with his own supplanter, Vitellius, led the assassination of Galba, earns distinction for instigating what was perhaps the most pathetic scene in all of antiquity before he came to power. He had been one of Emperor Nero's chief cohorts during that reign, arranging, for example, the murder of Nero's mother. Because of his close connection to the throne, Otho must have considered himself immune from Nero's wrath. How else to explain what happened next?

He was put in charge of protecting Poppaea Sabina, whom Nero had stolen from her husband to have for himself. Otho, however, fell madly in love with her and decided to steal her from the boss. Ordinarily this would have been a fatal mistake, but for some reason he got away with it. As Suetonius reports, instead of ordering the rival suitor killed, Nero stood outside the locked door of the room where Otho and Poppaea were staying and pleaded for his girl. He was ignored. Like Galba, Otho didn't last long as emperor; defeated in the civil war by his rival to the throne, Vitellius, he stabbed himself to death.

Rounding out this triumverate of flash-in-the-pan emperors, all of whom were deposed in the year A.D. 69, Vitellius came from a family of professional bootlickers. He distinguished himself by kissing the behinds of four emperors in a row, in one case quite literally, before coming to power himself. According to Suetonius, Vitellius spent his boyhood and adolescence as a member of Emperor Tiberius's stable of male prostitutes, earning in the process public promotions for his equally obsequious father. A debauchee himself, Vitellius naturally was a hit with Caligula, who admired his chariot-racing skills, and Claudius, who loved tossing dice with him. Nero in particular was a big fan, for Vitellius rendered a service near and dear to this emperor.

Fancying himself quite a musician, Nero was always eager to compete in musical contests, but had to feign modesty. That's where good old Vitellius came in. While Nero would leave the theater and pretend to disappear, Vitellius would rev up the audience with the idea of convincing their emperor to play for them. Then Vitellius would chase down the apparently reluctant Nero and, on behalf of the people, beg him to play.

After he won the throne from Otho, Vitellius became decadent in his gluttony. Surviving coins from his era faithfully reproduce the fat rings overwhelming the back of his head. One of his favorite dishes, with ingredients shipped in from all over the Roman empire, consisted of pike livers, pheasant and peacock brains, flamingo tongues, and lamprey milt, which are the male reproductive organs of the fish. But Vitellius would eat just about anything, snatching sacrificial foods off altars or devouring half-eaten food scraps left over from the day before.

Like those of his two predecessors, Vitellius's reign was very brief. He was captured trying to escape the forces of future Emperor Vespasian, trapped like a dog in his hiding place—a janitor's closet with a bed and mattress jammed against the door. Yanked out by rebels looting the palace, Vitellius at first tried to deny he was the emperor but was quickly recognized. His hands were tied behind his back and a noose was flung around his neck. Then, amid a jeering crowd, he was dragged away half-naked to the Forum, his remaining clothes in tatters. Excrement was thrown at him, while people screeched "glutton" and similar insults. Finally, he was tortured by the soldiers with little sword cuts, *à la* Caligula, before he was at last dispatched and tossed into the Tiber River.

After almost a century of imperial depravity, something strange happened. Rational rule came to Rome with the Flavian Dynasty. Suetonius gave the Emperor Vespasian and his son and heir Titus the ultimate compliment when he wrote: "There is no cause to be ashamed of their record." That ringing endorsement was the end of an era of sorts. Certainly there would be many other horrendous reigns before the Roman Empire in the west finally collapsed several centuries later, but the worst was over. It would not be until the popes firmly established themselves in Rome that a renaissance of scandal would begin.

PART VIII

Papal Vice

All was not lost after the decline and fall of the Roman Empire. Though the long parade of evil emperors did eventually pass forever out of the Eternal City, a succession of equally rotten popes eventually stepped in to carry on the legacy. "The Papacy," wrote Thomas Hobbes, "is no other than the Ghost of the deceased Roman Empire sitting around upon the grave thereof."

For centuries, the popes were the ultimate royals, claiming to be not only Christ's representatives on earth, but the rulers of kings as well. "All princes are obliged to kiss [the pope's] feet," Gregory VII decreed in the eleventh century. And though many monarchs resented this intrusion of papal authority over them, few could rival the least "Holy Fathers" when it came to bad behavior.

Gregory VII: "All princes are obliged to kiss [my] feet."

1

Not So Dear Johns

Hundreds of men—and one woman of legend—have occupied the throne of St. Peter, but only a blessed few did the great apostle proud. John XXIII was certainly a good and holy man—one of several great popes of the twentieth century, and perhaps the best ever—but twenty-two Johns preceded him.[1] And most of them weren't so hot. In the tenth century, John XIII, for one, had a nasty habit of ordering the eyes of his enemies plucked out; John XXII condemned a number of poor and humble Franciscan monks to be burned at the stake for adopting the "heresy" that Jesus and his apostles lived in poverty; and John XXIII—the original John XXIII, that is—was deposed in 1415 for piracy, murder, rape, sodomy, and incest. Other charges against him were apparently dropped for decency's sake.

Perhaps the worst John of all was John XII, who came to the throne in 955 at the ripe old age of eighteen. He has been called "the Christian Caligula," an apt moniker for this papal bad boy. Elected at the urging of his dying father, Alberic II, absolute ruler of Rome, John immediately adopted a lifestyle that shocked even the jaded Romans who were used to all manner of vice. A teenager with unlimited power, he turned his residence at

---

[1]Because of an historical glitch in the numbering of popes, there was no Pope John XX. There was, however, another (discredited) John XXIII in the fifteenth century.

the Lateran Palace into a brothel. He gambled with pilgrims' of-
ferings and bestowed rich gifts, including golden chalices from
St. Peter's, on his endless succession of lovers. With John and his
pals always on the prowl, women were warned away from the
church at the Lateran Palace lest they fell prey to the lusty young
pope.

Though the people of Rome were too divided among themselves to take any action against John, he did face a threat from
Berengar, king of Italy, who was eager to help himself to the
wealth of the papal states stretching across central Italy. The desperate pope appealed to the mighty German ruler, Otto of Sax-
ony, who had recently smashed the invading Huns. In return for
the coveted blessing and crown from the pope as Christian Emperor and protector of Rome, which John gladly gave, thus
establishing the Holy Roman Empire, Otto repelled Berengar.

With this new relationship between pope and emperor established, Otto took the opportunity to rebuke John for all his mis-
deeds. The stern lecture was not appreciated, and like the insolent
child he was, John offered the crown of the empire to his erstwhile
enemy Berengar just as soon as Otto returned to Germany. Needless to say, the emperor was not pleased and immediately headed
back to Rome to confront the disloyal pope. Terrified, John plundered what was left of the treasure of St. Peter's and fled to Tivoli.

In his absence, Otto summoned a synod of the church to
sort out the situation. Individuals were called, under oath, to
provide specific and substantiated evidence of the pope's mis-
conduct. The charges were stunning: that he had copulated with
a long list of ladies, including his father's mistress; that he
charged money for priestly ordinations; blinded his spiritual ad-
viser; and castrated a cardinal!

Regretting that the pope was not present to confront his accusers or defend himself against the charges, Otto wrote John in

Tivoli urging his return: "Everyone, clergy as well as laity, accuses you, Holiness, of homicide, perjury, sacrilege, incest with your relatives, including two of your sisters, and with having, like a pagan, invoked Jupiter, Venus, and other demons." John was unimpressed by the charges, as well as Otto's plea to return to Rome and face them. "To all the bishops," he wrote in response. "We hear that you wish to make another Pope. If you do I excommunicate you by Almighty God and you have no power to ordain [any]one or celebrate Mass." The synod then sent an emissary to Tivoli declaring that unless John presented himself in Rome immediately, he, not the bishops, would be excommunicated. The pope again dismissed them and was deposed as a result.

Otto put a new pope, Leo VIII, on the throne but could not remain in Rome to protect him. As bad as John had been, the Romans resented even more the foreign emperor daring to bring down one of their own and replace him with a pontiff not of their choosing. No sooner did Otto depart than John returned. He quickly exacted his revenge against the bishops who had testified against him. One had his tongue torn out and his nose and fingers cut off; another was scourged, and the hand of a third was hacked off. John also excommunicated his replacement, Leo, who had fled Rome upon his return.

A jealous husband ultimately spared Emperor Otto from having to make yet another trip to Rome to restore order. Finding the pope in bed with his wife, the enraged husband beat John so severely that he died three days later.[2]

---

[2]Other sources say the young pope died of a stroke while having sex.

2

A Matter of Grave Consequence

John XII reigned during one of the lowest points in papal history, when vice-infected pontiffs ruled at the whim of powerful Roman families and murdered, raped, and plundered their way to infamy. A third of the popes enthroned between A.D. 872 and 1012 died violently, sometimes killed by other popes. Others were deposed for their wickedness and fled Rome for their lives. One pope, Stephen VIII, was so horribly mutilated after having his nose, lips, and ears lopped off that he never showed his face in public again. No pontiff, however, was ever subjected to the abuse Pope Formosus endured under his successor, Stephen VI in A.D. 897—even if he was already dead.

Stephen, quite possibly the craziest pope who ever ruled, ordered the corpse of Formosus dug out of its grave to stand trial on a number of charges—nine months after it was buried. In what became known as the Cadaver Synod, the dead pope's rotting body was dressed in full papal vestments and propped up on a throne while Pope Stephen, presiding over the "trial," shouted questions at it.

Formosus was found guilty of perjury and other crimes for which all his papal acts and ordinations were declared null and void. The three fingers of his right hand, by which he had sworn oaths and given blessings, were hacked off and his body was tossed into the Tiber River. Stephen then ordered all clergy ordained by Pope Formosus to submit letters renouncing their ordinations as invalid. Several months after that, Stephen VI was himself deposed, imprisoned, and then strangled to death by supporters of Formosus.

The much-abused body of Pope Formosus, meanwhile, had been fished out of the Tiber and given a decent burial. All his papal acts were restored under subsequent pontiffs loyal to his memory. But the ordeal wasn't over yet. Formosus still had to contend with Pope Sergius III, who came to the throne in A.D. 904 after murdering the previous pope, Leo V, and Leo's rival, the antipope[1] Christopher.

Having participated in the Cadaver Synod under Stephen VI, Sergius reaffirmed his condemnation of Formosus and once again nullified all his acts. For good measure, he ordered Formosus's corpse exhumed yet again and had it beheaded. In addition to this important work of the Church, Sergius III made his own contribution to the legend of a female pope when he started sleeping with a fifteen-year-old mistress by the name of Marozia.

---

[1]Antipopes are individuals whose claim to the papacy has been rejected by the Church, though certain tumultuous periods in papal history have made it sometimes difficult to distinguish between valid and invalid claimants. There are thirty-nine listed antipopes. Some, like the original John XXIII, have the same name as officially recognized popes.

3

Her Holiness?

For centuries, many people believed that in the ninth century a female pontiff known as "Pope Joan" had occupied the throne of St. Peter disguised as a man. Her secret was revealed, the story went, only when she gave birth to a son on the way to Mass one day and died on the spot. After that, subsequent popes were said to go out of their way during papal processions to avoid the blamphemous site.

It has been suggested that the legend, or satire, of Pope Joan, which was finally disproved in the seventeenth century by a French Calvinist named David Blondel, almost certainly arose from the true story of two women—a mother and daughter from the powerful Theophylact family—who virtually ruled the papacy during a period in the tenth century known as "The Reign of Harlots."

During her affair with Pope Sergius III, Marozia, the daughter, gave birth to the pope's bastard son, who would later become Pope John XI. Marozia's mother Theodora, meanwhile, was sleeping with the bishop of Bologna. Not satisfied with his relatively lowly status, Theodora plotted a much grander office for her boyfriend. As Liutprand, bishop of Cremona, wrote at the time, "Theodora, like a harlot, fearing she would have few opportunities of bedding her sweetheart, forced him to abandon his bishopric and take for himself—Oh, monstrous crime! —the Papacy of Rome." He became Pope John X in A.D. 914.

This was three years after the death of Sergius III. Seeing that the dead pope would no longer be requiring Marozia's services, Theodora married her daughter off to an up-and-coming soldier of fortune named Alberic. Theodora and her lover John X found Alberic's skill as a soldier useful in consolidating their power, but Alberic—perhaps at wife Marozia's urging—eventually tried to seize power for himself. He was killed as a result, and Pope John ordered Marozia to look upon her husband's mutilated corpse and learn from it. It was a lesson that went unheeded, and when the pope's lover and protector Theodora died in A.D. 928, Marozia sought her revenge. With the help of her second husband, Guy, a feudal lord of Tuscany, Marozia knocked John X off his throne and had him strangled to death in prison. Thus the pope made by the mother was destroyed by her daughter.

Marozia had papal ambitions for her bastard son by Sergius III, but alas the lad was too young—even by the loose standards of the day—so she allowed two other insignificant pontiffs of her choosing to keep her son's future throne warm for him. Then, in A.D. 931, when he was about twenty years old, the boy was deemed ready to rule as Pope John XI.

With this ambition satisfied, Marozia next determined to marry Hugo, king of Italy, who happened to be the half brother of her second husband, Guy, and who was himself already married. These marital ties were simple to untangle with her son sitting at the head of the Church. John XI dutifully proffered the necessary dispensations and then presided over his mom's third marriage to Hugo. Everything would have been perfect except for one problem. In addition to the pope, Marozia had another son, by her first husband Alberic. Alberic Junior, bitter at having been left out of his family's good fortune, stormed Rome and put his half brother Pope John in prison, where he died four years later. Alberic also jailed his mother. Marozia would remain in a dark cell in the papal fortress of Castel Sant'Angelo for the next half century, though she did live to see her grandson, Alberic Junior's son, installed as the infamous John XII.

4

King of Kings

*L*ooking back on the dark century of his predecessors, Gregory VII might have hung his head in shame. He didn't. Instead, he exalted the papacy to levels it had never dared claim before. "The Roman Church has never erred, nor can it err until the end of time," the dwarfish pope boldly asserted after he came to the throne in 1073. As if the likes of Sergius III and John XII had never existed, Gregory further pronounced that "a rightly elected pope is, without question, a saint, made so by the merits of Peter."

Gregory clearly felt himself set above ordinary monarchs, decreeing that they could be dethroned at the pope's command. Christendom could have only one boss, and he was it. "Who does not know that kings and rulers are sprung from men who are ignorant of God," Gregory thundered, "who by pride, robbery, perfidy, murder, in a word, by almost every crime at the prompting of the devil, who is the prince of this world, have striven with blind cupidity and intolerable presumption, to dominate over their equals, that is over mankind? . . . Who can doubt that the priests of Christ are to be considered the fathers and masters of kings and princes and all the faithful?"

The papacy had long been dominated by the powerful Holy Roman Emperors who ruled over Germany and Northern Italy, manipulating popes and deposing them at will. Gregory, who had seen his own hero and namesake Gregory VI driven into exile by Emperor Henry III, was determined to bring these arrogant monarchs to their knees. He got his chance with Henry IV, whom he accused of interfering in the affairs of the Church. In an unprecedented demonstration of papal power, Gregory deposed the emperor: "On the part of God the omnipotent, I forbid Henry to govern the kingdom of Italy and Germany. I absolve all his subjects from every oath they have taken or may take; and I excommunicate every person who shall serve him as king."

To Henry's surprise, the edict was actually having an effect as his vassals began to withdraw their allegiance. He quickly saw he would have to come to an accommodation with the pope, though perhaps he never realized just how humiliating it would be. Humbling himself before Gregory at a castle outside Parma, the emperor was stripped of all his imperial insignia and ordered to remove his clothes as well. In the midst of the severe winter, Henry IV stood shivering and naked as a coarse woolen tunic was tossed to him by the pope who did not deign to speak to him. With a broom in one hand and a pair of shears in the other—symbols of his willingness to be whipped and shorn—the degraded monarch stood out in the cold for three days waiting for the pope to show some mercy.

"Henry was the first prince to have the honor of feeling the sharp thrust of spiritual weapon," Machiavelli wrote. He would not be the last. Though Henry IV eventually prevailed over Pope Gregory, deposing him and sending him into exile, a new precedent of papal dominance over kings had been set. Gregory was canonized for his efforts in 1606.

5

Innocent Proven Guilty

A century after the reign of Gregory VII, Innocent III took the concept of a monarchical papacy to even greater heights. The richly adorned pope—who reportedly suggested to Francis of Assisi, the great saint of the poor, that he go root along in a pig pen with his fellow swine—declared himself to be not only master of Christendom, but ruler of the world as well.

When King John of England had the audacity to defy him on a number of issues, including the appointment of the archbishop of Canterbury, Innocent excommunicated the surly monarch and deprived him of his throne. He also put England under an interdict that lasted more than six years. The churches of England were all shut down, babies went unbaptized, the dead were buried without ceremony, and the people were denied sacramental comfort.

Although King John profited from the harsh penalty his kingdom endured, absorbing for himself Church property and revenue, he came to realize that an excommunicated monarch was particularly vulnerable when King Philip II of France prepared an invasion of England with the pope's encouragement and blessing. With his throne at stake, John submitted to the pontiff. In 1213, he signed a document handing over his kingdom "to God and to our Lord Pope Innocent and his Catholic successors." The agreement made John a mere vassal and he had to pay a steep annual rent for the privilege of ruling Innocent's new domain.

The pope was indignant when two years later John was forced to put his seal on the Magna Carta, considered to be the very foundation of English liberty. How dare these English barons interfere with *his* kingdom! "By Saint Peter, we cannot pass over this insult without punishing it," Innocent roared before condemning the Magna Carta as "contrary to moral law." The king, he explained, was answerable only to the pope—not these foolish Englishmen. In a papal decree, Innocent, "From the plentitude of his unlimited power and authority, which God has committed him to bind and destroy kingdoms, to plant and uproot," annulled the Magna Carta and absolved King John from observing it. He also warned that excommunication awaited "anyone who should continue to maintain such treasonable and iniquitous pretensions."

Besides humbling kings and threatening nobles, Innocent III presided over an era of Christian intolerance that was approaching its most murderous. His targets were infidels and heretics. Christians had long been called to slaughter Muslims since Pope Urban II launched the First Crusade in 1095 to force them out of the Holy Land. More than 70,000 people were massacred when Jerusalem was taken in that venture. Succeeding popes enticed the flock with promises of a special place in heaven and the automatic absolution of sins on earth if they would join the holy cause.

Innocent III continued the tradition, instigating the Fourth Crusade in 1202. This particular venture was highlighted by the sacking of Constantinople and the destruction of the old cathedral of Santa Sophia. The tombs of emperors were desecrated, relics stolen, and women, including nuns, raped and murdered. The Eastern Orthodox Church had split with Rome a century before, so from Rome's point of view, they got what they deserved.

The Children's Crusade was a particularly inspired movement against the infidels during Innocent's reign. Tens of thousands of faith-filled tykes embarked on a vast, unsupervised mission across Europe to free Jerusalem. The first group of some 30,000 little ones, led by a French shepherd boy named Stephen, fell victim to a gang of disreputable merchants before they ever left France. They were shipped off to the slave markets in North Africa. A second group of 20,000 made it all the way over the Alps and as far as Italy before they too were captured. Some were killed; others sold. Innocent graciously released the few survivors from their crusade vows.

Though crusades against Muslims were nothing new, Innocent III became the first pope to order one against fellow Christians. The Cathars, or Albigensians as they also are known, were a well-established sect in the southeast corner of France with a different take on Christian doctrine.[1] Innocent hated them and wanted them eradicated. "Death to heretics," he thundered as he inaugurated the holy war against the Cathars, offering the same indulgences crusaders were promised for fighting Muslims. Inspired by the pope, his eager generals embarked on a grotesque massacre.

The papal army first attacked the town of Beziers, a Cathar stronghold. Catholics there had been warned to hand over any heretics in their midst lest they be killed, too. Many resisted and took their Cathar brethren into the age-old sanctuary of the church. Then came the command: "Kill them all; the Lord will look after His own." Inside the church of Mary Magdalene,

---

[1] The Cathars were ascetics with a strict moral code who believed in the duality of life—that good and evil were actually separate creations.

thousands of Catholics and Cathars huddled together as their town was destroyed outside. Two priests were saying Mass when the doors of the church were smashed open and the papal army poured in. Not one soul was spared—not even the priests performing the sacred service.

With Beziers in ruins, the papal legate on the scene wrote the pope. "Today, Your Highness, twenty thousand citizens were put to the sword, regardless of age or sex." Far from being offended or outraged by the sheer brutality of the cleansing, Innocent rejoiced and called for more. In the town of Bram, the noses of Cathars were chopped off and their eyes cut out. One of them was allowed to keep an eye to lead the blinded and bloody remainder to Cabaret to serve as a warning to the people there.

Next came the town of Minerve, where 140 Cathar religious leaders were led out of town into a meadow. There a giant funeral pyre awaited them. As a chronicler loyal to the pope noted, "There was no need for our men to cast them in; nay, all were so obstinate in their wickedness as to cast themselves in of their own free will." Thus, the grand tradition of burning heretics had begun.

For Innocent, there was no irony in the fact that he was now responsible for more accumulated Christian deaths than the most savage Roman emperor. He was tickled with the outcome. In a letter to a knight in his service, the pope wrote "praise and thanks to God for that which He hath mercifully wrought and through these others whom zeal for the orthodox faith hath kindled to his work against His most pestilential enemy."

6

Feel the Burn

*I*nnocent III's nephew, Pope Gregory IX, made his uncle's persecution of heretics an official function of the church when he established the Inquisition in 1232. "It is the duty of every Catholic to persecute heretics," he proclaimed. For centuries to come, legions of merciless inquisitors would promulgate this campaign of terror against anyone who strayed from official church teaching or dared question it.

Catholics were encouraged, on pain of excommunication, to expose any heresy in their midst. Children were made to testify against parents; mothers against children. Anyone holding a grudge could make an accusation and efficiently do away with an enemy. The accused were dragged before papal inquisitors to answer charges in total secrecy. No defense witnesses were permitted and prosecution witnesses remained anonymous. Acquittals were rare and there was no appeal. Once condemned, a victim was handed over to the secular authorities to be burned at the stake.

To get his fledgling Inquisition off to a good start, Gregory IX personally issued verdicts in open meetings for almost a year. He also appointed the first two full-time inquisitors, Peter Seila and William Arnald, the forerunners of a long line of papally blessed murderers like Tomas de Torquemada, the infamous enforcer of the Spanish Inquisition. Another inquisitor, Robert le Bougre, went to Champagne in France to investigate charges that the local bishop there was allowing heresy to prosper in his diocese. The whole town was put on trial and 180 people, including the bishop, were condemned to the stake.

Not long after Gregory's death in 1241, Pope Innocent IV added his own imprint on the Inquisition when he approved the use of torture. Now confessions could be elicited from even the most stubborn heretic. Witnesses could be tortured, too, although boys under fourteen years of age and girls under twelve were exempt. The pope benevolently forbade inquisitors to maim or kill when applying torture, but mistakes were made. He also mandated that a person could be tortured only once, but that was subject to interpretation. One torture session could last for weeks.

A guide for inquisitors, popularly known as the *Book of the Dead*, was eventually published. It was not a hallmark of jurisprudence:

"Either the person confesses and he is proved guilty from his own confession, or he does not confess and is equally guilty on the evidence of witnesses. If a person confesses the whole of what he is accused of, he is unquestionably guilty of the whole; but if he confesses only a part, he ought still to be regarded as guilty of the whole since what he has confessed proves him to be capable of guilt as to the other points of the accusation. . . .

"Bodily torture has ever been found the most salutary and efficient means of leading to spiritual repentance. Therefore, the choice of the most befitting mode of torture is left to the Judge of the Inquisition, who determines according to the age, the sex, and the constitution of the party. . . .

"If, notwithstanding all the means employed, the unfortunate wretch still denies his guilt, he is to be considered as a victim of the devil; and, as such, deserves no compassion from the servants of God, nor the pity and indulgence of Holy Mother Church: he is a son of perdition. Let him perish among the damned."

7

Papal Bully

Cardinal Benedict Gaetani was not an especially religious man, but this never stopped anyone from becoming pope, and he desperately wanted the job. The papal throne was the most glorious in the world and Gaetani was determined to have all the power and wealth that went along with it. After the death of Pope Nicholas IV in 1292, he saw his chance.

There was at the time a bitter rivalry between the two leading families of Rome, the Orsinis and the Colonnas, and the sharp divisions were reflected in the College of Cardinals who gathered to elect the next pope. Half of them wanted an Orsini pope; the other half a Colonna. With the electors hopelessly deadlocked, months went by without a new pontiff emerging.

Benedict Gaetani was loyal to neither Orsini nor Colonna and positioned himself as an alternative to both. Biding his time as the cardinals squabbled endlessly among themselves, he was convinced they would eventually turn to him as a compromise. But what happened next stunned him. One of the cardinals, perhaps facetiously, suggested that they end the standoff once and for all and elect a renowned hermit known as Peter of Morone. Whether the proposal was made in jest or not, the idea quickly caught on among the other cardinals, who were by this time absolutely sick of one another. Trudging up to the mountain cave that was Peter's home, they proclaimed the bewildered man pope.

After a long history of worldly pontiffs plucked from the richest Roman families, many people believed the Holy Spirit may have actually had a hand in the election of this simple and holy man. Not Benedict Gaetani. Denied the plum he felt sure was his, he was outraged by the farce he saw unfolding. Nevertheless, he had no choice but to go along with it. But he did have a plan.

Peter of Morone, who took the name Celestine V, was clearly out of his element amidst the cynical papal politics that swirled around him. He was used to living in a cave, not ruling Christendom. In his confusion he turned to Gaetani, a trained lawyer, who was only too eager to help him navigate his way—right out of the papacy. By some accounts, Gaetani installed a hidden tube in Celestine's room. During the night as the pope slept, he would whisper into it, "Celestine, Celstine, lay down your office. It is too much for you." Only too glad to oblige what he believed was the voice of God, Celestine V dutifully resigned and Benedict Gaetani was immediately elected Pope Boniface VIII.

Before he could enjoy his new throne, Boniface had to do away with his predecessor. The ex-pope Celestine—now just plain old Peter of Morone again—enjoyed wide support even after his abdication and Boniface could not afford to have him around as the focus of any misplaced loyalty. Though Peter wanted nothing more than to retire quietly to his cave and pray in peace, he was arrested and imprisoned. He died several months later in the filthy hole that was his cell.

Peter's followers made much of the fact that while their hero was rotting away in his squalid prison, "he to whom he had left the Papacy reposed like a god on a couch adorned with purple and gold." Peter himself made a remarkably accurate prophecy after his capture. "You have entered like a fox," he told Boniface. "You will reign like a lion and you will die like a dog."

Boniface wasn't listening. With his rival out of the way, the new pope was ready to enjoy life as the greatest monarch in the world. He certainly played the part well, dressing in the finest robes of purple and erecting statues of himself all over Rome. His imperial arrogance alienated nearly everyone who came into contact with him. "The cardinals all desire his death and are weary of his devilries," wrote Gerald of Albalato, an envoy from the king of Aragon. "Cardinal Lanbulf says that it is better to die than to live with such a man. He is all tongue and eyes but as the rest of him is rotten, he won't last much longer."

As the last of the great medieval popes in the line of Gregory VII and Innocent III, Boniface VIII made claims of papal supremacy that rivaled his predecessors in sheer pomposity. "The breast of the Roman Pontiff is the repository and fount of all law," he decreed. "This is why blind submission to this authority is essential to salvation." But the pope who could say without blushing, "We declare, announce and define that it is altogether necessary for salvation for every creature to be subject to the Roman Pontiff," was lacking in any religious or moral beliefs himself. What he had to say privately was in distinct contrast to his grand public pronouncements.

"Why, there is no more to going to bed with women and boys than in rubbing one hand against the other," he said on the subject of sexual morality, and his true feelings about the immortality of the soul would have gotten him burned at the stake if he weren't pope: "A man has as much hope of survival after death as that roast fowl on the dining table there."

Spiritual salvation was not high on Boniface's agenda—getting rich was. A Spanish diplomat summed him up well: "This pope cares for only three things: a long life, a rich life, and a well-endowed family around him." To achieve these ends—at least the last two—Pope Boniface used the treasure of the Church to snatch up land and cities all around Rome. He planned for a Gaetani dynasty that would rival any of Rome's greatest families. The aggrandizement of the Gaetanis, however, came at the expense of the Colonnas, whose property and ancient prerogatives were ruthlessly trampled. The ensuing conflict would result in Boniface's total humiliation and the end of the imperial papacy.

It started with a bold robbery. Stephen Colonna, a younger member of the clan, hijacked a wagon carrying a hoard of gold the pope intended to use to buy even more land for his family. When two Colonna cardinals heard of this dangerous affront to the pope, they appeared before him and begged his forgiveness. Boniface's answer was a demand that the loot be returned, which seemed more than reasonable. But his further demand that all Colonna possessions around Rome be put under the control of papal garrisons was an outrage.

Instead of bowing to this term, the Colonnas declared war. Leaflets were spread all over Rome calling into question the legitimacy of Boniface's pontificate and accusing him of stealing it from the hermit pope, Celestine V. The pope was up to their challenge. He excommunicated the entire clan, "even unto the fourth generation." This was not simply a spiritual weapon. Excommunication meant that a person was outside the protection of the law, and his life and property were fair prey for anyone who wished to take them. Doing so, in fact, was considered a blessed virtue.

Boniface went even further. He actually called for a holy crusade against the Colonnas. Though few ended up joining the pope's transparent effort to benefit himself, there were enough supporters to crush the family and devastate their lands and cities. All that was left was the ancient city of Palestrina, where the entire clan gathered in their defeat. It was clear that they could hold out indefinitely behind Palestrina's impenetrable walls, but Boniface was able to entice them out. He tricked them into believing that all would be forgiven if they would simply yield the city and submit to him.

Throwing themselves down before the pope, the leaders of the family kissed his feet and begged for pardon. Boniface, however, wasn't through with them yet. As a final blow, he committed an act that would be bitterly recalled in Dante's *Inferno* (where Boniface ended up, along with several other popes, in the eighth circle of hell—face first in a fissure). The pope ordered the entire city of Palestrina annihilated. Nothing was spared of this magnificent town filled with priceless antiquities and noble history—not even the palace of Julius Caesar. With a wave of the pope's hand it was all flattened and salt was thrown into its furrows to leave it irretrievably barren. Boniface VIII had won—or so he thought. The Colonnas would get their revenge with a little help from Philip IV of France.

The clash between the pope and King Philip was all about money. Both of them needed lots of it—Philip to strengthen his hold on a kingdom just beginning to emerge from feudal divisions, and Boniface to fund his ever-expanding territorial ambitions. The pope tried to stop the king from pillaging the coffers of the French Church that they both relied so heavily upon for cash, and grew enraged at Philip's continual defiance. "Our predecessors have deposed three kings of France," Boniface warned. "Know we can depose you like a stable boy if it prove necessary."

What the pope failed to realize, however, was that the era of papally controlled monarchs was coming to a rapid close. Instead of meekly bowing to Boniface's threats and commands, Philip called a council to condemn him as a criminal and funded a secret expedition against him. In September 1306, a band of armed men entered the town of Anagni, the birthplace of the pope and his favored retreat from Rome. Led by a senior member of the Colonna family, the gang stormed the papal palace there and confronted Boniface as he sat regally upon his throne waiting for their arrival.

The sight of the arrogant pope who had destroyed his family enraged Colonna and he moved to strike his nemesis with a dagger. He was restrained at the last moment by a companion who no doubt feared the Divine wrath that would have resulted in such a sacrilege. Boniface's life was saved, but not his dignity. Colonna and his cohorts stripped the pope of all his vestments and led him away in chains. For three days he was held prisoner, during which time it was said that he lost his mind. And though he was eventually freed by Gaetani family forces, Boniface was not the same. Broken and in despair, the last of the mighty medieval popes died a month later.

8

Will the Real Pope Please Rise?

Having crushed Boniface VIII, King Philip IV was now master. With a French pope, Clement V, as his virtual puppet, he commenced what came to be known as the Babylonian Captivity. The papacy was moved from its ancient seat in Rome—the burial place of St. Peter, the first pope—to the fortified city of Avignon in France.

For nearly a century, a succession of popes ruled from the luxurious papal palace on the Rhone River, which came complete with its own state-of-the-art torture chamber. The great scholar Petrarch described the court there as "the shame of the world." Maybe he was just upset that that Pope Benedict XII was reportedly sleeping with his sister. Avignon, after all, was no worse than Rome.

Eventually the Eternal City beckoned home the papacy, leading to the Great Western Schism that lasted from 1378 to 1417. The returning cardinals, who were mostly French, were terrorized by the Roman mob into electing an Italian pope. Anxious to quell the mob's fury, they quickly settled on Bartolemeo Prignano, who became Pope Urban VI in 1378. He was not a good choice.

The man the cardinals elected happened to be a madman with a drinking problem. "I can do anything, absolutely anything

I like," Urban barked after donning his new papal vestments. This self-ordained license included the torture and murder of six cardinals who dared defy him. Realizing they had a complete maniac on their hands, the princes of the Church elected a new pope to replace Urban, Clement VII.[1] The French cardinals then scurried back to Avignon with Clement. The only problem was, Urban had no intention of budging from his throne in Rome. Instead, he appointed his own cardinals and ruled from there.

Now there were two duly elected popes and two colleges of cardinals: one in France, one in Italy. With the Great Schism, all of Christendom was divided in loyalty. France and Scotland, for example, officially submitted to Clement VII, while England, Germany, and the kingdoms of central Europe declared their allegiance to Urban VI. Even saints took sides. St. Catherine of Sienna supported Urban and St. Vincent of Ferrar went with Clement. It was a mess that was about to get even messier.

When Urban VI died in 1389, the Roman side chose Boniface IX, who promptly excommunicated Clement VII. Then Clement died and a new Avignon pope was elected in his place. And so on it went—pope versus antipope—until finally the cardinals on both sides had enough. Gathering together in 1409, they deposed Gregory XII (the Roman pope at the time) and Benedict XIII (the Avignon pope). In their place, the united cardinals elected Pope Alexander V. Only hitch was, neither of the old popes was willing to step down. Now there were THREE popes!

The situation was ultimately resolved at the Council of Constance, where everybody was deposed in favor of Martin V in 1417—just in time for the papacy to freshen itself, gather its strength, and face the coming Renaissance.

---

[1]This Clement VII is now considered an antipope, while the Clement VII who reigned two centuries later (and who denied Henry VIII his divorce from Katherine of Aragon) is officially recognized. Benedict XIII and Alexander V are other antipopes listed in this section.

9

Double, Double, Toil and Trouble

The rebirth of culture and learning that was sweeping Europe in the fifteenth century was not entirely lost on the papacy. It's just that many popes found it difficult to completely let go of the Dark Ages. Sixtus IV, for example, commissioned the magnificent Sistine Chapel—right around the time he gave his blessing to the Spanish Inquisition and anointed the murderous Torquemada to run it. His nephew, Julius II, patronized Michelangelo and Raphael—when he wasn't dressed in full armor and slaughtering his enemies. "Now let's see who has the bigger balls," Julius once hollered on the battlefield, "the king of France or the pope."

Innocent VIII seemed poised to modernize the papacy when he became the first pontiff to openly acknowledge his illegitimate children. Before he came along, papal bastards were always euphemistically referred to as "nephews." Any promise Innocent may have shown as a modern son of the Renaissance, however, was quickly extinguished when he gave his seal of approval to what may be the most destructive book in history.

His papal bull entitled *Summis Desiderantes Affectibus* gave new life to the persecution of witches and served as the preface to *Malleus Maleficarum*, or *The Witches Hammer*, a handbook for the discovery and punishment of witches written by two of the Church's most ruthless Inquisitors, Heinrich Kraemer and Johann Sprenger.

"Men and women straying from the Catholic faith have abandoned themselves to devils, *incubi* and *succubi* [demonic male and female sexual partners]," Innocent wrote, "and by their incantations, spells, conjurations, and other accursed offenses, have slain infants yet in the mother's womb . . . they hinder men from performing the sexual act and women from conceiving, whence husbands cannot know their wives nor wives receive their husbands."

If it hadn't been used for centuries to come as a key instrument in the torture and burning of thousands, *The Witches Hammer* might have gone down in history as one of the more laughable studies in stupidity. A memorable passage from the book concerns "a venerable Father from the Dominican House of Spires, well known for the honesty of his life and for his learning."

"One day," the priest says, "while I was hearing confessions, a young man came to me and, in the course of his confession, woefully said that he had lost his member. Being astonished at this, and not being willing to give it an easy credence, since in the opinion of the wise it is a mark of light-heartedness to believe too easily, I obtained proof of it when I saw nothing on the young man's removing his clothes and showing the place. Then, using the wisest counsel, I asked whether he suspected anyone of having so bewitched him. And the young man said that he did suspect someone but that she was absent and living in Worms. Then I said: 'I advise you to go to her as soon as possible and try your utmost to soften her with gentle words and promises,' and he did so. For he came back after a few days and thanked me, saying that he was whole and had recovered everything. And I believed his words, but again proved them by the evidence of my eyes."

After his zealous advocacy of witch hunting, Innocent VIII must have had a moment of clarity at the end of his life, perhaps realizing all the misery and harm he had caused with it. As he lay dying in 1492, the pope reportedly prayed that a better man than he would succeed him. Alas, the prayer went unanswered as Rodrigo Borgia charged his way to the throne.

10

All the Holiness Money Can Buy

The Borgia clan of the fifteenth century could very well qualify as the prototypical Mafia family. Like any good Gambino or Genovese, they looked out for their own, used ill-gained wealth to get whatever they wanted, and killed without blinking. Of course there was also the religious hypocrisy. Few mobsters ever missed a Mass. Rodrigo Borgia became the pope. As Alexander VI, he ruled as the ultimate godfather, and his reign—marked by murder, greed, and unbridled sex—was one of the most infamous in papal history. But it was his rise to power that provided the most lurid chapter of Alexander's checkered career.

Rodrigo Borgia indicated early on that he had the makings of a great Renaissance pontiff. He was only twelve when he reportedly committed his first murder, stabbing to death another boy his age. His uncle, Pope Callistus III, assured Rodrigo's place in the Church by making him a cardinal when he was twenty-five and vice-chancellor of the Holy See a year later. Thanks to the offices provided by Uncle Cal, Rodrigo soon became a very rich man.

"He is enormously wealthy," a contemporary wrote, "and through his connections with kings and princes, commands great influence. He has built a beautiful and comfortable place for himself between the bridge of Sant' Angelo and the Campo di Fiori. His revenues from his papal offices, his abbeys in Italy and Spain, his three bishoprics of Valencia, Portus, and Cartagena, are vast. . . . His plate, his stuffs embroidered with silk and gold, his books are all of such quality as would befit a king or pope. I hardly need mention the sumptuous bed-hangings, trappings for his horses and similar things of gold, silver, and silk, nor the vast quantity of gold coin which he possesses."

Rodrigo Borgia's money would later come in handy when he set out to buy himself the papacy. In the meantime, he settled into his luxurious lifestyle as a prince of the Church with his mistress, Vannozza de' Catanei. In addition to the children he had from previous affairs, Vannozza bore him four more illegitimate children over the next twenty years. Two of them, Cesare and Lucrezia Borgia, would become as infamous as their dad.

Much as he loved Vannozza, however, Rodrigo eschewed monogamy as vigorously as he had celibacy. His extravagant sex life was greeted with a wink by his uncle Pope Callistus, but after Callistus died in 1458, his successor Pius II took a less favorable view. No slouch in the sack himself, having sired two children of his own, Pius was nevertheless shocked by Cardinal Borgia's behavior.

"Beloved Son," the pope wrote Rodrigo after hearing of a particularly lusty evening. "We have heard that, four days ago, several ladies of Sienna—women entirely given over to worldly frivolities—were assembled in the gardens of Giovanni di Bichis and that you, quite forgetful of the high office with which you are invested, were with them from the seventeenth to the twenty-second hour. With you was one of your colleagues whose age alone, if not the dignity of his office, ought to have recalled him to his duty. We have heard that the most licentious dances were indulged in, none of the allurements of love were lacking and you conducted yourself in a wholly worldly manner. Shame forbids mention of all that took place—not only the acts themselves but their very names are unworthy of your position. In order that your lusts might be given free rein the husbands, fathers, brothers and kinsmen of the young women were not admitted. . . . All Sienna is talking about this orgy. . . . Our displeasure is beyond words. . . . A cardinal should be beyond reproach."

Between the orgies, Cardinal Borgia continued to accumulate vast wealth. He made lots of money selling pardons for all manner of crimes, even the most heinous. After hearing protests over his paid reprieve of a father who murdered his daughter, he retorted, "It is not God's wish that a sinner should die, but that he should live—and pay!"

Borgia had more than enough money to take a stab at the papacy. Although popes were no longer elevated to the office by powerful Roman families or Christian emperors, the palms of the cardinals who elected them took plenty of greasing. In the conclave of 1484, after the death of Sixtus IV, Borgia lost the coveted crown to Innocent VIII, the great witch hunter. After Innocent died in 1492, however, Borgia was determined that he would not be cheated of the world's ultimate throne again. He nearly bankrupted himself in the process.

It was a tight race, but Borgia had plenty of money. He even boasted that he had sacks of gold enough to fill the Sistine Chapel. And though he was a hated foreigner (both Borgia and his uncle Callistus III were Spanish), the price was right for many of the obdurate Roman cardinals.

One persistent rival stood in his way, however. Cardinal Ascario Sforza was also enormously wealthy and came from the ruling dynasty of the Duchy of Milan, which would give him much support. Taking Sforza aside, Borgia bluntly asked him what it would take to withdraw. Sforza settled for the lucrative office of vice chancellor and a huge cash payment. The next day, four mule-loads of bullion were on their way to Sforza's palace. Now Borgia needed only one more vote, which was purchased from the cardinal of Venice. Though the amount was a pittance compared to what Borgia had spent on the others, it was certainly more than the ninety-six-year-old cardinal could ever hope to spend in the time he had left.

The election was held and, as expected, Rodrigo Borgia won. The new Alexander VI could barely contain his glee. "I am pope, I am pope," he exclaimed as he donned his sumptuous new papal vestments. "We are now in the clutches of perhaps the most savage wolf the world has ever seen," remarked Giovanni di Medici, the future Pope Leo X. "Either we flee or he will, without a doubt, devour us."

After an extravagant, debauched coronation ceremony that bordered on the pagan, Alexander VI settled right into his new position. He traded his long-term mistress Vannozza for the much younger and fresher Giulia Farnese, who was about sixteen at the time; the pope was pushing sixty. Giulia was immediately dubbed "the Pope's Whore" and "the Bride of Christ" by the snickering Roman populace, but her position garnered power and she was able to get her brother, the future Pope Paul III, a plush position as a cardinal.

Usually the office was very expensive to acquire, and Alexander VI fed his coffers by constantly making new cardinals. After they paid for the position, the pope was known to have them poisoned to make room for more. (One exception was Alexander's teenage son, Cesare, who got his post for free.) Ironically, Pope Alexander himself fell victim to a deadly potion, most probably intended for someone else. His grotesque demise in 1503, at age seventy-three, was vividly recorded by his aide John Burchard.

As the pope lingered on his bed, unable to swallow, his face turned the color of mulberry and his skin started to peel off. The fat of his belly liquified, while his bowels bled. Alexander finally died after hours of agony, but the indignity he faced was only just beginning. As the pope's blackened corpse started to putrefy, the tongue swelled and forced open the mouth, which, according to Burchard, was foaming like a kettle over a fire. The bloated body, growing as wide as it was long, finally burst, emitting sulphurous fumes from every orifice. It was, the Venetian ambassador wrote, "the ugliest, most monstrous and horrible dead body that was ever seen, without any form or likeness of humanity." The same could be said of the Church that was by now ripe for Reformation.

11

Indulge Me If You Will

Pope Leo X ignored all the signs of the Church fraying around him. He was too busy having fun. "Now I can really enjoy myself," the pope wrote to his cousin right after his election in 1513. And indeed he did. A lavish entertainer, Leo spent enormous sums on food, wine, and after-dinner diversions. He loved the company of young men, indulging in "those pleasures which cannot, with decency, be mentioned," as the Florentine statesman Francesco Guicciardini wrote. Maybe that's why this pope never had any "nephews."

He was a grand patron of the arts, who "would have been a perfect pope," one contemporary historian wrote, "if to these [artistic] accomplishments he had added even the slightest knowledge of religion." This assessment of Leo's spirituality was not entirely fair, however. After all, he was sensitive enough to know that he could never order a Christian to execute a cardinal who had conspired against him. In a great display of piety, he hired a Muslim to do the job.

Leo had elaborate building plans to monumentalize his papacy. The greatest of all was the rebuilding of St. Peter's, which had been razed by his predecessor Julius II. He wanted the new structure to be the biggest and grandest church in all the world. His ambitions, however, required a constant influx of cash, and Leo was always short. To remedy the situation, he settled on an age-old papal prerogative—the sale of indulgences to fill his coffers.

The notion that people could actually buy their way into heaven by paying off the pope enraged a German monk by the name of Martin Luther. In an act of bold defiance against this form of papal abuse, Luther took a hammer and nailed his *Ninety-Five Theses Upon Indulgences* to the doors of the cathedral at Wittenberg in 1517. "The Pope's wealth far exceeds that of all other men," Luther wrote. "Why does he not build the Church of St. Peter with his own money instead of the money of poor Christians?" Leo X recognized the danger to the papacy Luther represented, excommunicating him and ordering him burned in effigy, but he died without doing anything to reform the Church that was continuing to unravel by dissent.

12

In the Ghetto

*U*nlike Leo, Paul IV wasn't about to sit around the Vatican pleasuring himself while kings and commoners alike gave Rome the collective finger. Elected at age seventy-nine, this vile-tempered, foul-mouthed Vicar of Christ was probably too old—and way too mean—to enjoy himself anyway. Instead, this pope was a fierce reactionary determined to reassert the supreme power of the papacy.

Paul started with a little house cleaning. He was so disgusted by the nudes Michelangelo had created in the Sistine Chapel that he ordered clothes painted on a swath of them. The artist who completed this task, Daniele da Volterra, became known as "The Britches Maker." In his fury at the Reformation that was sweeping Christendom, Paul reignited the fires of the Roman Inquisition. Often presiding over heresy trials himself, the pope dared anyone to challenge him or his authority. Even Ignatius Loyola, the great soldier turned saint, "trembled in every bone" at the thought of crossing Paul.

In his drive to maintain orthodoxy, the pope created the *Index of Forbidden Books*, a landmark in thought control that would linger well into the twentieth century. Among the first entries were the works of the Dutch scholar Erasmus and all Bibles not written in Latin. In time, authors added to the list would include everyone from Boccaccio to Galileo, who was persecuted by Pope Urban VIII in the next century for daring to suggest that the earth revolved around the sun—not the other way around.

As much as Paul IV hated dissent, though, he hated Jews even more. While the papacy had never been a model of tolerance—cursing the Jews for having killed Christ—Paul took to persecuting them with an unprecedented ferocity. In a preview of Nazi policy still almost four hundred years away, he herded all the Jews of Rome into ghettos and forced them to sell their property to Christians at ridiculously low prices. He also ordered them to wear distinctive yellow headgear and forbade them to marry Christians or attend to them as physicians. Jewish synagogues were destroyed and sacred texts burned.

And though he was the most despised pope of the century—upon his death in 1559, joyful crowds rampaged through Rome smashing his statues—Paul IV's legacy of intolerance lingered for centuries. It took a far greater pope in the twentieth century to begin to atone for all the hatred and injustice that had been sown. "The Mark of Cain is stamped upon our foreheads," the gentle and beloved Pope John XXIII wrote in a prayer. "Across the centuries, our brother Abel has lain in blood which we drew, and shed tears we caused by forgetting Thy Love. Forgive us, Lord, for the curse we falsely attributed to their name as Jews. Forgive us for crucifying Thee a second time in their flesh. For we knew not what we did."

PART IX

Death Be Not Dignified

*For God's sake, let us sit upon the ground
And tell sad stories of the death of kings.*

—*Richard II*, Act III, scene ii

All things must pass, it is true, but it seems the Grim Reaper got a little giddy when it came to swatting down royalty. With all that pomp and pretense just begging to be punctured, how could he resist? Certainly Death was diabolically inventive in the variety of undignified demises he concocted for his royal victims, but, clever as he was, there were some notable occasions when the Great Leveler truly outdid himself.

OCCIDERE NOLITE TIMERE

EDWARDVS II REX ANG

At bottom, Edward II meets a ghastly end.

1

A Tight Squeeze

William the Conqueror was an impressive figure at the turn of the last millennium, a fearsome warrior whose life seemed to be one spectacular triumph after another. He defied the taint of illegitimacy at an early age—back when they still called him William the Bastard—to become the Duke of Normandy. Out-maneuvering dangerous relatives, subduing restless nobles, and checking the territorial ambitions of neighboring states, Duke William consolidated his power and then set his sights on Britain. There he easily defeated the English King Harold at the Battle of Hastings in 1066 and became the first of the long line of monarchs who have ruled Britain ever since. But two decades later he died, and things didn't go so well after that.

With his last breath in 1087, the once awesome ruler was instantly transformed into a bloated corpse destined for a series of indignities he could never have imagined during his lifetime. Actually, the humiliation began shortly before William expired—with the wound that killed him. While fighting in France, the warrior king was felled not by an enemy's ax or sword, but by his own saddle—gouged on its horn when his horse reared at a burning ruin. History does not record exactly where on his person William was ruptured. One can only imagine.

The stricken king was taken by his retainers to the priory of Saint-Gervais, where he died several days later. With their sovereign dead, William's loyal companions immediately raced off to secure their own interests, leaving the body alone with the servants. William the Conqueror was now ripe for the picking. Seizing the opportunity, the greedy staff started hauling away all his possessions, even his clothes, and the dead king was left on the floor nearly naked.

The Norman chronicler Ordericus Vitalis recorded the whole ghastly episode a generation later: "Behold this mighty prince who was lately obsequiously obeyed by more than a hundred thousand men in arms, and at whose nod nations trembled, was now stripped by his own attendants, in a house which was not his own, and left on the bare ground from early morn to almost noon."

And yet the ordeal wasn't over. Eventually King William's body was collected by a group of monks and given a funeral. When it came time to place the corpse in its coffin, however, the gathered were stunned to find it didn't quite fit. William had to be crammed in. He had grown a bit obese after his glory days, so this was difficult. Suddenly the church was filled with a horrible stench. Ordericus Vitalis concludes the story: "His corpulent stomach, fattened with so many delicacies, shamefully burst, to give a lesson, both to the prudent and the thoughtless, on what is the end of fleshy glory."

2

A Royal Pain in the Ass

 Tall, strong, and golden-haired, Edward II looked every inch the medieval ideal of kingly splendor. And were it not for his penchant for perfumed male lovers and the utter contempt he felt for his wife and his royal duties, the image might have been complete. As it stood, though, this English king spent most of his time fawning over one Piers Gaveston, whom Edward's macho father, Edward I, had banished from the kingdom during the previous reign for unseemly behavior with his son.

Showering Gaveston with land, titles, and sexual treats when he inherited the throne in 1307, King Edward managed to alienate his queen, Isabella of France, and England's most powerful magnates. Isabella could not have been too pleased, in fact, when Edward gave Gaveston all their wedding presents and indicated from the beginning that he far preferred Gaveston's bed to hers. And the nobles found it more than a little irritating that the king ignored them while bestowing fortune and honors upon this upstart who openly mocked them.

Fed up, the barons wrenched Gaveston away from the king and chopped off his head. Like an oversexed hydra, however, new favorites immediately sprang up in his place. Now it was Isabella who had finally had enough. Fleeing to her native France, the queen took herself a lover, Roger Mortimer, and raised an army to invade her wayward husband's kingdom.

In September 1326, they arrived in England without meeting any resistance. The king was forced to abdicate in favor of his son, Edward III, and was kept starving in the dungeon of Berkeley Castle. Isabella and Mortimer wanted Edward dead, but killed in a way that would leave no mark on his body. Accordingly, he met a ghastly demise involving the insertion of a red-hot iron poker.

3

※❦※

Spinning in Her Grave

As the last of Henry VIII's six wives, Katherine Parr was fortunate enough to outlive the dangerously fickle old king. Afterwards, she even got to marry the love of her life, Thomas Seymour, who happened to be her late husband's former brother-in-law. Life was bliss for the thirty-nine-year-old Queen Dowager, but it was suddenly cut short soon after she gave birth to her only child in 1547. Though she was interred at the chapel of her Sudely Castle estate, she would not rest in peace for centuries to come.

The chapel holding Katherine Parr's remains began to fall into neglect after some years, and by the 1700s it had crumbled to such an extent that no one was really sure where exactly the late queen rested. Then, in 1782, the occupant of the Sudely property, a man named John Lucas, came across her coffin amidst the rubble of the old chapel. His morbid curiosity overwhelming any respect he may have had for dead royalty, Lucas hacked open the casket. In it he found the almost perfectly preserved remains of the queen who had been dead for more than two hundred years.

The pristine corpse didn't retain its freshness for long, though. People were reporting a sickening stench emanating from it a year later. A stone slab was placed on the tomb to discourage further sightseeing, but ten years after that, Queen

Katherine was disturbed yet again. A group of drunken men decided she needed a proper burial and proceeded to dig a grave. Unfortunately, they tossed her in upside down.

In the early nineteenth century, the ivy-choked tomb was rediscovered. This time it was sealed shut once and for all. A marble effigy of the queen was placed in the restored chapel at Sudely, and an altar there was dedicated to her memory. Nearly three centuries after her death, Katherine Parr was finally at rest.

4

Strike Three

Mary Queen of Scots had a real knack for getting herself into trouble. She married a jerk just because he looked good, and then eloped with the chief suspect in his murder.[1] After abdicating the throne and fleeing her disgusted Scottish subjects, she was kept prisoner in England by her cousin Elizabeth I for almost twenty years. During this time she was involved in no fewer than four dangerous plots designed to free her and place her on the English throne, one of which finally sealed her doom. It seems the Scottish queen was a genius at making bad choices. Still, no matter what kind of mess Mary had made of her life, it didn't compare to the mess an inexperienced executioner made of her.

After Queen Elizabeth reluctantly signed her cousin's death warrant, events moved quickly. None of her counselors wanted the English queen, who despaired at the idea of executing a fellow monarch, to suddenly change her mind as she often did. On the morning of February 8, 1587, Mary Queen of Scots was led into the Great Hall of Fotheringhay Castle. Eyes straight ahead, back rigid, and head held high, she paused at the foot of the steps leading to the black-draped scaffold upon which she was to

---

[1]Mary's miserable marriage to Henry Stuart, Lord Darnley, is recounted in Part III, Chapter 3.

die. Her once magnificent looks had faded with age and years of imprisonment, but she still radiated royal dignity.

Reaching the platform, the forty-four-year-old queen was directed to sit in a chair as the warrant of her execution was read aloud. Looking about the Great Hall, she saw the crowd gathered to witness her demise. More than one hundred people were riveted by the unfolding spectacle. Nearby was the hooded executioner dressed entirely in black, the instrument of his trade lying on the floor.

As she faced the block where she was to lose her head, Mary saw herself as a martyr for her Catholic faith and she was proud. Suddenly, though, a man emerged from the crowd and interrupted the moment. "I am the Dean of Peterborough!" he shouted. "It is not too late to embrace the true faith! Yea, the Reformed Religion, which hath . . ." Mary, taken aback, interjected calmly, saying: "Good Mister Dean, trouble not yourself any more about this matter. I was born in this religion, have lived in this religion, and am resolved to die in this religion."

As the dean continued his exhortation, Mary turned away and prayed quietly in Latin. The headsman stepped forward and knelt before her. "Forgive me," he said, as decorum required. "I forgive you and all the world with all my heart," she answered gently, "for I hope this death will make an end to all my troubles."

Wishful thinking.

Rising, the executioner offered to help the queen disrobe in preparation for the ax. Declining politely, Mary turned instead to her ladies-in-waiting for assistance. They unbuttoned her black gown, revealing a vibrant crimson one underneath. Her veil and headdress were removed and set on a nearby stool. Taking out a gold-bordered handkerchief, she handed it to one of her ladies, whose hands were trembling so much that Mary had to help secure it as her blindfold.

Someone then led the queen to the block and helped her to kneel on the cushion before it. She reached out, groping for the cold wood, and placed her neck on it. "Into Thy hands, O Lord, I commend my spirit," she whispered in Latin, as the executioner raised his ax and brought it down hard.

THWACK!

A groan was heard coming from the victim. To his horror, the executioner had missed his target, grazing the side of the queen's skull instead. "Sweet Jesus," she was heard to mutter before the ax was lifted again. This time it nearly severed neck from body. Angry and exasperated, the executioner sawed through the remaining flesh. The head rolled away, while the body fell on its back, gushing blood. "God save Queen Elizabeth," the executioner shouted as he grasped the severed head by the hair and raised it to the crowd. Suddenly, it fell and rolled away, leaving in his hand only a red wig. Onlookers gasped, seeing the gray-haired head, suddenly old, facing them, lips still moving.

The executioner then lifted the queen's dress to remove her garters, his time-honored prerogative, but was startled as a small dog emerged from the folds. Mary's pet, Geddon, had been hidden in the dress. The little dog rushed to the corpse and circled, confused and distraught, then began to howl. The Protestant dean who had earlier confronted Mary leapt to the platform and pushed the dog's face into the pool of blood. "Remember what [John] Knox prophesied about the dogs drinking her blood!" he screeched. "Drink, you cur!" But Geddon resisted, instead sinking his teeth into the dean's hand.

Mary's head was displayed on a velvet cushion before an open window at Fotheringhay Castle. Her crucifix, prayer book, bloodstained clothes, the execution block and anything she had touched were taken to the courtyard and burned, obliterating all traces of the mutilated queen.

5

Prescription for Disaster

After Charles II suffered what was probably a minor stroke in 1685, twelve physicians were summoned to the royal chambers and immediately set upon a course intended to rid the English king's body of all poisons. They extracted a full quart of his blood. They drained him of liquids by administering powerful emetics and enemas. Charles, not surprisingly, remained ill.

The doctors were on top of the situation, though. Over the next few days, they shaved the king's scalp and singed it with burning irons, filled his nose with sneezing powder, covered him with hot plasters and then ripped them off. After Charles complained of a sore throat, body aches, and cold sweats, the medics rubbed his feet with a mixture of resin and pigeon feces.

The king was sinking rapidly. The doctors pulled out all the stops. It was time to exercise the most sophisticated techniques known to modern practitioners. They drilled holes in the royal noggin to drain off the bad humors. But it was no use. Five days after treatment began, "The Merry Monarch" breathed his last, apologizing for taking so long to die, and thanking his physicians for the heroic efforts to save him.

6

A Look
of Detachment

Charles II left lots of bastards when he died, but no legitimate heirs to succeed him on the throne. This didn't stop his eldest son, James, Duke of Monmouth, from making an armed grab for the crown anyway. The revolt was a flop, easily squashed by the forces of Monmouth's uncle, King James II, who ordered his ambitious nephew beheaded. What happened next is an irresistible tale, frequently told by the Yeoman Warders at the Tower of London.

After the duke's execution, someone remembered that no official portrait of him existed. Treasonous bastard though he may have been, he was still the son of a king and it seemed only proper that his image be preserved. With his head now hacked off, it would be difficult for Monmouth to pose for an artist. But not impossible. All it took was a little ingenuity. The severed head was simply sewn back on the body, which was then propped up for its sitting. It should be noted for the record that certain authorities dispute the Beefeaters' story of the reattached head, but what fun are they?

7

❦

Eat Your Heart Out

When a king of France died, he was subject to a fairly rigorous post-mortem. His body was sliced open from throat to hips, after which his internal organs were removed and preserved. This ritual wasn't so bad. After all, it was part of an old tradition going back to the ancient Egyptians. The procedure took an odd twist with Louis XIV, however. While the hearts of most French kings were placed in gilded urns to rest for eternity, the Sun King's ended up in the stomach of an English eccentric. Or so the story goes.

Blame it on the French Revolution. Sure, Louis XIV had been dead for decades before the popular uprising even started, but he was royal, and as his descendent Louis XVI discovered on the guillotine, royalty wasn't going over very well at the time. Even dead royalty. At the Cathedral of St. Denis, an angry mob raided the tomb of the king who had gloriously wallowed in absolute monarchy for more than half a century.[1] They stole his embalmed heart.

The organ was then sold to an English nobleman, Lord Harcourt, who in turn sold it to the dean of Westminster, Rev. William Buckland. When the good dean died, the heart passed by inheritance to his son, Francis Buckland. Frank, as he was called

---

[1]Louis XIV's career as the center of attention at Versailles is explored in Part II, Chapter 2.

by his friends, was a scientifically minded man, but nevertheless a bit bizarre. He was among the founders of the Society for the Acclimatization of Animals in the United Kingdom, whose goal it was to import and raise exotic animals to increase the national food supply.

For a while Buckland was satisfied devouring kangaroo, ostrich, and the like, but soon his palate became more adventurous. Almost anything organic would do. And here's where Louis XIV's heart came in. According to one report, Buckland produced the dried organ at dinner one evening. "I have eaten many strange things in my lifetime," a startled guest recalled him saying, "but I have never before eaten the heart of a king."

In a few gulps, the Sun King became a gourmet snack.

8

Royal Flush

George II never did get much respect. Although he was a brave warrior—the last British monarch to lead his troops into battle, in fact—the German-born king seemed unable to shake the aura of absurdity that surrounded him. His British subjects, led by his own son, laughed at his thick accent, stifling court, and drooling lechery.[1] Even his death in 1760 lacked dignity. Poor George died straining on the toilet.

---

[1] See Part I, Chapter 3, for details about George II's busy love life, and Part V, Chapter 5, for the account of his unpleasant relationship with his son, Frederick.

9

A Lot Off the Top

$\mathcal{M}$arie Antoinette's enduring reputation for decadent extravagance is not entirely unearned. Even if she never actually dismissed reports of widespread bread shortages with the infamous line, "Let them eat cake," her lavish lifestyle nevertheless flew smack in the face of the abject poverty and hunger that surrounded her. The puffed and powdered queen blithely ignored the misery, immersing herself instead in a cycle of elaborate ceremony, obsessive spending, and absurd fashion.

"The queen is a pretty woman," her brother, the Austrian emperor Joseph II, wrote during a visit to France in 1777, "but she is empty-headed, unable as yet to find her advantage, and wastes her days running from dissipation to dissipation, some of which are perfectly allowable but nonetheless dangerous because they prevent her from having the thoughts she needs so badly."

Maybe it was the big hair. Piles and piles of it. The enormous coiffures the queen so fancied—hours spent in their construction, reaching several feet high, and elaborately decorated with fruits, feathers, jewels, and figurines—seemed to sum up her entire vacuous existence. The head that carried this frivolous mass would eventually be lopped off amid the screeches of revolutionary madness, but it was the degrading existence Marie Antoinette was forced to endure just prior to her public execution that offered the starkest contrast to her former life as France's over-pampered queen.

Whereas she once amused herself amid the glitter and luxury of Versailles with hundreds of fawning nobles eagerly competing to attend to her every whim, she was now held in a blackened prison cell that dripped with moisture and was kept frigid in the absence of a fireplace. The rich gowns and adornments were all gone, replaced by a single frayed black dress. Deprived of her children, or even the comfort of a single candle at night, the former queen—now known as prisoner number 280—suffered illness and severe anxiety all alone on a narrow, filthy cot.

She was taken from her cell to appear before the Revolutionary Tribunal, which was an utter travesty. Absurd accusations of murder, treason, and even incest with her own son were hurled at "the Austrian Bitch," as she was called, without any consideration for the truth. It was here, however, that the once flighty and spoiled queen proved her mettle. She addressed the court with dignity and honor, seeming to transcend the deadly spectacle that engulfed her.

"One saw sadness in the faces of the honest spectators," an eyewitness of the trial recorded, "and madness in the eyes of the crowd of men and women placed in the room by design—madness which, more than once, gave way to emotions of pity and admiration. The accusers and judges did not succeed in hiding their anger, or the involuntary confusion they felt at the Queen's noble firmness."

The preordained verdict was death—the same fate her husband Louis XVI had met nine months earlier.[1] The ex-queen

---

[1] Louis XVI's execution also was a degrading public spectacle. After being mangled by the guillotine, the king's severed head was seized by a young guard who, according to one eyewitness, paraded it around the scaffold "with the most atrocious and indecent gestures."

was brought back to her miserable cell to await the guillotine. On the appointed day, October 16, 1793, she sent farewells to her children and in her prayer book wrote, "My God have pity on me! My eyes have no more tears to shed for you, my poor children. Adieu. Adieu!"

She then had to prepare herself for the execution scheduled for midday. When she was queen, Marie Antoinette always had a giddy coterie on hand as she picked out the day's wardrobe and took her luxurious bath behind a screen for modesty. Now there was only one woman assigned to her. Bleeding heavily, she asked the maid to stand in front of her while she undressed and changed her soiled undergarments. "The [guard] came up to us at once," the woman recalled, "and, standing by the headrest, watched her change. She put her fichu up to cover her shoulders, and with great sweetness said to the young man, 'In the name of decency, monsieur, let me change my linen in private.'" The guard, claiming he had orders to watch the prisoner's every movement, refused to look away, so the former queen was forced to take off her stained petticoat with as much modesty as she could manage and stuff it into a chink in the wall.

Soon it was time to go. The executioner, who happened to be the son of the man who had beheaded Louis XVI, came in to tie up her hands and cut off her hair. She had hoped that she would be carried to the execution site in a coach, as her husband had been, but saw when she left the prison that a cart awaited her—a cart used to carry common criminals to their deaths. Feeling her bowels loosen, the former queen of France had to request that her hands be unbound so she could relieve herself against the prison wall.

Riding backwards on the cart to the Place de la Revolution, she stoically endured the jeers of the inflamed crowds that lined the route. It was a festive occasion all around. In the square where the guillotine stood, people were selling fruits and wine to the excited onlookers who closed in around the scaffold to watch "the Widow Capet" lose her head.

In the middle of this horrific circus, Marie Antoinette—looking old well beyond her years, with her white hair shorn—remained calm and dignified. Accidentally stepping on the executioner's foot as she ascended the scaffold, she apologized gently. "Pardon, monsieur. I did not mean to do it." She was then tied down on the beheading machine and the wooden collar was snapped around her neck. In an instant the head was severed and held aloft for all to see. The crowd roared its approval.

10

The Case of the Purloined Penis

A man deserves some measure of dignity when he dies, but Napoleon Bonaparte seems to have ended up a few inches short. If the provenance of the small, shriveled object preserved in a New York hospital is correct, the little emperor is buried in Paris without a key part of his anatomy.

While age has obviously taken its toll on the missing member, which is about the size of a pinkie finger, there apparently wasn't much to begin with. "His reproductive organs were small and apparently atrophied," a physician attending Napoleon's autopsy in 1821 later noted. "He is said to have been impotent for some time before he died."

It was after this autopsy, performed on the remote South Atlantic island of St. Helena, where Napoleon had been exiled under British military supervision after plunging most of Europe into war, that a Corsican chaplain named Vignali reportedly swiped the imperial penis with a quick slice of the knife. "Voila! I have it!" he is said to have written.

The cleric's motivation was simple, according to New York urologist and Napoleon collector John Lattimer, who now owns the dried-up piece of history and keeps it preserved in its own little casket. Napoleon was abusive and insulting to his fellow

Corsican, typical behavior for the obnoxious emperor, and Vignali became enraged.

"The Corsicans are a very emotional lot," notes Lattimer, who says Vignali would have had time "to get his revenge and nip off his bit" after the autopsy was over. In the tropical heat, Lattimer offers from experience that the stench from the postmortem would have been almost unbearable. As soon as the body was sewn back up, the British officers overseeing the procedure would have been glad to take their leave, allowing a brief opportunity for Vignali to emasculate the emperor.

As to whether the tiny object in his possession is the real thing, Lattimer has no doubt. It was part of a larger collection of Napoleonana, ownership of which can be traced right back to Vignali. "I have not seen anything that undermines its credibility," he says. "There are no obvious holes in the continuity of ownership."

The doctor has treated Napoleon's most private of parts with utmost respect since he acquired it in the early 1970s. He never puts it on display and will not allow it to be photographed. He even offered to return it to the Invalides in Paris, where Napoleon is buried, but has not received an official response so far. Perhaps the French are not eager to acknowledge, as *The Washington Post* so eloquently put it, that "their noble heritage may derive, in part, from a legacy that is not so much gilded, but gelded."

11

Extreme Overkill

*T*he Bolsheviks ended three hundred years of Romanov rule in Russia when they murdered Tsar Nicholas II and his family in 1918, but they were not especially proud of the way they did it. Many details of the killings remained shameful state secrets for decades, giving rise to rumors that some members of the family may have actually survived the slaughter. Romantic legends and clever imposters would further obscure the truth. It was only after the fall of communism and the disintegration of the Soviet Union that the complete picture started to emerge. Long-hidden reports of chief executioner Yakov Yurovsky, the discovery of the Romanovs' bones, and major advances in forensic science all served to expose just how hideous these murders really were.

During the night of October 16–17, 1918, the deposed emperor and his family were wakened, told to dress and to assemble quickly in the basement of the mansion in the Siberian town of Ekaterinburg, where they had been kept prisoners for the past seventy-eight days. On the walls, filthy graffiti mocked the doomed family as they walked by. Nicholas carried his only son, thirteen-year-old Alexis, who was crippled by hemophilia. The tsar was followed by his ailing wife, Empress Alexandra, and his four beautiful daughters: Olga, twenty-two; Tatiana, twenty-one; Marie, nineteen; and, carrying her pet spaniel, Anastasia, seventeen. Accompanying the family were four loyal members of the staff who had stayed with them during their imprisonment: Nicholas's personal physician, Dr. Botkin, and his valet, Alouzy Trupp; Alexandra's maid, Anna Demidova; and the cook, Ivan Kharitonov.

Arriving in the designated room, suspecting nothing, the group was told to line up against a wall to have their picture taken. But instead of a photographer, twelve armed men entered the room. Yurovsky, the lead executioner, stood in front of the tsar and read from a piece of paper. "In view of the fact that your [German] relatives are continuing their attack on Soviet Russia," he declared, "the Ural Executive Committee has decided to execute you."

Stunned, Nicholas barely had time to react before Yurovsky shot him dead at point blank range. With that, the rest of the men started firing wildly. Empress Alexandra, who had been sitting in a chair provided for her, died instantly, as did the eldest daughter, Olga, the doctor, and two of the staff.

For the others, however, death did not come so quickly. The killers were shocked to find their bullets ricocheting off the three other daughters, the tsarevitch, and the maid, Demidova. Confused, they attacked them with bayonets, which failed to penetrate, causing the executioners to stab them all the more ferociously. The tsarevitch was brutally kicked in the head and shot twice in the ear. The bloody and gunsmoke-filled room was then quiet as the killers started carrying the bodies out in sheets. Suddenly, one of the daughters stirred and cried out. The men quickly set on her, savagely attacking her until she was still.

The bodies were tossed in a waiting truck and taken to an abandoned mine shaft about twelve miles away. Near the site, the corpses were unloaded and undressed. Immediately it became clear why the bullets and bayonets had been so ineffective on some of them. Sewn into corsets and other undergarments were row upon row of diamonds that had helped deflect the on-slaught. "No one is responsible for their death agonies but them-selves," Yurovsky recorded. "There turned out to be eighteen pounds of such valuables. By the way, their greed turned out to be so great that on Alexandra Fyodorovna there was a simply huge piece of gold wire bent into the shape of a bracelet of around a pound in weight. All these valuables were immediately ripped out so that we wouldn't have to drag the bloody clothing with us."

As their clothes were burned, the naked bodies were laid out on the grass. The once beautiful faces of the daughters were now unrecognizable after having been smashed and battered by rifle butts. Some of them were violated. "I felt the empress myself and she was warm," one of the killers said. "Now I can die in peace because I have squeezed the empress's——," said an-other. The last word was deleted from the report.

All the bodies were then tossed into the mine shaft. Yurovsky dropped in several hand grenades to collapse the structure, but they were largely ineffective. He soon realized that the burial site was too exposed and subject to discovery by the approaching White Army, which was loyal to the tsar and from whom the Bolsheviks wished to keep the murders hidden. It was decided that the corpses of the Romanovs and their staff would have to be moved. Yurovsky returned to the site and ordered the man-gled bodies pulled out of the shaft. All the White Army inves-tigators later found there were bits and pieces of the family's possessions, including a child's military belt buckle, which the tsarevitch had worn, and the decaying corpse of Anastasia's pet dog. They also found a severed finger thought to have been Alexandra's.

Yurovsky moved the bodies to a more remote location. Two were burned, one of which was Alexis. Scientists differ on whether the other was Anastasia or Marie. The rest were tossed into a hastily dug grave. Yurovsky attempted to disfigure them further by pouring on sulfuric acid. When the bones were discovered decades later, scientists examining them were shocked at how much damage had been so brutally inflicted on them. Faces had been completely crushed and bones looked like a truck had rolled over them. Dr. Ludmilla Koryakova had exhumed plenty of skeletons in the course of her work. "But never," she told the Sunday *Times*, "so many that were so badly damaged—so violated. I was ill."

On July 17, 1998, eighty years after the murders, the remains of the Romanov family and staff were finally laid to rest at the eighteenth-century Cathedral of St. Peter and St. Paul, a mausoleum for the tsars since the time of Peter the Great. Russian president Boris Yeltsin paid tribute to the family with a stirring apology. "All these years, we were silent about this horrible crime," he said. "Those who perpetrated this crime and those who for decades have been finding excuses for it are guilty. All of us are guilty. One cannot lie to oneself and explain away wanton cruelty as political necessity. . . . We are all responsible to the historic memory of the people. That's why I should come here as a person and as president. I bow my head before the victims of a senseless murder."

12

*It's Not Nice
to Kill the King*

*O*ccasionally, in matters of death, royalty actually had the last laugh. Such was the case with Oliver Cromwell, the feisty parliamentarian who took over the government after the English Civil War and the execution of King Charles I in 1649. Cromwell ruled Britain as Lord Protector until he died in 1658, and was buried like royalty in Westminster Abbey. Shortly thereafter, the executed king's son, Charles II, was restored to the throne. Needless to say, he did not appreciate how his beheaded father had been treated by Cromwell, and soon got his revenge.

The Lord Protector's remains were disinterred from the Abbey and dragged through the streets of London. They were then taken to Tyburn, the execution place of common criminals, and hung all day. After the corpse was cut down, the head was lopped off and paraded on a stick, while the body was tossed in a pit. Cromwell's head finally was impaled on a spike atop Westminster Hall, where it remained for twenty-five years until a storm blew it down. It was not until 1960, after passing from owner to owner, that the rotted head was buried at Cromwell's alma mater, Sidney Sussex College in Cambridge.

As a final insult to the puritanical regicide, the British monarchy Cromwell so eagerly set out to destroy continues to thrive as Queen Elizabeth II sits firmly upon her throne.

APPENDIX I

British Monarchs
(1066–Present)

The Normans

William I (The Conqueror)
Born 1027
Ascended the throne 1066
Reigned 21 years
Married Matilda of Flanders
Died 1087, aged 60
Pages: 127, 261–262

William II ("Rufus")
Born 1056
Ascended the throne 1087
Reigned 13 years
Son of William the Conqueror
Never married
Died (murdered?) 1100, aged 44
Pages 20, 127

Henry I
Born 1069
Ascended the throne 1100
Reigned 35 years
Brother of William II
Married (1) Matilda of Scotland (2) Adela of Couvain
Died 1135, aged 66
Page: 127

Stephen
Born c. 1097
Ascended the throne 1135

Reigned 19 years
Nephew of Henry I
Married Matilda of Boulogne
Died 1154, aged about 57
Page: 127

The Angevins

Henry II

Born 1133
Ascended the throne 1154
Reigned 35 years
Grandson of Henry I
Married Eleanor of Aquitaine
Died 1189, aged 56
Pages: 127–128, 173–174

Richard I ("The Lion Heart")

Born 1157
Ascended the throne 1189
Reigned 10 years (killed in battle)
Son of Henry II
Married Berengaria of Navarre
Died 1199, aged 42
Pages: 20, 128

John

Born 1167
Ascended the throne 1199
Reigned 17 years
Brother of Richard I
Married (1) Isabel of Gloucester (2) Isabella of Angouleme
Died 1216, aged 48
Pages: 128, 233–234

Henry III

Born 1207
Ascended the throne 1216
Reigned 56 years
Son of King John
Married Eleanor of Provence
Died 1272, aged 65

Edward I

Born 1239
Ascended the throne 1272
Reigned 35 years
Son of Henry III
Married (1) Eleanor of Castile (2) Margaret of France
Died 1307, aged 68
Page: 263

Edward II

Born 1284
Ascended the throne 1307
Reigned 20 years (deposed and murdered)
Son of Edward I
Married Isabella of France
Died 1327, aged 43
Pages: 20, 129, 263–264

Edward III

Born 1312
Ascended the throne 1327
Reigned 50 years
Son of Edward II
Married Philippa of Hainault
Died 1377, aged 65
Pages: 129–131, 264

Richard II

Born 1367
Ascended the throne 1377
Reigned 22 years (deposed and murdered)
Grandson of Edward III
Married (1) Anne of Bohemia (2) Isabella of France
Died 1400, aged 33
Page: 130

House of Lancaster

Henry IV

Born 1367
Ascended the throne 1399 (usurper)
Reigned 14 years
Cousin of Richard II
Married (1) Mary Bohun (2) Joan of Brittany
Died 1413, aged 46
Pages: 130, 133

Henry V

Born 1387
Ascended the throne 1413
Reigned 9 years
Son of Henry IV
Married Catherine of Valois
Died 1422, aged 35
Pages: 130, 133

Henry VI

Born 1421
Reigned 1422–1461 and 1470–1471
Reigned a total of 40 years (deposed and murdered)

Son of Henry V
Married Margaret of Anjou
Died 1471, aged 50
Pages: 130–137

House of York

Edward IV

Born 1442
Reigned 1461–1470 and 1471–1483
Reigned a total of 21 years
Cousin of Henry VI
Married Elizabeth Woodville
Died 1483, aged 41
Pages: 16–17, 133–137

Edward V

Born 1470
Ascended the throne 1483
Reigned two months (deposed and later murdered)
Son of Edward IV
Never married
Died 1483, aged 13
Page: 137

Richard III

Born 1452
Ascended the throne 1483
Reigned 2 years (killed in battle)
Brother of Edward IV; uncle of Edward V
Married Anne Neville
Died 1485, aged 33
Pages: 137–138

House of Tudor

Henry VII
Born 1457
Ascended the throne 1485
Reigned 24 years
Remote Lancastrian lineage
Married Elizabeth of York (Edward IV's daughter)
Died 1509, aged 52
Pages: 59–60, 138

Henry VIII
Born 1491
Ascended the throne 1509
Reigned 38 years
Son of Henry VII
Married (1) Katherine of Aragon (2) Anne Boleyn (3) Jane Seymour
(4) Anne of Cleves (5) Catherine Howard (6) Katherine Parr
Died 1547, aged 56
Pages: 17, 31, 59–80, 81, 83, 101–107, 108, 109, 138–139, 140–142, 265

Edward VI
Born 1537
Ascended the throne 1547
Reigned 6 years
Son of Henry VIII and Jane Seymour
Never married
Died 1553, aged 16
Pages: 31, 72, 107, 109, 140–141

Mary I ("Bloody Mary")
Born 1516
Ascended the throne 1553
Reigned 5 years
Daughter of Henry VIII and Katherine of Aragon
Married Philip II of Spain

Died 1558, aged 42
Pages: 18, 31, 60, 66, 72, 101–111, 140–147

Elizabeth I ("The Virgin Queen")

Born 1533
Ascended the throne 1558
Reigned 44 years
Daughter of Henry VIII and Anne Boleyn
Never married
Died 1603, aged 70
Pages: 17–19, 29–33, 68, 83, 85, 103–104, 109, 140–146, 267

House of Stuart

James I (VI of Scotland)

Born 1566
Ascended the throne 1603
Reigned 22 years
Son of Mary Queen of Scots (cousin of Elizabeth I)
Married Anne of Denmark
Died 1625, aged 59
Pages: 19–20, 84

Charles I

Born 1600
Ascended the throne 1625
Reigned 24 years (deposed and executed)
Son of James I
Married Henrietta Maria of France
Died 1649, aged 48
Page: 285

Commonwealth (No Monarchy) 1649–1660

Charles II

Born 1630

Ascended the throne 1660
Reigned 25 years
Son of Charles I
Married Catherine of Braganza
Died 1685, aged 55
Pages: 20, 270, 271, 285

James II
Born 1633
Ascended the throne 1685
Reigned 3 years (deposed)
Brother of Charles II
Married (1) Anne Hyde (2) Mary of Modena
Died (in exile) 1701, aged 68
Pages: 20, 147–150, 271

William III and Mary II (comonarchy)
William: Born 1650
Ascended the throne 1689
Reigned 13 years
Nephew of James II
Died 1702, aged 52 years
Pages: 20, 147–148, 150
Mary: Born 1662
Ascended the throne 1689
Reigned 5 years
Daughter of James II
Married William III
Died 1694, aged 32
Pages: 20–21, 147–150

Anne
Born 1665
Ascended the throne 1702
Reigned 12 years
Sister of Mary II; second daughter of James II
Married Prince George of Denmark

Died 1714, aged 49
Pages: 21, 147–150

House of Hanover

George I
Born 1660
Ascended the throne 1714
Reigned 13 years
Great-grandson of James I
Married Princess Sophia of Zelle
Died 1727, aged 67
Pages: 21–22, 151–152

George II
Born 1683
Ascended the throne 1727
Reigned 33 years
Son of George I
Married Caroline of Anspach
Died 1760, aged 76
Pages: 22–23, 114, 152–154, 274

George III
Born 1738
Ascended the throne 1760
Reigned 59 years
Grandson of George II
Married Charlotte of Mecklenburg-Strelitz
Died 1820, aged 81
Pages: 23, 43, 95–97, 154–155, 186–190

George IV
Born 1762
Ascended the throne 1820
Reigned 9 years
Son of George III

Married (1) Mrs. Maria Fitzherbert (invalidated) (2) Caroline of Brunswick
Died 1830, aged 67
Pages: 23, 41–45, 94–97, 154–155, 187

William IV
Born 1765
Ascended the throne 1830
Reigned 6 years
Son of George III; brother of George IV
Married Adelaide of Saxe-Coburg
Died 1837, aged 71
Pages: 23–24, 156–157

Victoria
Born 1819
Ascended the throne 1837
Reigned 63 years (longest in British history)
Niece of George IV and William IV
Married Prince Albert of Saxe-Coburg-Gotha
Died 1901, aged 81
Pages: 24–25, 120–123, 156–157, 195

House of Saxe-Coburg-Gotha to Windsor

Edward VII
Born 1841
Ascended the throne 1901
Reigned 9 years
Son of Queen Victoria
Married Alexandra of Denmark
Died 1910, aged 68
Pages: 120–123

George V
Born 1865
Ascended the throne 1910

Reigned 25 years
Son of Edward VII
Married Princess Mary of Teck
Died 1936, aged 70
Pages: 46, 157

Edward VIII

Born 1894
Ascended the throne 1936
Reigned for 11 months (abdicated)
Son of George V
Married Mrs. Wallis Warfield Simpson
Died 1972, aged 78
Pages: 25–26, 48–51

George VI

Born 1895
Ascended the throne 1936
Reigned 15 years
Son of George V; brother of Edward VIII
Married Lady Elizabeth Bowes-Lyon
Died 1952, aged 56
Page: 49

Elizabeth II

Born 1926
Ascended the throne 1952
Currently reigning
Daughter of George VI
Married Philip Mountbatten (formerly Prince Philip of Greece), Duke of Edinburgh
Page: 285

APPENDIX II

French Monarchs (1515–1814)

House of Valois

Francis I
Born 1494
Ascended the throne 1515
Reigned 32 years
Married (1) Claude, daughter of Louis XII (2) Eleanor of Spain
Died 1547, aged 52
Pages: 8, 61

Henri II
Born 1519
Ascended the throne 1547
Reigned 12 years (killed in a jousting tournament)
Son of Francis I
Married Catherine de Medici
Died 1559, aged 40
Pages: 8–9, 11

Francis II
Born 1544
Ascended the throne 1559
Reigned 1 year
Son of Henri II
Married Mary Queen of Scots
Died 1560, aged 16
Page: 81

Charles IX
Born 1550
Ascended the throne 1560
Reigned 13 years
Brother of Francis II

Married Elizabeth of Austria
Died 1574, aged 23
Page: 12

Henri III

Born 1551
Ascended the throne 1574
Reigned 15 years (assassinated)
Brother of Charles IX and Francis II
Married Louise of Lorraine
Died 1589, aged 37
Pages: 9–11

House of Bourbon

Henry IV

Born 1553
Ascended the throne 1589
Reigned 20 years (assassinated)
Married (1) Marguerite (Margot) of Valois (2) Marie de Medici
Died 1610, aged 56
Pages: 11–14

Louis XIII

Born 1601
Ascended the throne 1610
Reigned 33 years
Son of Henry IV
Married Anne of Austria
Died 1643, aged 41

Louis XIV ("The Sun King")

Born 1638
Ascended the throne 1643
Reigned 72 years (longest in European history)
Son of Louis XIII

Married (1) Marie Therese of Austria (2) Mme. de Maintenon
Died 1715, aged 77
Pages: 14, 34–38, 180–181, 272–273

Louis XV
Born 1710
Ascended the throne 1715
Reigned 58 years
Great-grandson of Louis XIV
Married Marie Leszcynska of Poland
Died 1774, aged 64
Pages: 14–15, 93

Louis XVI
Born 1754
Ascended the throne 1774
Reigned 18 years (deposed and executed)
Grandson of Louis XV
Married Marie Antoinette of Austria
Died 1793, aged 38
Pages: 14, 93, 272, 276–277

First Republic (No Monarchy) 1792–1804

Empire

Napoleon I
Born 1769
Crowned himself emperor 1804
Reigned 14 years (twice abdicated)
Married (1) Josephine de Beauharnais (2) Marie Louise of Austria
Died 1821, aged 51
Pages: 96, 158–169, 279–280

Appendix III

Russian Monarchs (1682–1917)
The Romanovs

Peter I (The Great)
Born 1672
Ascended the throne 1682 (shared with half brother Ivan V until 1696)
Reigned 43 years
Married (1) Eudoxia Lopukhin (2) Marta Skowronska
   (later Empress Catherine I)
Died 1725, aged 52
Pages: 115–119, 182–185

Catherine I
Born 1684
Ascended the throne 1725
Reigned 2 years
Second wife of Peter the Great
Died 1727, aged 43

Peter II
Born 1715
Ascended the throne 1727
Reigned 2 years
Grandson of Peter the Great
Never married
Died 1730, aged 14

Anna
Born 1693
Ascended the throne 1730
Reigned 10 years
Niece of Peter the Great
Married Frederick William of Courland
Died 1740, aged 47
Pages: 39–40

Ivan VI

Born 1740
Ascended the throne 1740
Reigned 13 months (deposed and later murdered)
Great nephew of Empress Anna
Never married
Died 1764, aged 23

Elizabeth

Born 1709
Ascended the throne 1741
Reigned 20 years
Daughter of Peter the Great
Never married
Died 1762, aged 52
Pages: 86–87

Peter III

Born 1728
Ascended the throne 1762
Reigned six months (deposed and murdered)
Grandson of Peter the Great; nephew of Empress Elizabeth
Married Sophie Frederike Auguste of Anhalt-Zerbst
   (later Catherine II)
Died 1762, aged 34
Pages: 3, 86–88, 93, 191–192

Catherine II (The Great)

Born 1729
Ascended the throne 1762
Reigned 34 years
Married Peter III
Died 1796, aged 67
Pages: 3–7, 86–88, 93, 191–192

Paul I

Born 1754
Ascended the throne 1796
Reigned 4 years (assassinated)
Son of Catherine II (paternity remains uncertain)
Married (1) Wilhelmina of Darmstadt (2) Sophia Dorothea of Wurttemberg
Died 1801, aged 46
Pages: 191–193

Alexander I

Born 1777
Ascended the throne 1801
Reigned 24 years
Son of Paul I
Married Princess Louise of Baden-Durlach
Died 1825, aged 47
Page: 192

Nicholas I

Born 1796
Ascended the throne 1825
Reigned 29 years
Brother of Alexander I
Married Princess Charlotte of Prussia
Died 1855, aged 58

Alexander II

Born 1818
Ascended the throne 1855
Reigned 26 years (assassinated)
Son of Nicholas I
Married Marie of Hesse-Darmstadt
Died 1881, aged 62

Alexander III

Born 1845
Ascended the throne 1881
Reigned 13 years
Son of Alexander II
Married Princess Dagmar of Denmark
Died 1894, aged 49

Nicholas II

Born 1868
Ascended the throne 1894
Reigned 22 years (deposed and murdered)
Son of Alexander III
Married Alexandra (granddaughter of Britain's Queen Victoria)
Died 1918, aged 50
Pages: 194–197, 281–284

APPENDIX IV

Timeline

Chronological Index of Monarchs featured in this book

Concurrent events in the Western World

27 B.C.–A.D. 80

Tiberius—Roman Emperor
(reigned A.D. 14–37)
Pages: 203–206, 218

Caligula—Roman Emperor
(reigned 37–41)
Pages: 206–212, 218, 219

Claudius—Roman Emperor
(reigned 41–54)
Pages: 211–214, 218

Nero—Roman Emperor
(reigned 54–68)
Pages: 215–217, 218–219

Galba—Roman Emperor
(reigned 68–69)
Pages: 217–218

Otho—Roman Emperor
(reigned 69)
Pages: 217–219

Vitellius—Roman Emperor
(reigned 69)
Pages: 217–219

• The Roman Empire, approaching the height of its power and prestige, rules over the entire Mediterranean, much of Europe, and parts of the Middle East. The empire brings to its territories law, language, government, and infrastructure.

• Great Writers: Virgil, Horace, Livy, and Ovid

• The Pax Romana, or Roman Peace, begins during the reign of Augustus and marks nearly two centuries of relative tranquillity in the empire.

• Jesus Christ is crucified, c. A.D. 30

• Fire destroys much of Rome, A.D. 64

• First recorded persecution of Christians, A.D. 64

Vespasian—Roman Emperor
(reigned 69–79)
Page: 219

• Construction begins on the Roman Colosseum, c. A.D. 70

Titus—Roman Emperor
(reigned 79–81)
Page: 219

890–999

Formosus—Pope
(reigned 891–896)
Pages: 226–227

Stephen VI—Pope
(reigned 896–897)
Pages: 226–227

Leo V—Pope
(reigned 903)
Page: 227

Christopher—Antipope
(reigned 903–904)
Page: 227

Sergius III—Pope
(reigned 904–911)
Pages: 227–229

John X—Pope
(reigned 914–928)
Page: 229

John XI—Pope
(reigned 931–935)
Pages: 228–230

• The Dark Ages that came over Europe after the fall of the Roman Empire in A.D. 476 continue. Existence for the average person is often brutal, dirty, and short. Life expectancy averages about 30 years, with an infant mortality rate of 40 percent.

• About 90 percent of the population lives on the land— often poor, malnourished, and bound to a feudal lord. Cities are small and underpopulated. Decay of the once extensive Roman infrastructure is evident almost everywhere.

• The Christian Church is the wealthiest and most influential force in Europe, permeating almost every aspect of life with intertwined spiritual and temporal powers. As a rule, only clerics and monks are educated.

Otto I—Holy Roman Emperor
(reigned 962–973)
Pages: 224–225

Stephen VIII—Pope
(reigned 939–942)
Page: 226

John XII—Pope
(reigned 955–964)
Pages: 223–225, 230, 231

Leo VIII—Pope
(reigned 963–965)
Page: 225

John XIII—Pope
(reigned 965–972)
Page: 223

• Europe consists of mostly small feudal states, with unified kingdoms yet to emerge. A loosely affiliated collection of German and Italian states form the Holy Roman Empire.

• Fierce Viking raids that terrorized the region for centuries are diminishing, allowing powerful monasteries to establish themselves as centers of community.

1000–1099

Gregory VI—Pope
(reigned 1045–1046)
Page: 232

Henry III—Holy Roman Emperor
(reigned 1046–1056)
Page: 232

William I (The Conqueror)—
King of England
(reigned 1066–1087)
Pages: 127, 261–262

Gregory VII—Pope
(reigned 1073–1085)
Pages: 221, 231–233, 241

• Leif Ericson leads what was probably the first European expedition to the Atlantic coast of North America and establishes a short-lived settlement there, c. 1000.

• A schism permanently divides Christendom into the Roman Catholic and Eastern Orthodox Churches, 1054.

• Wresting power away from the feudal lords, King William I

Henry IV—Holy Roman Emperor
(reigned 1084–1108)
Page: 232

William II ("Rufus")—King of England
(reigned 1087–1100)
Pages: 20, 127

Urban II—Pope
(reigned 1088–1099)
Page: 234

builds Europe's first nation-state after conquering England, 1066.

• Construction begins on the Tower of London, 1078.

1100–1199

Henry I—King of England
(reigned 1100–1135)
Page: 127

Stephen—King of England
(reigned 1135–1154)
Page: 127

Henry II—King of England
(reigned 1154–1189)
Pages: 127–128

Philip II—King of France
(reigned 1180–1223)
Page: 233

Richard I ("The Lion Heart")—King of England
(reigned 1189–1199)
Pages: 20, 128

Innocent III—Pope
(reigned 1198–1216)
Pages: 233–237, 241

• Gothic art and architecture begin to emerge, c. 1150.

• The first paper mill is constructed in Europe, 1150.

• The cornerstone is laid for Notre-Dame Cathedral, Paris, 1163.

• Vikings make the last recorded voyage to North America, 1189.

John—King of England
(reigned 1199–1216)
Pages: 128, 233–234

1200-1299

Gregory IX—Pope
(reigned 1227–1241)
Page: 237

Edward I—King of England
(reigned 1272–1307)
Page: 263

Innocent IV—Pope
(reigned 1243–1254)
Page: 238

Philip IV—King of France
(reigned 1285–1314)
Pages: 243–245

Nicholas IV—Pope
(reigned 1288–1292)
Page: 239

Celestine V—Pope
(reigned 1294)
Pages: 240–242

Boniface VIII—Pope
(reigned 1294–1303)
Pages: 240–244

• King John of England is forced to sign the Magna Carta, which serves as the earliest foundation for constitutional government in England and, later, much of the world, 1215.

• Linen is first manufactured in England, 1253.

• Thomas Aquinas, a leader in the emerging scholastic movement, outlines Catholic theology and reconciles Aristotelian rationalism with Christian faith, 1258–1273.

• English House of Commons is founded when elected representatives from towns and shires are first called to Parliament, 1260.

• Marco Polo journeys to China, 1271.

• Jews are expelled from England, 1290.

• Spectacles are invented, 1290.

• First mechanical clocks in Europe, late 1200s.

Appendix IV

1300–1399

o━━━━━━━━━━━━━━━━━━━━━━━━━━━━━o

Clement V—Pope
(reigned 1305–1314)
Page: 245

Edward II—King of England
(reigned 1307–1327)
Pages: 20, 129, 263–264

John XXII—Pope
(reigned 1316–1334)
Page: 223

Edward III—King of England
(reigned 1327–1377)
Pages: 129–130, 264

Benedict XII—Pope
(reigned 1335–1342)
Page: 245

Richard II—King of England
(reigned 1377–1399)
Page: 130

Urban VI—Pope
(reigned 1378–1389)
Pages: 245–246

Boniface IX—Pope
(reigned 1389–1404)
Page: 246

Benedict (XIII)—Antipope
(reigned 1394–1417)
Page: 246

• Dante Alighieri writes *Divine Comedy*, c. 1308–1321.

• Hundred Years' War begins when Edward III of England claims French throne, 1337.

• Plague, or the Black Death, kills about one quarter of Europe's population, 1347–1352.

• Giovanni Boccaccio, *Decameron*, c. 1349–1353.

• Large cannons are first used in warfare, c. 1350.

• Legend of Robin Hood first appears in literature, c. 1378.

• Geoffrey Chaucer writes *Canterbury Tales*, c. 1386–1400.

Henry IV—King of England
(reigned 1399–1413)
Pages: 130, 133

1400-1499

Gregory XII—Pope
(reigned 1406–1415)
Page: 246

Alexander V—Antipope
(reigned 1409–1410)
Page: 246

John (XXIII)—Antipope
(reigned 1410–1415)
Page: 223

Henry V—King of England
(reigned 1413–1422)
Pages: 130, 133

Martin V—Pope
(reigned 1417–1431)
Page: 246

Henry VI—King of England
(reigned 1422–1461 and 1470–1471)
Pages: 130–137

Callistus III—Pope
(reigned 1455–1458)
Pages: 250–252

Pius II—Pope
(reigned 1458–1464)
Pages: 131, 251–252

• Prince Henry the Navigator of Portugal organizes over fifty explorations of the West African coast, 1419–1460.

• Joan of Arc is burned at the stake two years after defeating the English in the siege of Orleans, 1431.

• Fra Angelico paints *The Annunciation*, c. 1450.

• Johannes Gutenberg perfects his printing press, c. 1450.

• Ottoman Turks capture Constantinople (now Istanbul, Turkey), ending the East Roman, or Byzantine Empire, 1453.

• Calais is England's last possession in France when the Hundred Years' War ends, 1453.

• Lorenzo de Medici ("The Magnificent") presides over the Renaissance in Florence, 1469–1492.

Edward IV—King of England
(reigned 1461–1470 and 1471–1483)
Pages: 16–17, 133–137

Sixtus IV—Pope
(reigned 1471–1484)
Pages: 247, 252

Ferdinand and Isabella (co-monarchy)—King and Queen of Spain
(reigned Ferdinand: 1474–1516;
Isabella 1474–1504)
Pages Ferdinand: 55–57, 59
Pages Isabella: 55–57, 59

Edward V—King of England
(reigned 1483)
Page: 137

Richard III—King of England
(reigned 1483–1485)
Pages: 137–138

Innocent VIII—Pope
(reigned 1484–1492)
Pages: 247–249, 252

Henry VII—King of England
(reigned 1485–1509)
Pages: 59–60, 138

Alexander VI—Pope
(reigned 1492–1503)
Pages: 250–254

• Thomas Malory's *Le Morte D'Arthur* becomes the most complete version of the legend of King Arthur and the Knights of the Round Table, c. 1469.

• Kingdoms of Aragon and Castile are united, bringing almost all of what is now Spain under one rule, 1479.

• First European manual of navigation is produced in Portugal, 1484.

• Sandro Botticelli paints *Birth of Venus*, c. 1485.

• Christopher Columbus arrives in the New World, 1492.

• Jews are expelled from Spain, 1492.

• Leonardo da Vinci draws plans for a flying machine, 1493.

• Pope Alexander VI divides the New World between Spain and Portugal, 1493.

• John Cabot claims Newfoundland for England, 1497.

• Michelangelo carves the *Pieta*, 1498.

• Vasco da Gama discovers sea route to India, 1498.

1500–1599

Julius II—Pope
(reigned 1503–1513)
Pages: 247, 255

Henry VIII—King of England
(reigned 1509–1547)
Pages: 17, 31, 59–80, 81, 83, 101–107,
108, 109, 138–139, 140–142, 265

Francis I—King of France
(reigned 1515–1547)
Pages: 8, 61

Charles V (I of Spain)—Holy
Roman Emperor
(reigned 1519–1556)
Pages: 64, 73, 102, 175–176

Leo X—Pope
(reigned 1513–1521)
Pages: 65, 253, 255–256

Clement VII—Pope
(reigned 1523–1534)
Pages: 64–65

Paul III—Pope
(reigned 1534–1549)
Page: 253

Mary Queen of Scots—Queen of
Scotland
(reigned 1542–1567)
Pages: 81–85, 267–269

• Leonardo da Vinci paints the
Mona Lisa, 1503.

• Other great artists: Titian,
Raphael, Correggio, El Greco,
Tintoretto, Durer, and Holbein.

• "America" appears on a map
of the world for the first time,
1507.

• First shipment of African
slaves to the New World, 1450.

• Desiderius Erasmus writes
Praise of Folly, 1511.

• Juan Ponce de Leon claims
Florida for Spain, 1513.

• Niccolo Machiavelli writes
The Prince, 1513.

• Vasco Nunez de Balboa finds
Pacific Ocean, 1513.

• Thomas More writes *Utopia*,
1516.

• Ferdinand Magellan sets sail
for the first voyage around the
globe, 1519.

Edward VI—King of England
(reigned 1547–1553)
Pages: 31, 72, 107, 109, 140–141

Henri II—King of France
(reigned 1547–1559)
Pages: 8–9, 11

Mary I ("Bloody Mary")—Queen of England
(reigned 1553–1558)
Pages: 18, 31, 60, 66, 72, 101–111, 140–147

Paul IV—Pope
(reigned 1555–1559)
Pages: 257–258

Philip II—King of Spain
(reigned 1556–1598)
Pages: 111, 143, 175–177

Elizabeth I ("The Virgin Queen")—Queen of England
(reigned 1558–1603)
Pages: 17–19, 29–33, 68, 83, 85, 103–104, 109, 140–146, 267

Francis II—King of France
(reigned 1559–1560)
Page: 81

Charles IX—King of France
(reigned 1560–1574)
Page: 12

Henri III—King of France
(reigned 1574–1589)
Pages: 9–11

• Hernando Cortes conquers the Incas in Mexico, 1521.

• William Tyndale translates the Bible into English, 1522.

• Augsburg Confession forms the basic statement of faith for the emerging Lutheran Church, 1530.

• Ignatius Loyola founds the Society of Jesus, or the Jesuits, 1534.

• Protestant reformer John Calvin publishes *The Institutes of the Christian Religion*, 1536.

• Hernando de Soto leads first European exploration of the Mississippi River, 1541.

• Nicolaus Copernicus, the founder of modern astronomy, asserts that the sun—not the earth, as previously believed—is the center of the universe in *On the Revolution of Heavenly Spheres*, 1543.

• Andreus Vesalius's *On the Structure of the Human Body* becomes the first detailed work on anatomy, 1543.

• England loses Calais, its last possession in France, 1558.

Henry IV—King of France
(reigned 1589–1610)
Pages: 11–14

Philip III—King of Spain
(reigned 1598–1621)
Page: 177

• Jean Nicot introduces tobacco use in France, 1560.

• Philip II sends out the failed Spanish Armada against England, 1588.

• Edmund Spenser writes *The Faerie Queene*, 1590.

• Henry IV of France grants freedom of religion with the Edict of Nantes, 1598.

1600–1699

James I (VI of Scotland)—King of England
(reigned 1603–1625)
Pages: 19–20, 84

Philip IV—King of Spain
(reigned 1621–1665)
Page: 177

Urban VIII—Pope
(reigned 1623–1644)
Page: 258

Charles I—King of England
(reigned 1625–1649)
Page: 285

Louis XIV ("The Sun King")—
King of France
(reigned 1643–1715)
Pages: 14, 34–38, 180–181, 272–273

• William Shakespeare writes *Hamlet*, c. 1601.

• Other Great Writers: Milton, Jonson, Moliere, Congreve, Dryden, Donne, and Bunyan.

• The English Poor Law of 1601 establishes the concept of government welfare.

• The Gunpowder Plot devised by Guy Fawkes and others to blow up the English Houses of Parliament fails, 1605.

• Jamestown, Virginia, becomes the first permanent English settlement in North America, 1607.

• Johannes Kepler discovers the three laws of planetary motion, 1609–1619.

Charles II—King of England
(reigned 1660–1685)
Pages: 20, 270, 271, 285

Carlos II—King of Spain
(reigned 1665–1700)
Pages: 177–178

Peter I (The Great)—Tsar of
Russia
(reigned 1682–1725)
Pages: 115–119, 182–185

James II—King of England
(reigned 1685–1688)
Pages: 20, 147–150, 271

**William III and Mary II (co-
monarchy)**—King and Queen of
England
(reigned William: 1689–1702;
Mary: 1689–1694)
Pages William: 20, 147–148, 150
Pages Mary: 20–21, 147–150

• Pilgrims arrive at Plymouth, Massachusetts, 1620.

• William Harvey discovers blood circulation, 1628.

• Great Artists: Rembrandt, Rubens, Bernini, Van Dyck, and Vermeer.

• Rene Descartes, one of the greatest philosophers of the Enlightenment, publishes *Discourse on Method* with its famous passage, "I think, therefore I am," 1637.

• World's first public opera house opens in Venice, 1637.

• Civil War in England begins, 1642.

• The Peace of Westphalia settles the Thirty Years' War, which had involved much of Europe, 1648.

• Isaac Newton, perhaps the greatest scientific mind of all time, proves gravitation, discovers the secrets of light and color, invents calculus, and arrives at the three laws of motion, 1665–1689.

• Christopher Wren begins plans for the rebuilding of St. Paul's Cathedral after it was destroyed in the Great Fire of London, 1666.

• Anton van Leeuwenhoek first records observations of microscopic life, 1674.

1700-1799

Anne—Queen of Great Britain
(reigned 1702–1714)
Pages: 21, 147–150

Frederick William I—King of
Prussia
(reigned 1713–1740)
Pages: 112–114

George I—King of Great Britain
(reigned 1714–1727)
Pages: 21–22, 151–152

Louis XV—King of France
(reigned 1715–1774)
Pages: 14–15, 93

George II—King of Great Britain
(reigned 1727–1760)
Pages: 22–23, 114, 152–154, 274

Anna—Empress of Russia
(reigned 1730–1740)
Pages: 39–40

Frederick II (The Great)—King of
Prussia
(reigned 1740–1786)
Pages: 88, 112–114, 191–192

Maria Theresa—Empress of Austria
(reigned 1740–1780)
Pages: 89–92

Elizabeth—Empress of Russia
(reigned 1741–1762)
Pages: 86–87

• Act of Union joins England and Scotland to form Great Britain, 1707.

• Industrial Revolution begins, c. 1730.

• Benjamin Franklin conducts experiments with lightning, 1752.

• Great Writers: Johnson, Rousseau, Fielding, Pope, Swift, Voltaire, Locke, Wordsworth, Coleridge, Defoe, and Diderot.

• Henry Cavendish discovers the properties of hydrogen and identifies it as an element, 1766.

• The American colonies declare their independence from Britain, 1776.

• Adam Smith's *The Wealth of Nations* becomes the foundation of modern capitalism, 1776.

• Great Composers: Handel, Bach, Haydn, Mozart, and Beethoven.

• The French Revolution begins with the attack on the Bastille, 1789.

• Anton Laurent Lavoisier, the founder of modern chemistry, publishes *Elementary Treatise on Chemistry*, 1789.

• Mary Wollstonecraft's *A Vindication of the Rights of Women* becomes one of the earliest feminist manifestos, 1792.

• Edward Jenner gives the world's first vaccine, for smallpox, 1796.

1800–1899

• Great Inventions and Discoveries: telegraph, sewing machine, mechanical calculation, atomic theory, elevator, automobile, photosynthesis, speed of light, pasteurization, law

William IV—King of Great Britain
(reigned 1830–1837)
Pages: 23–24, 156–157

Victoria—Queen of Great Britain
(reigned 1837–1901)
Pages: 24–25, 120–123, 156–157, 195

Francis Joseph I—Emperor of
Austria/Hungary
(reigned 1848–1916)
Pages: 178–179

Wilhelm II—Kaiser of Germany
(reigned 1888–1918)
Page: 157

Nicholas II—Tsar of Russia
(reigned 1894–1917)
Pages: 194–197, 281–284

of heredity, antiseptic surgery, bicycle, typewriter, dynamite, assembly line manufacturing, celluloid, food canning, telephone, electric light, phonograph, skyscraper, X-rays, radio, rocket propulsion, radium, and motion pictures.

• Karl Marx publishes *The Communist Manifesto*, 1848.

• Charles Darwin publishes *The Origin of Species*, 1859.

• Civil War begins in the United States, 1861.

• Great Writers: Hawthorne, Melville, Flaubert, Conrad, Proust, Twain, Dostoevsky, Ibsen, Shaw, R.L. Stevenson, Hardy, Wilde, Whitman, James, Bronte, Thackery, Dickens, Poe, Tennyson, Austen, Byron, Hugo, Tolstoy, Turgenev, and Chekhov.

• The first impressionist painting exhibition is held in Paris. It features Claude Monet's *Impression: Sunrise*, which gives the art movement its name, 1874.

• Great Composers: Schubert, Tchaikovsky, Liszt, Verdi, Brahms, Strauss, Mahler, Dvorak, Chopin, Berlioz, and Wagner.

1900–1958

Edward VII—King of Great Britain
(reigned 1901–1910)
Pages: 120–123

George V—King of Great Britain
(reigned 1910–1936)
Pages: 46, 157

Edward VIII—King of Great
Britain
(reigned 1936)
Pages: 25–26, 48–51

George VI—King of Great Britain
(reigned 1936–1952)
Page: 49

Elizabeth II—Queen of Great
Britain
(reigned 1952–present)
Page: 285

John XXIII—Pope
(reigned 1958–1963)
Pages: 223, 258

• The Wright brothers first take flight, 1903.

• The *Titanic* sinks, 1912.

• World War I occurs, 1914–1918.

• Russian Revolution begins, 1917.

• Influenza epidemic kills an estimated 20 million people worldwide, 1918.

• Prohibition begins in U.S., 1920.

• Charles Lindbergh makes the first solo, nonstop flight across the Atlantic Ocean, 1927.

• First experimental television broadcast, 1927.

• Stock market crash heralds the beginning of the Great Depression, 1929.

• World War II occurs, 1939–1945.

• Era of space exploration begins when U.S.S.R. launches the first artificial satellite, 1957.

Select Bibliography

Appleby, John T. *Henry II: The Vanquished King.* 1962. Macmillan. New York

Bernier, Olivier. *Louis the Beloved: The Life of Louis XV.* 1984. Doubleday. Garden City, New York

Bolitho, Hector. *Victoria: The Widow and Her Son.* 1934. D. Appleton-Century. New York-London

Bryan, J., III and Charles J. V. Murphy. *The Windsor Story: An Intimate Portrait of Edward VIII and Mrs. Simpson.* 1979. Morrow. New York

Chamberlin, E. R. *The Bad Popes.* 1969. Dorset. New York

Cronin, Vincent. *Louis XIV.* 1965. Houghton Mifflin/Riverside Press. Cambridge

Davies, Norman. *Europe: A History.* 1996. Oxford University Press. Oxford-New York

De Rosa, Peter. *Vicars of Christ: The Dark Side of the Papacy.* 1988. Crown. New York

Donaldson, Frances. *Edward VIII: A Biography of the Duke of Windsor.* 1974/75. Lippincott. Philadelphia and New York

Duffy, Eamon. *Saints and Sinners: A History of the Popes.* 1997. Yale University Press. New Haven and London

Erickson, Carolly. *Bloody Mary.* 1978. Doubleday. Garden City, New York

———. *To the Scaffold: The Life of Marie Antoinette.* 1991. Morrow. New York

Fraser, Antonia. *Mary Queen of Scots.* 1969. Delacorte. New York

———, ed. *The Lives of the Kings and Queens of England.* 1975. Knopf. New York

———. *The Wives of Henry VIII.* 1994. Vintage. New York

Fulford, Roger. *The Wicked Uncles: The Father of Queen Victoria and His Brothers.* 1933/1968. Books for Libraries Press. Freeport, New York

Gramont, Sanche de. *Epitaph for Kings.* 1967. G. P. Putnam's Sons. New York

Green, David. *Queen Anne.* 1970. Charles Scribner's Sons. New York

Green, V. H. H. *The Hanoverians.* 1948. Edward Arnold. London

Haldane, Charlotte. *Queen of Hearts: Marguerite of Valois.* Bobbs-Merrill. Indianapolis-New York

Hamilton, Elizabeth. *William's Mary: A Biography of Mary II.* 1972. Taplinger. New York

Hatton, Ragnhild. *George I: Elector and King.* 1978. Harvard University Press. Cambridge, Massachusetts

Hibbert, Christopher. *George IV: Prince of Wales.* 1972. Longman. London

————. *George IV: Regent and King.* 1973. Harper & Row. New York, Evanston, San Francisco, London

Langdon-Davies, John. *Carlos: The King Who Would Not Die.* 1962. Prentice-Hall. Englewood Cliffs, New Jersey

Liss, Peggy K. *Isabel the Queen.* 1992. Oxford University Press. Oxford-New York

Longford, Elizabeth, ed. *The Oxford Book of Royal Anecdotes.* 1989. Oxford University Press. Oxford, New York

Luke, Mary M. *Gloriana: The Years of Elizabeth I.* 1973. Coward, McCann, Geoghegan. New York

————. *The Nine Days Queen: A Portrait of Lady Jane Grey.* 1986. Morrow. New York

Mahoney, Irene. *Madame Catherine: Matriarch, Mother of Kings, Mistress to an Era—The Life of Catherine de Medici.* 1975. Coward, McCann, Geoghegan. New York

Massie, Robert K. *Nicholas and Alexandra: An Intimate Account of the Last of the Romanovs and the Fall of Imperial Russia.* 1967. Atheneum. New York

————. *Peter the Great: His Life and World.* 1986. Knopf. New York

McBrien, Richard P. *Lives of the Popes: The Pontiffs from St. Peter to John Paul II.* 1997. HarperCollins. San Francisco

McGuigan, Dorothy Gies. *The Hapsburgs.* 1996. Doubleday. Garden City-New York

Mitford, Nancy. *The Sun King: Louis IV at Versailles.* 1966. Harper & Row. New York

Morand, Paul. *Sophia Dorothea of Celle: The Captive Princess.* 1968. American Heritage Press. Trans. Anne-Marie Geoghegan. New York, St. Louis, San Francisco, Toronto

Murphy, Edwin. *After the Funeral: The Posthumous Adventures of Famous Corpses.* 1995. Citadel Press/Carol. New York

Redman, Alvin. *The House of Hanover.* 1960. Alvin Redman Limited. London

Rose, Kenneth. *King George V.* 1984. Knopf. New York

Rubin, Nancy. *Isabella of Castile: The First Renaissance Queen.* 1991. St. Martin's Press. New York

Saint-Simon, Duke De. *The Age of Magnificence: The Memoirs of the Duke De Saint-Simon.* Ed. and trans. Sanche de Gramont. 1963. G. P. Putnam's Sons. New York

Schom, Alan. *Napoleon Bonaparte.* 1997. HarperCollins, New York

Sedillot, Rene, trans. Gerard Hopkins. *An Outline of French History.* 1961. Knopf. New York

Seward, Desmond. *The Wars of the Roses.* 1995. Viking. New York

Somerset, Anne. *Elizabeth I.* 1991. St. Martin's Press. New York

St Aubyn, Giles. *Edward VII: Prince and King.* 1979. Atheneum. New York

———. *Queen Victoria: A Portrait.* 1992. Atheneum. New York

Steinberg, Mark D., and Vladimir M. Khrustalev. *The Fall of the Romanovs.* 1995. Yale University Press. New Haven and London

Suetonius, trans. Robert Graves. *The Twelve Caesars.* 1957. Penguin Classics. London

Troyat, Henri. *Catherine the Great.* Trans. Joan Pinkham. 1980. E. P. Dutton. New York

Warren, W. L. *Henry II.* 1973. University of California Press. Berkeley and Los Angeles

Ziegler, Gilette, trans. Simon Watson Taylor. *At the Court of Versailles: Eye Witness Reports from the Reign of Louis XIV.* 1966. E. P. Dutton. New York

Ziegler, Philip. *King Edward VIII.* 1991. Knopf. New York

Acknowledgments

I want to thank all my wonderfully supportive family and
friends, especially my mom, dad, and sister Mary,
Melissa O'Neill Alshab, Jamie Beidleman, Anne Hennessey
Conway, Mike Curtin, Mary Jane and Bill Foote,
Mike Grimpus, Nancy and Pip Lisas, and Tom O'Neil.

I also want to thank my outstanding agent, Jenny Bent,
and editor, Caroline White, as well as the folks at Penguin
who put this book together, and Erik Falkensteen of the
Granger Collection who spent so many hours finding the
illustrations.

Many of my current and former colleagues at *The
Washington Post* helped me in numerous and diverse ways,
especially Marty Barrick, Mike Drew, Bill Elsen, Mary Hadar,
Marla Harper, Melissa McCullough, Olwen Price,
Boyce Rensberger, Curt Suplee, Mary Lou White, and
Tom Wilkinson.

Finally, I am most grateful to Ann Marie Lynch, who
defines the word friendship, and Gene Weingarten of *The
Washington Post* whose twisted genius is a gift from God.